THE 2007 TOUR DE FRANCE

JOHN WILCOCKSON & THE EDITORS OF *VELONEWS*

BOULDER, COLORADO

Front cover photographs: Getty Images

Maps by Charles Chamberlin

Photography credits for 16-page insert, with respective page numbers and positioning:
Getty Images: 1 *(bottom)*, 5 *(top)*, 6 *(bottom)*, 7, 8 *(top)*, 10 *(bottom)*, 11 *(bottom)*, 12 *(top)*
Casey B. Gibson: 1 *(top)*, 4, 6 *(top)*, 10 *(top)*, 12–13, 14, 15, 16
Cor Vos Photography: 5 *(bottom)*
Graham Watson: 2–3, 8 *(bottom left and right)*, 9, 11 *(top)*

Rider diary headshots by Don Karle (Vande Velde) and Graham Watson (Gerrans)

Distributed in the United States and Canada by Publishers Group West.

VeloPress®, a division of Inside Communications, Inc.
1830 North 55th Street
Boulder, Colorado 80301–2700 USA
303/440-0601; Fax: 303/444-6788; E-mail: velopress@insideinc.com

Cover and interior design by Erin Johnson Design

Library of Congress Cataloging-in-Publication Data

Wilcockson, John.
  The 2007 Tour de France / John Wilcockson and the editors of VeloNews
VeloPress.
    p. cm.
  ISBN-13: 978-1-934030-10-3 (pbk. : alk. paper)
  ISBN-10: 1-934030-10-4 (pbk. : alk. paper)
  1. Tour de France (Bicycle race) (2007) I. Velonews. II. Title.
  GV1049.2.T68W547 2007
  796.6'20944—dc22
                          2007039763

To purchase additional copies of this book or other VeloPress books, call 800/234-8356 or visit us at www.velopress.com.

Printed in the United States of America
07 08 09 / 10 9 8 7 6 5 4 3 2 1

Contents

Acknowledgments

A s the world of sports becomes more media focused each year, so the Tour de France becomes more complicated to report. And as cycling makes strides in clearing dopers from the sport, so antidoping measures play a larger role at the Tour. Because all of these factors add to the complexity of reporting the race, along with the multitude of events that influence its outcome in the months before the Tour even starts, it takes a whole team to produce this book. This year, besides enjoying their companionship through three weeks of another intensive, suspenseful Tour de France, I want to thank all of the *VeloNews* editors for their help in producing this absorbing story of a spectacular race. European correspondent Andrew Hood supplied much of the reporting and background details on the Spanish-speaking athletes and the continuing fallout from Operación Puerto; senior writer Neal Rogers provided daily feedback and quotes from many sources; editor Ben Delaney gave reporting assistance and insight through the middle part of the Tour; and technical editor Matt Pacocha provided details and writing about special bikes and new equipment used at the Tour. The exclusive story about Michael Rasmussen and the shoebox in Chapter 9 came from velonews.com editor Charles Pelkey. Adding to the depth of this volume are the Tour diaries of Australian rider Simon Gerrans of Ag2r, and American veteran Christian Vande Velde of CSC. Thanks also to Chas Chamberlin for the excellent course maps; to photographers Casey Gibson and Graham Watson for providing most of the images in the photo section; to the staff of VeloPress, including Iris Llewellyn, Renee Jardine, and Ted Costantino, for their encouragement and expertise; and most of all to all the athletes that made the 2007 Tour another one to remember.

John Wilcockson
August, 2007

2007 Tour de France Start List

Caisse d'Épargne
11. Oscar Pereiro (Sp)
12. David Arroyo (Sp)
13. José Garcia Acosta (Sp)
14. José Ivan Gutierrez (Sp)
15. Vladimir Karpets (Rus)
16. Francisco Perez (Sp)
17. Nicolas Portal (F)
18. Alejandro Valverde (Sp)
19. Xabier Zandio (Sp)

T-Mobile
21. Michael Rogers (Aus)
22. Marcus Burghardt (G)
23. Mark Cavendish (GB)
24. Bernhard Eisel (A)
25. Linus Gerdemann (G)
26. Bert Grabsch (G)
27. Kim Kirchen (Lux)
28. Axel Merckx (B)
29. Patrik Sinkewitz (G)

Team CSC
31. Carlos Sastre (Sp)
32. Kurt-Asle Arvesen (N)
33. Fabian Cancellara (Swi)
34. Iñigo Cuesta (Sp)
35. Stuart O'Grady (Aus)
36. Frank Schleck (Lux)
37. **Christian Vande Velde (USA)**
38. Jens Voigt (G)
39. **David Zabriskie (USA)**

Predictor-Lotto
41. Cadel Evans (Aus)
42. Mario Aerts (B)
43. Dario David Cioni (I)
44. **Chris Horner (USA)**
45. Leif Hoste (B)
46. Robbie McEwen (Aus)
47. **Fred Rodriguez (USA)**
48. Johan Vansummeren (B)
49. Wim Vansevenant (B)

Rabobank
51. Denis Menchov (Rus)
52. Michael Boogerd (Nl)
53. Bram De Groot (Nl)
54. Thomas Dekker (Nl)
55. Juan Antonio Flecha (Sp)
56. Oscar Freire (Sp)
57. Grischa Niermann (G)
58. Michael Rasmussen (Dk)
59. Pieter Weening (Nl)

Ag2r Prévoyance
61. Christophe Moreau (F)
62. José Luis Arrieta (Sp)
63. Sylvain Calzati (F)
64. Cyril Dessel (F)
65. Martin Elmiger (Swi)
66. John Gadret (F)
67. Simon Gerrans (Aus)
68. Stéphane Goubert (F)
69. Ludovic Turpin (F)

Euskaltel-Euskadi
71. Haimar Zubeldia (Sp)
72. Igor Anton (Sp)
73. Mikel Astarloza (Sp)
74. Jorge Azanza (Sp)
75. Iñaki Isasi (Sp)
76. Iñigo Landaluze (Sp)
77. Ruben Perez (Sp)
78. Amets Txurruka (Sp)
79. Gorka Verdugo (Sp)

Lampre-Fondital
81. Alessandro Ballan (I)
82. Daniele Bennati (I)
83. Paolo Bossoni (I)
84. Marzio Bruseghin (I)
85. Claudio Corioni (I)
86. Danilo Napolitano (I)
87. Daniele Righi (I)
88. Tadej Valjavec (Slo)
89. Francisco Javier Vila (Sp)

Gerolsteiner
91. Stefan Schumacher (G)
92. Robert Förster (G)
93. Markus Fothen (G)
94. Heinrich Haussler (G)
95. Bernhard Kohl (A)
96. Sven Krauss (G)
97. Ronny Scholz (G)
98. Fabian Wegmann (G)
99. Peter Wrolich (A)

Crédit Agricole
101. Thor Hushovd (N)
102. William Bonnet (F)
103. Alexandre Botcharov (Rus)
104. Anthony Charteau (F)
105. Julian Dean (NZ)
106. Dmitriy Fofonov (Kaz)
107. Patrice Halgand (F)
108. Sébastien Hinault (F)
109. Christophe Le Mével (F)

Discovery Channel
111. **Levi Leipheimer (USA)**
112. Alberto Contador (Sp)
113. Vladimir Gusev (Rus)
114. **George Hincapie (USA)**
115. Egoï Martinez (Sp)
116. Benjamin Noval (Sp)
117. Sergio Paulinho (P)
118. Yaroslav Popovych (Ukr)
119. Tomas Vaitkus (Lit)

Bouygues Telecom
121. Pierrick Fedrigo (F)
122. Stef Clement (Nl)
123. Xavier Florencio (Sp)
124. Anthony Geslin (F)
125. Laurent Lefèvre (F)
126. Jérôme Pineau (F)
127. Matthieu Sprick (F)
128. Johann Tschopp (Swi)
129. Thomas Voeckler (F)

Agritubel

131. Juan Miguel Mercado (Sp)
132. Freddy Bichot (F)
133. Moises Duenas (Sp)
134. Romain Feillu (F)
135. Eduardo Gonzalo (Sp)
136. Cédric Hervé (F)
137. Nicolas Jalabert (F)
138. Benoît Salmon (F)
139. Nicolas Vogondy (F)

Cofidis

141. Sylvain Chavanel (F)
142. Stéphane Augé (F)
143. Geoffroy Lequatre (F)
144. Cristian Moreni (I)
145. Nick Nuyens (B)
146. Ivan Ramiro Parra (Col)
147. Staf Scheirlinckx (B)
148. Rik Verbrugghe (B)
149. Bradley Wiggins (GB)

Liquigas

151. Filippo Pozzato (I)
152. Michael Albasini (Swi)
153. Manuel Beltran (Sp)
154. Kjell Carlström (Fin)
155. Murilo Fischer (Bra)
156. Aleksandr Kuchynski (Blr)
157. Manuel Quinziato (I)
158. Charles Wegelius (GB)
159. Frederik Willems (B)

Française des Jeux

161. Sandy Casar (F)
162. Sébastien Chavanel (F)
163. Mickael Delage (F)
164. Rémy Di Grégorio (F)
165. Philippe Gilbert (B)
166. Lilian Jégou (F)
167. Mathieu Ladagnous (F)
168. Thomas Lövkvist (S)
169. Benoît Vaugrenard (F)

Quick Step-Innergetic

171. Tom Boonen (B)
172. Carlos Barredo (Sp)
173. Steven De Jongh (Nl)
174. Juan Manuel Garate (Sp)
175. Sébastien Rosseler (B)
176. Gert Steegmans (B)
177. Bram Tankink (Nl)
178. Matteo Tosatto (I)
179. Cédric Vasseur (F)

Team Milram

181. Erik Zabel (G)
182. Alessandro Cortinovis (I)
183. Ralf Grabsch (G)
184. Andriy Grivko (Ukr)
185. Christian Knees (G)
186. Brett Lancaster (Aus)
187. Alberto Ongarato (I)
188. Enrico Poitschke (G)
189. Marcel Sieberg (G)

Astana

191. Alexander Vinokourov (Kaz)
192. Antonio Colom (Sp)
193. Maxim Iglinskiy (Kaz)
194. Serguei Ivanov (Rus)
195. Andrey Kashechkin (Kaz)
196. Andreas Klöden (G)
197. Daniel Navarro (Sp)
198. Grégory Rast (Swi)
199. Paolo Savoldelli (I)

Saunier Duval-Prodir

201. David Millar (GB)
202. Iker Camano (Sp)
203. David Cañada (Sp)
204. Juan José Cobo (Sp)
205. David De La Fuente (Sp)
206. Ruben Lobato (Sp)
207. Iban Mayo (Sp)
208. Christophe Rinero (F)
209. Francisco José Ventoso (Sp)

Barloworld

211. Alexander Efimkin (Rus)
212. Félix Cardenas (Col)
213. Giampaolo Cheula (I)
214. Enrico Degano (I)
215. Geraint Thomas (GB)
216. Robbie Hunter (SA)
217. Paolo Longo (I)
218. Kanstantin Siutsou (Blr)
219. Juan Mauricio Soler (Col)

Note: Because there was no
defending champion (Floyd
Landis) or team (Phonak),
the numbers 1 through 9 were
not allocated.

2007 Tour de France Route Map

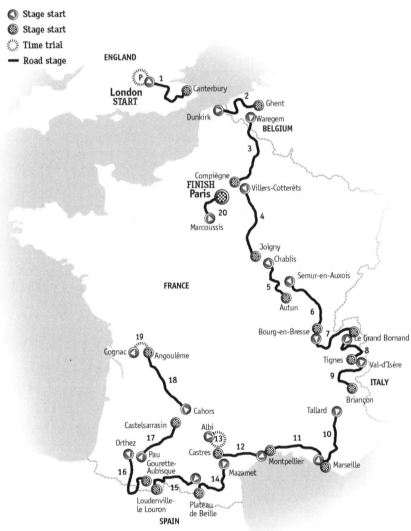

- Stage start
- Stage start
- Time trial
- Road stage

ENGLAND

London
START

P

1

Canterbury

2

Ghent

Dunkirk

Waregem

BELGIUM

3

Compiègne

FINISH
Paris

Villers-Cotterêts

20

4

Marcoussis

FRANCE

Joigny

Chablis

Semur-en-Auxois

5

Autun

6

Bourg-en-Bresse

7

Le Grand Bornand

19

8

Cognac

Angoulême

Tignes

Val-d'Isère

9

ITALY

Briançon

18

Cahors

Tallard

Castelsarrasin

Albi

13

11

10

Orthez

17

Pau

Castres

12

Gourette-
Aubisque

Mazamet

Montpellier

Marseille

16

14

15

Loudenville-
le Louron

Plateau
de Beille

SPAIN

1

Truth and Consequences

*After months of doping headlines, the 2007
Tour de France kicked off under a cloud of suspicion.*

Bjarne Riis is a deeply complex character. The balding, smooth-skinned Dane talks in hushed tones, like an archetypal mafia *capo*. He often answers journalists with a shrug, or challenges them on the competency of their questions, or replies with a question of his own. He is highly intelligent, a knowledgeable coach and trainer, a smart tactician, and a successful businessman. He has an enormous capacity for multitasking.

All of these qualities helped him create and build a highly successful professional cycling team, ranked number 1 on the Union Cycliste Internationale (UCI) ProTour in both 2005 and 2006 and sponsored by one of the world's leading information technology companies, CSC. And before retiring from racing in early 2000, Riis had been instrumental with his leadership, both on and off the bike, in building a small German team sponsored by Deutsche Telekom into what became an institution in pro cycling and a part of Germany's sporting fabric.

Riis won the 1996 Tour de France almost insolently to end Miguel Induráin's five-year reign over the world's greatest bike race. In particular, he toyed with the opposition riding to the summit finish at Lourdes-Hautacam on that Tour's 16th stage. At one point on the 12km climb, he eased off on the pedals and slowly drifted to the back of the lead group, looking at each rival to ascertain his state of fatigue. Satisfied that they were all suffering, he then bolted up the road to defeat runner-up Richard Virenque by almost a minute; Induráin struggled to the mountaintop in 12th place two and a half minutes back. People immediately started questioning the athletic authenticity of Riis's coup.

Riis added to Induráin's humiliation on the next stage—a marathon 262km grind over the Pyrénées to the Spaniard's hometown of Pamplona—by driving an eight-man breakaway on a day of tremendous heat that arrived at the finish eight minutes ahead of Induráin's 15-man chase group. In the final standings, Riis's youthful German protégé Jan Ullrich was second, followed by the Festina team's Virenque and Laurent Dufaux. When Riis returned home, he was greeted by what is said to have been the biggest party in honor of one person ever held in Denmark. But even the Danes wondered if their hero's performance was totally legitimate.

Two years later, the Festina riders were busted for teamwide doping. Virenque and his teammates eventually admitted to using the blood booster erythropoietin (EPO) and a variety of other banned drugs. In a subsequent tell-all book, *Breaking the Chain,* Festina team soigneur Willy Voet, who did jail time for transporting the team's drugs across the Belgian-French border on his way to the 1998 Tour, wrote that if EPO gave Virenque a hematocrit reading of up to 55 percent (the level of oxygen-carrying red blood cells that was the Festina team's self-imposed limit), then, to beat him, Riis must have raced at 60 percent. Following that hypothesis, Riis was dubbed "Mr. 60 percent," even though there was no proof that the 1996 Tour champion's hematocrit ever approached such a death-threatening level.

It would be a decade before rumors about Riis became facts.

On May 25, 2007, six weeks before the Tour kicked off in London, and following similar confessions in Germany by six of his former Telekom teammates, Riis held a press conference at the headquarters of his company, Riis Cycling A/S, in Lyngby, Denmark. He revealed that he did indeed dope in the mid-1990s. "I have taken banned substances, I have taken EPO. I bought it and took it myself," he said, explaining that the Telekom team doctors were not responsible for his actions. "It is ultimately the cyclists themselves who must take responsibility."

Besides EPO, Riis said he used human growth hormone and cortisone when he was racing for Italian squad Gewiss-Ballan (1993–1995) and Telekom (1996–1998), including the 1996 season when he won the Tour. When asked by the Danish media if he should be stripped of his title (an action subsequently taken by Tour organizer Amaury Sports Organisation (ASO), Riis replied, "That's up to you guys. I've got my winner's jersey in a cardboard box in my garage. You can come and get it if you want. That's okay by me. [But] you can't take away my experience and my pride of winning."

Explaining his reasons for coming forward with these details ten years after the transgressions, Riis said in a prepared statement: "First of all, I'm doing this to keep the focus on the work we are doing today that keeps cycling in the right perspective. The massive steps we have taken to fight doping, and the ways in which we have secured that, the team rests on the right and proper foundations.

"I think if we are to talk about doping, we should talk about what to do now and not about the mistakes in the past. The recent developments in Germany have taken the balance out of this and therefore I want to set the record straight. And I want to do this, because the future of cycling needs the right focus.

"Second of all, I'm doing this to get rid of the endless discussions about things that are truly in the past and that I personally have put behind [me] a long time ago. I don't want my personal past to overshadow the work and brilliant effort that Team CSC is doing today. We are the number 1 team in the world for the second year running and I want my riders and sponsors to be proud of that. They work, within the rules, with passion, professionalism, and commitment, and I want them to keep on doing that. When I was a rider in the 1990s, I worked extremely hard to get my results. I worked extremely hard, day in, day out, and I sacrificed a lot just even to be part of the best. In that time, the perspective on doping and preparation was wrong and misguided.

"That also means that I did things that I shouldn't have and I have regretted that ever since. Those were mistakes that I take the full responsibility for, and I don't have anyone to blame but myself. We all make mistakes, and I think my biggest mistake was to let my ambition get the better of me. *That* I have had to deal with a long time ago, and I am glad to say that I am a lot wiser now, both in my personal and in my professional life."

The mixed reception to Riis's confession summed up the feelings of cycling insiders. The CSC team's Spanish captain, Carlos Sastre, said, "I can only say that Bjarne has my total confidence and support. He's someone who made a mistake in the past and, since that time, has fought hard to show young riders the values of determination, training, and sacrifice. In reply to [his confession], so difficult and hard for Bjarne, I just want to say that, despite what the rest of the world might think, this team owes him a lot."

Taking the opposite tack, ASO's new Tour de France race director Christian Prudhomme commented, "Bjarne Riis said it himself: He's not worthy of having won the Tour de France because he cheated. He soiled the Tour. I ask myself: Is he worthy of directing a big cycling team?"

Prudhomme would later say that he didn't want Riis at the 2007 Tour. Accordingly, although the 43-year-old Dane traveled to the start in London, he decided not to remain with the race; instead, he let his directeurs sportifs, Kim Andersen and Alain Gallopin, manage the team in his absence.

— ⊙ —

Besides Bjarne Riis, also absent from the Tour would be the rider he helped win the Tour in 1997, his former Telekom teammate Ullrich, and the rider he hoped could win the Tour for CSC, Ivan Basso. A year earlier, both riders had been prevented from starting the Tour at the last minute because of their alleged inclusion on a list of 58 riders implicated in the Spanish blood-doping ring, Operación Puerto.

Ullrich's exclusion was based on intercepted phone conversations between the doctor at the center of the investigation, Eufemiano Fuentes, and Ullrich's coach and mentor, Rudy Pevenage. Ullrich was first suspended, then sacked by his T-Mobile team, and then became the subject of a German sports fraud investigation. On August 17, 2006, the BKA, Germany's FBI, searched the office and home of doctor-anesthetist Markus Choina, who was believed to have supplied drugs to Dr. Fuentes, and on September 13 searched the homes of Ullrich and Pevenage, the Hamburg offices of Ullrich's agent Wolfgang Strohband, and the Bonn HQ of the T-Mobile team. Ullrich was away on his honeymoon when the investigators came to his house in Switzerland, but they still collected various materials for DNA sampling.

Despite months of denying any connection to Puerto, Ullrich finally gave up the fight and announced his retirement from cycling on February 26, 2007. "Today I'm ending my career as a professional cyclist," he said. "I never once cheated as a cyclist."

Referring to his exclusion from the 2006 Tour 24 hours before the start, Ullrich said, "My life as a cyclist collapsed that day. I've been painted as a criminal while I've done nothing wrong."

There remained, however, the bags of blood and plasma that Spanish police had confiscated from Madrid apartments used by Dr. Fuentes and his accomplice, hematologist José Luis Merino Batres. The determined prosecutors in Bonn, Germany, finally got court orders to compare Ullrich's DNA samples with the blood contained in nine bags that Fuentes labeled with the codenames "No. 1," "Hijo de Rudicio" (Son of Rudy), and "Jan." On April 4, 2007, it was confirmed that "without a doubt" the blood was Ullrich's.

As for Basso, he had seemed untouchable. The 2006 Giro d'Italia champion calmly denied allegations he worked with the controversial Fuentes. He insisted that the code name "Birillo" mentioned in the Operación Puerto papers had nothing to do with him, and he retreated to his home near Varese in northwest Italy to patiently wait out the storm.

In late August 2006, Basso methodically presented his case before Italy's antidoping commission in Rome, hauling along a 35-page dossier of evidence with his attorney, Massimo Martelli, to face down allegations. When, on October 27, the Italian Olympic Committee (CONI) and his national cycling federation formally shelved the case and dropped any immediate possibility of sanctions for lack of concrete evidence, Basso felt vindicated.

A week before the CONI decision, Basso and CSC team manager Riis had cut their ties, leaving the Italian free to join another squad. "It was difficult to see Ivan leave the team because we worked so hard, but we took the decision and I am still confident with it," Riis told *VeloNews.* "I have no regrets. I couldn't do anything else than what I did. It was my decision."

Then, on November 9, Discovery Channel, eager to sign a Tour contender to replace seven-time winner Lance Armstrong, announced that Basso would ride for the U.S. team under a two-year deal. The wagons were drawn and Basso grew comfortable behind a formidable circle of allies that included RCS, the powerful Giro d'Italia organizer that wanted Italy's top star in its *corsa rosa*; the Italian cycling federation; a sycophantic national press; Discovery Channel officials; and Armstrong himself who, in addition to owning a share of the Discovery Team, wields significant power and influence on his own.

While the similarly implicated Ullrich slunk into retirement, Basso came through smelling pretty rosy. Decked out in the blue and black uniform of Discovery Channel, he returned to competition at the Amgen Tour of California in February without much fanfare. He then started Italy's Tirreno-Adriatico in March as part of his pre-Tour buildup. His career seemed to be back on track. But Basso's wall of defense started to show chinks in the days following the startling discovery in early April that DNA samples taken from Ullrich matched blood in bags confiscated the previous May from Fuentes's apartments in Madrid.

> **"The team is trying to find a new sponsor and win bike races, and my situation is a distraction to both of those goals. It is important that everyone knows this was 100 percent my decision. Nobody asked me to leave."**

Suddenly everyone asked, What about Basso? Among those asking questions were the antidoping prosecutors at CONI who had cleared Basso of any charges six months earlier. Fueled by the Ullrich news, prosecutors called the 29-year-old Basso to testify at a new hearing. Instead of racing the Ardennes classics in Belgium, Basso was suspended by the Discovery Channel. The weight of the news overwhelmed the usually stoic Basso, who collapsed into tears according to a report in *La Gazzetta dello Sport.*

A few days later, Basso resigned from the Discovery team. "This was a very difficult decision, for me and my family, but I think it is the right thing to do," Basso said. "The team is trying to find a new sponsor and win bike races, and my situation is a distraction to both of those goals. It is important that everyone knows this was 100 percent my decision. Nobody asked me to leave."

Then, at his May 7 hearing, Basso admitted his involvement in the Puerto scandal. That confession, however, wasn't quite a full mea culpa, as Basso explained at a news conference the following day. "I have never taken banned substances, and I have never employed blood doping," he told reporters in a prepared statement. "I did admit having *attempted* to use doping for the [2006] Tour de France, and I am ready to pay the penalty for that. All my wins have been achieved in a proper and clean manner, and I have every intention of returning to action and continuing with the job I love once I have paid the penalty." Basso was later handed a modified two-year suspension by CONI that was due to end on October 24, 2008.

Following the Basso and Ullrich cases, the UCI, under the leadership of President Pat McQuaid, continued to push for the Puerto blood bags to be made available for DNA sampling, though cycling's governing body had no legal authority to force the matter. "The UCI wants to ensure that all the blood that was found in relation to the Puerto affair is identified," McQuaid wrote in a letter to Spanish authorities in April. "The whole cycling community, and indeed the whole sports world, is waiting for the identification of all athletes who are apparently or possibly involved in the affair."

Tour de France officials said they were determined to keep Puerto-linked riders out of the 2007 edition. "We have asked the teams not to bring the Puerto riders," Tour director Prudhomme told *L'Équipe.* "We cannot have a repeat of last year, and we must work together to rid the sport of doping."

— ◉ —

It wasn't Puerto that snared defending Tour champion Floyd Landis. It was an elevated testosterone-to-epitestosterone ratio—and a subsequent test for artificial testosterone that proved positive—that led to his downfall. But a year after he supplied that urine sample at Morzine on July 20, 2006, the American was still proclaiming his innocence and still awaiting the verdict of a three-man arbitration panel convened by the U.S. Anti-Doping Agency (USADA) in May 2007.

Landis's high-profile defense began in September 2006 after his lawyers received some 370 pages of documents from USADA—the paper trail produced by the French laboratory that conducted the A and B tests of his sample. A retired doctor and Landis's onetime coach, Arnie Baker, examined the documents and put together a slide show of alleged lab mistakes that later became the basis of a presentation given by Baker and Landis on a four-month, nationwide fund-raising and publicity tour for the Floyd Fairness Fund, which was established on January 4, 2007.

At more than a dozen venues, each attended by between 75 and 300 faithful fans, Landis swapped his cycling uniform for a suit and tie, gave his side of the doping story, answered questions, signed autographs, and auctioned items such as signed yellow jerseys. The reason for the traveling slideshow was twofold: to raise money for his arbitration hearing, which took place at Pepperdine University in Malibu, California, May 14 to 23; and to advocate athletes' rights in what Landis claims is the World Anti-Doping Agency's (WADA) self-serving, shotgun-spray fight against doping.

In his 45-minute presentation, Baker claimed that the Laboratoire National de Dépistage du Dopage (LNDD) in Châtenay-Malabry, France, made numerous mistakes. In particular, for Landis's positive sample, four testosterone breakdown products were measured using isotope ratio mass spectrometry. All four metabolites, Baker said, should measure abnormal if their origin is exogenous—from outside Landis's body. Given the LNDD's positive criteria as any value below -3.0, with an uncertainty level of ±0.8 as positive of endogenous testosterone, Baker said only one of Landis's metabolites examined arguably met the criteria to determine a positive result, with a measurement of -6.39. The other three metabolite levels came in at -2.02, -3.51, and -2.65.

Further, Baker said, an Australian WADA-accredited lab sets its positivity criteria beyond -4.0 and claims that all four metabolites must fall beyond the positivity range for a sample to be called positive. "The LNDD does not publish its positivity criteria, but the Australian lab does," Baker said. "So does the WADA-accredited lab at UCLA [in California], which is three times as large as the next biggest WADA lab, in Germany. Australia would not call this a positive test, and UCLA would not call this a positive test. I've spoken with people who work at the UCLA lab that have told me they would not call this a positive test. One of the fundamental missions of WADA—to ensure uniformity of its laboratories—has failed."

At the hearing, one of the key expert witnesses was Wolfram Meier-Augenstein, a researcher in isotope ratio testing at Queen's University, Belfast, in Northern Ireland. The German scientist was critical of the chromatography, the graphic representation of the test data. He said flaws made it impossible to interpret the results with any certainty. "By anybody's standards, that's not accurate enough," he said.

A second Landis witness, Dr. John Amory of the University of Washington, who treats patients with low doses of testosterone, also said that Landis's test results were too inconsistent to be trustworthy. "I don't think they can be used to confirm doping occurred," he said.

Similar testimony was given by the defense team's final witness, Simon Davis, an authority on the instrument used to confirm the presence of synthetic testosterone in a urine sample. Davis, who was at the French lab during testing operations, said that LNDD technicians did not follow the manufacturer's guidelines in calibrating and operating the instrument. He was also critical of the data-processing procedures adopted at LNDD, claiming that the two female technicians who testified earlier in the Landis hearing "clearly did not understand the instrument." As a result, Davis opined that the Landis results were "totally unreliable."

In their closing arguments, USADA's lawyers said, "The Paris lab technicians have been called [by the defense team] either incompetent on one hand or skilled, evil geniuses on the other. What [Landis] would like the panel to believe is they are both. The panel has had the opportunity to judge their credibility. They take great pride in their work."

Landis's lawyer Maurice Suh contested that statement in his closing argument, saying, "We have never claimed they are evil geniuses. We don't think they are evil. They aren't geniuses. They are incompetent. It does surprise us that a tech with six months on the job and little proper training was testing the samples of the winner of the Tour de France."

Landis, who was bolstered by the presence of his Mennonite parents in the courtroom, remained calm during the nine days of testimony—except when USADA witness Greg LeMond revealed that Landis's former Chevy Trucks mountain bike teammate turned business manager Will Geoghegan called him the night before his testimony and threatened to expose the fact that LeMond was sexually abused as a child. Of that witness-tampering scandal, Suh said, "We were shocked and felt terrible about Geoghegan. It was wrong and disgusting. But there should be no guilt by association."

The crux of the case, however, remained the scientific minutiae that dominated the hearing. And Landis remained confident, even as he conceded that the majority of damage had already been done. He spent an estimated $2 million on his defense—a quarter of which came from the Floyd Fairness Fund—besides losing all of the potential endorsements a Tour winner can expect. "We know we will never be 100 percent cleared," Landis said. "It's not possible to prove your innocence. You can never go back. That is why we're trying to change the system. I was convicted by governing-body officials and the press long before I was even told what happened. We're trying to prevent that from happening in the future."

A few hours after the Landis USADA hearing wrapped up in California, a nationally televised news conference convened by T-Mobile team general manager Bob Stapleton got under way at the Deutsche Telekom headquarters in Bonn, Germany. This was the same venue where, six months earlier, T-Mobile introduced its zero-tolerance doping policy, which was to be overseen by Stapleton and his new team director Rolf Aldag, a former Telekom rider.

Sitting next to Stapleton and Aldag at this May 24 meeting was a surprise guest, Erik Zabel, who raced for Telekom/T-Mobile for 13 seasons before joining his current team, Milram. The lasting image for the event's huge TV audience was the teary-eyed Zabel, the pro peloton's most respected racer, saying he doped 11 years ago. Zabel said that in the first week of the 1996 Tour de France—the race in which he won the first of his six green-jersey titles as best sprinter—he asked his Belgian soigneur, Jeff D'Hondt, to give him a course of EPO injections. "There were rumors about EPO, that you couldn't win anything without this product," Zabel recounted. "I wanted to try it like everyone else, but it made me sick. I was waking up in a sweat, my pulse was very weak. I got scared as they said that some riders had died. So I told Jeff D'Hondt to stop giving it to me."

Zabel, 36 and in his 16th pro season, said that was the only time he ever cheated. "We would have very likely kept quiet about [doping] and continued to say that we knew nothing in the hope that they would leave us in peace till the end of our days," Zabel added. "But today we can't think about our successes of the past, that perhaps we didn't deserve it. We have to admit that we'll remain in the annals of our sport as the EPO generation."

Before Zabel spoke, his former team colleague and roommate Aldag— who Stapleton said would remain in his post as team director—gave details of his extensive abuse of EPO from 1995 through 2002. With his voice trembling, Aldag said, "I had a bad conscience in 1997. I was thinking about the risks to my health, but when the UCI brought in a maximum hematocrit level of 50 percent, that got rid of my guilt. I bought a centrifuge so I could control my own level. No one else knew what I was doing."

Zabel and Aldag, like Riis at his news conference the following day, said they doped on their own volition. They said they were influenced by neither their Belgian team director Walter Godefroot nor the Telekom team's German physicians, Dr. Lothar Heinrich and Dr. Andreas Schmid.

Perhaps they were trying to save the medical careers of the two sports doctors who worked for the University of Freiburg, the city where Ullrich lived during his years with Telekom. They were both alleged to have engaged in doping practices by Belgian soigneur D'Hondt, who worked for Telekom from 1992 to 1996, in his tell-all book, *Memoirs of a Bike Racing Soigneur*, extracts of which were published by *Der Spiegel* on April 28. After ex-Telekom racer Bert Dietz, today a bike shop owner, went on German TV to confirm the book's accusations, the doctors changed their tune. The doctors were later suspended by the T-Mobile squad and then fired by the university after they admitted giving riders EPO injections.

Following Dietz's confession, another teammate, Brian Holm of Denmark, said he twice used EPO when he was a Telekom rider. Like Aldag, Holm kept

his job as a directeur sportif at T-Mobile. Other ex-Telekom riders came forward. Gerolsteiner team director Christian Henn said EPO use was part of the
culture. "It was like that then," he said about the mid-1990s. Gerolsteiner did
not fire Henn, but the German team's part-time assistant director Udo Bölts
voluntarily resigned after telling German TV he was tempted to use EPO in
1996 and 1997, despite his riding (and finishing) 12 Tours.

There were calls from the German government and Tour director
Prudhomme for teams to sack the men who broke cycling's code of silence
on doping. Others said that the sport should not forget what happened in the
past but had to forgive those who have the courage to admit their mistakes.
This was the attitude of the Milram team management, which kept Zabel on
its roster for the Tour. Like a crusader, Zabel said, "I've been lying for 11 years
but enough is enough. I don't want my son, who loves the sport of cycling, to
go through the same as I did. I have to imagine what the cycling of our children will be like and do everything to make it better. We can't do it alone; we
need some help."

— ⊙ —

While the cathartic confessions of Zabel, Aldag, Riis, and the other former
Telekom team riders gave the public a peek into the mentality of pro
cyclists in the 1990s, some insight on the current doping culture in cycling
was coming from other sources.

On June 19, at a meeting in Switzerland with all the ProTour teams, UCI
president Pat McQuaid introduced an antidoping pledge that riders would be
asked to sign before they could start the 2007 Tour. The one-page document
committed riders to agree that they were "not involved in the Puerto affair
nor any other doping case," and that any infringement of the antidoping rules
would result in their paying the UCI "an amount equal to my annual salary in
2007 as a contribution to the fight against doping." The document also asked
the riders to give DNA to be "compared with the blood samples seized in the
Puerto affair."

Two days after that meeting, the UCI's director of antidoping programs,
Anne Gripper, told Agence France Presse that a half dozen big-name riders had been subject to surprise out-of-competition controls that had yielded
some "nonnegative" results. Gripper said that officials were waiting for the
results from the B sample tests before jumping to conclusions.

"We have targeted six, seven riders considered a high risk because of their
suspicious behavior and because they could perform very well in the Tour de
France," Gripper said. "Some have already had three or four surprise controls."

Gripper said the UCI controllers had dubbed three of these riders as the "men in black" because they "train in anonymous jerseys rather than in team kits so that they can avoid the UCI controllers trying to make the surprise controls."

The story prompted an immediate press release from the Astana team, which took offense at insinuations in some European media. The statement said that if riders sometimes trained in plain uniforms it's because they did not want to be bothered by cyclo-tourists, especially along France's Côte d'Azur, where its Kazakh team leader Alexander Vinokourov often trained. The team added that it was conducting a training camp in the Pyrénées riding in the Kazakh national jerseys, rather than the Astana team kit. "It's not because they are trying to avoid something," the team said.

Riders are typically subjected to one surprise out-of-competition test per season, but UCI officials can order more if they have suspicions. The UCI has been known to target suspect riders with more rigorous antidoping controls.

A week after the "men in black" revelations, Vinokourov, the top prerace favorite for the 2007 Tour, told *L'Équipe* that his trainer was the controversial Italian sports doctor Michele Ferrari, who was once accused of involvement in EPO doping. Ferrari was convicted of sporting fraud and malpractice in 2004 before winning an appeal two years later.

"Michele Ferrari is a physical trainer but not my doctor," said Vinokourov. "All I did was listen to people like Mario Cipollini who said great things. [Lance] Armstrong also worked with him. I didn't want to miss out on this experience. I contacted him [after Armstrong retired]."

Vinokourov, who lives in Monte Carlo, said that working with Ferrari was not that extraordinary. "Once a month I take a test to find out what kind of form I am in physically and my training depends on those results. His training plans are effective and precise. Since last year I've come on a lot in the mountains and also the time trials. Winning the Vuelta [a España] cemented my faith in him.

"Ferrari has never offered me any medication. He is just my physical trainer and if I'm talking as openly as this it's because I've nothing to hide."

Vinokourov added, "The day that the UCI establishes an official list of doctors that we are not allowed to work with, then I'll stop. But for the moment, this list doesn't exist." He added that none of his Astana teammates worked with Ferrari.

Vinokourov's revelation came on the heels of the suspension (and later dismissal) by the Astana team of two of his likely Tour de France teammates. German Matthias Kessler tested positive for synthetic testosterone, which he later admitted to, and Italian Eddy Mazzoleni was being questioned by CONI about his implication in the 2003 "oil for drugs" doping investigation.

Vinokourov told *L'Équipe* he believed that the doping accusations against his teammates, along with the "men in black" insinuations, were part of a conspiracy to disrupt his Tour plans. "They're really trying to tarnish our image," he said. "It's really difficult to concentrate on the Tour de France in these conditions."

The same day, one of Vino's 2006 Astana teammates, Jörg Jaksche, became the first rider to admit to blood doping with Puerto doctor Fuentes. Referring to the Puerto code name "Bella Jörg," Jaksche told *Der Spiegel* in a lengthy article, "I'm Bella. It's my blood that was found in three bags. I was a client of Dr. Fuentes from 2005 to 2006 in Madrid. Fuentes was a master of concealment. None of his clients knew each other. Even within our team, you weren't really sure if the other riders went to him."

Jaksche, who raced for Liberty Seguros (later Astana) in 2005 and 2006, was one of the 13 riders, including Basso, Ullrich, and Alberto Contador, who were prevented from starting the 2006 Tour de France because of being implicated in the Puerto affair. Jaksche's lawyer, Michael Lehner, said that his client was now ready to give evidence before the World Anti-Doping Agency, the UCI, and legal authorities—a fact that could potentially create new revelations in the months following the 2007 Tour.

The German claimed in the article that he started taking EPO and human growth hormone while racing for the Italian team Polti in 1997 and 1998. "That was my crash course," Jaksche said. "A soigneur injected me with EPO in my room. The logic is you adjust your performance level to the rest, because everyone is doing it. In cycling, you live in a parallel universe."

Whether more doping revelations would emerge from this alternative world at the Tour itself was just one of the ongoing fears harbored by the 21 teams, the millions of fans, the UCI, and race organizer ASO. Certainly the international media, fueled by an almost continuous diet of doping stories since the 2006 Tour, would be on the lookout for any tidbit of controversy.

That's why Bjarne Riis, who knew that his CSC team's independent medical monitoring program was the most stringent in the peloton, decided not to hang around after the start of the Tour. He didn't want his personal history to affect the collective interests of his team. He wanted Sastre and his team riders to focus on the race.

2

The Clean Crusaders

*With the Tour and the UCI fighting cheats harder than ever before,
the CSC and T-Mobile teams lead the antidoping crusade.*

The cycling world was stunned when the Discovery Channel team announced in November 2006 that it was signing Ivan Basso as its team leader. Only two weeks earlier UCI ProTour teams had made a verbal agreement not to sign riders implicated in doping investigations. The move by Discovery team director Johan Bruyneel went in the face of the current accelerated campaign to clean up professional cycling. After all, Basso had been excluded from the 2006 Tour de France because his name appeared on the Operación Puerto blacklist. Although he was temporarily cleared to race by the Italian Olympic Committee, Basso was considered such a hot property that Team CSC boss Bjarne Riis, cognizant of his sponsors' concerns and the ProTour code of ethics, let Basso go in October.

One of Basso's former teammates at CSC, Jens Voigt, was so incensed by Discovery picking up Basso that he said on Eurosport, "The return of Ivan Basso to bike racing isn't good for its image. The public will think that nothing has changed." The popular German rider then added, "The attitude of the riders has changed. A small minority will not be allowed to ruin the reputation of the majority any longer."

Voigt's views were backed by the T-Mobile team's new team director, Rolf Aldag, and the sport's most respected pro, Erik Zabel. Others were concerned that Discovery had ignored the ProTour teams' agreement not to sign riders unless they agreed to DNA testing—the measure that could clear up any doubts of a rider's implication in the Puerto blood-doping ring.

As a result of the furor, Discovery issued another press release in which Bruyneel said, "There has never been a DNA issue. Ivan agreed through his lawyer even before we signed him to give a sample." Regarding the ethical questions, Bruyneel said, "We believe . . . an athlete is innocent until proven guilty." He then added, "The Code of Conduct creates some issues that we will have to work together to resolve."

It was the ProTour's code of conduct that led T-Mobile to part ways with its former directeur sportif Rudy Pevenage, along with star riders Jan Ullrich and Oscar Sevilla, who were all implicated in Operación Puerto. The German team went even further, firing team manager Olaf Ludwig and releasing another dozen riders, before appointing the former director of its women's team, Californian Bob Stapleton, as the overall manager. Pevenage and another Belgian directeur sportif, Frans Van Looy, were replaced with two younger men, Australian Allan Peiper from Davitamon-Lotto and the just retired Dutch rider Tristan Hoffman from CSC.

Stapleton was not the type of person Europeans expected to see put in charge of the Continent's biggest-budget cycling team. He was not a former pro cyclist, but a successful entrepreneur. He cofounded the American mobile phone company VoiceStream Wireless, which was sold to Deutsche Telekom (T-Mobile's parent company) for $24 billion in 2001. In introducing him to a skeptical German media, T-Mobile International's director of sports communication, Christian Frommert, said, "T-Mobile believes that sport should be kept clean and will actively play a role in helping restore cycling's credibility. The goal, alongside sporting success, is to make an efficient and lasting contribution to resolving cycling's current difficulties."

With that mission to clean up the sullied image shared by his team and the sport of cycling, Stapleton went to work, appointing the recently retired Aldag as team director, hiring respected new directeurs sportifs like Peiper, and recruiting exciting young prospects such as Germany's world under-23 champion, Gerald Ciolek, and 21-year-old British sprinting phenom, Mark Cavendish.

Besides the new staff and riders, Stapleton introduced a stringent antidoping policy, which involved not only more out-of-competition testing but also a comprehensive training and medical program. All the riders on T-Mobile's 2007 roster agreed to submit to DNA testing and to forgo the use of personal coaches and sports doctors.

Stapleton told *VeloNews* that his appointment had received "a very mixed reception." It was positive from his riders but mainly negative from other teams. "I think it's a threatening situation for the teams: an outsider with a very different view, very outspoken," he said. "I think that's perceived as more of a threat by most teams, and it hasn't been a warm welcome.

"I think there's been so much doping and concealment in the sport, that someone who's really willing to take those issues head on—it's risky. I mean, if you have had that in your personal paths, in the history of your team, or maybe currently in your team, this is a 'crazy guy' who could upset your situation. So there has been a certain element of that.

"My goal is to make change happen. It's not a popularity contest. I expected a lot of resistance. But I really want to create a good environment in the sport, for our athletes and all athletes. They all deserve a level playing field, so their personal accomplishments, their personal work, can advance them."

The T-Mobile riders' medical supervision was put in the hands of Andreas Schmid's medical team at the University of Freiburg. Schmid said that besides monitoring for anomalies in riders' blood profiles, his team would work closely with nutritionists and sports psychologists, who would conduct group and one-on-one therapy sessions.

"Our motto is to gain our achievements in a clean way," said Aldag. "Every rider who signs with us has to be aware what he's signing. There will be no deception anymore. The riders will be checked inside out."

And should a rider still come up positive in an internal test, Aldag said, "In case of a doping abuse . . . the riders will have to pay back their salaries for the damage suffered to the sponsor's and the team's image. If a rider gets tested positive we'll know the control system works."

The costly antidoping campaign lost some impetus in the spring of 2007 when the former Team Telekom riders—including Aldag and Zabel—confessed to having used performance-enhancing drugs in the 1990s during a 90-minute nationally televised news conference. The situation worsened when the two sports doctors at the University of Freiburg who were monitoring the riders' health program admitted complicity in providing banned substances to the team a decade ago. But Stapleton stayed centered. He stood by Aldag, spoke individually to all of his 30 athletes, and continued to enjoy the full backing of his sponsors, who later confirmed they would honor their commitment to back the team through 2010.

Asked about his endorsement of Aldag, Stapleton said, "I personally believe that it's never too late to come forward and acknowledge the problems in the sport, and I support these guys for doing it. And I think they're a part of the solution. I mean, it would be nice that we could change the sport, but it takes motivated people within it to do it. And you've got to decide person by person whether you think they believe. For example, Rolf Aldag, I know he believes. I've directly observed it for nine months. He believes in what the team's doing and his actions are totally consistent with [that]. He's as hard or harder than I am on personal conduct.

"He and Zabel and many of those athletes—and athletes now—are caught up in a fundamentally corrupt system that once you're in, it's really hard to get out. It's a slippery slope of doping once you're in it, and now you're part of it and you *have* to lie. You really do, or your career will be over. It's a cycle of fear.

"I was deeply impressed with the pressure these guys were under and to a certain extent the way they'd been tortured for years by this. There's no doubt in my mind that they're anything less than 100 percent sincere. And to those who were skeptical about [Aldag and Zabel's] tears in the press conference—they were absolutely genuine. I can't imagine anybody not believing it [if they] saw it live. And I think that's part of the problem.

"I mean, these guys carry this around and had enough strength to come out and tell a very detailed story, and they did it in front of one of the largest daytime television audiences in German history—five and a half million watching a live broadcast out of a population of 80 million in the middle of a business day. Stunning. This wasn't some benign press statement sent out with a lawyer next to you. This was a deeply personal, public vetting of a dark past. I give 'em huge credit for it.

"I was still disappointed, frankly, that Rolf didn't tell me more, sooner," Stapleton admitted. "We could have done more with it. It would've been a very positive start. Instead, it was a setback for us. I understand why he did it. I think he thought the one chance he had to really do something progressive with the team was jeopardized if he were to have come forward; and he really wanted to do something good and be judged by his good actions. But that didn't work.

"I think I understand a little bit better how it happens now. And it makes me more determined to fight it because I just don't want to see these young kids get hurt."

With his unfettered but sympathetic views on cycling and his team's stepped-up antidoping campaign, Bob Stapleton (no relation to Discovery Channel team co-owner Bill Stapleton) quickly established himself as a person who could help pull pro racing out of its morass.

As T-Mobile was launching its antidoping program, Riis's CSC team announced an even more stringent one in conjunction with the Bispebjerg University Hospital in Denmark. Starting with the team's December 2006 training camp in South Africa, the project claimed to be the most comprehensive test system in professional cycling. Close to 800 extra blood and urine tests, costing the team about $600,000, would be done throughout the 2007 season. The majority of the tests would be conducted out of competition and unannounced, supervised by the Danish hospital's antidoping crusader Rasmus Damsgaard. Test results would be shared with the UCI and positive tests would face the same scrutiny as WADA-sanctioned controls.

"Our ambition is to be pioneers in the work against doping, so we are very proud to initiate this program," Riis said. "We have worked closely with Rasmus Damsgaard to develop the program and we think it gives us a unique possibility to do something for the future of cycling and maybe sport in general."

"This program is . . . groundbreaking in both its shape and content," said Dr. Damsgaard. "Hopefully it will also create a stir within the world of sports . . . so that more programs like this will see the light of day. This project with Team CSC will help show just how serious and uncompromising antidoping work should be."

Team boss Riis added, "I have no qualms about submitting our riders to the most rigorous tests out there, because we want cycling to be a clean sport. I want to prove that my team can be clean and still be good. This is the proof and this is what I want to show the world. I believe in the team. I know they can do it. There's no hocus-pocus. I know there are some who still don't believe us, but we will prove it."

While Riis confessed to having doped in his racing career, no aspersions were placed on Danish medic Damsgaard, who has been crusading for many years against doping in sport. Indeed, a few weeks after Riis's shocking revelations, the strength of the CSC program was bolstered with the half-year announcement of the 2007 test results.

Damsgaard said that more than 400 urine and blood tests had been carried out on Team CSC's 28 riders, both in surprise out-of-competition controls and in races. None of the 198 urine tests returned a positive result and all of the 225 blood tests were within standards set by the UCI and even stricter criteria set by Damsgaard's medical team. To emphasize the program's transparency, full details of the test results were posted on the Team CSC Web site.

"We have created the most rigid testing system in the entire history of the sport and none of our results have indicated anything suspicious whatsoever," Damsgaard stated. "Both I and the UCI consider this program groundbreaking, and in the future it will hopefully gain a lot of support from the sports world in general.

"The program has three main objectives: to catch cheaters and detect doping; to set entirely new standards for the future fight against doping; and to maintain the health and integrity of the riders."

Shortly after the team's test results were published, another potential bombshell was thrown by the German racer Jörg Jaksche in his tell-all interview with *Der Spiegel*. Jaksche won Paris-Nice while riding for Team CSC in 2004 and said in the interview that he used banned doping products throughout his career.

To counteract Jaksche's intimation that CSC was involved in his doping practices, the team's three sports doctors issued a statement: "The medical staff of Team CSC has always been working in an ethical, professional way. In case of illness or injury we try to help our riders by treating them according to the rules of the UCI (i.e., medication and physiotherapy). No products were used that are on the prohibited list. The use of glucocorticosteroids for injuries (local infiltrations) and beta-2 agonists (by inhalation) is part of our treatment possibilities. We only use these when that treatment is medically appropriate, and the use of alternative medications, not on the prohibited list, would be unsatisfactory. In those cases, the UCI was always informed, and the Therapeutic Use Exemption was signed by the cyclist and one of our medical doctors."

The team's head doctor is Joost de Maeseneer, a Belgian, who has been an outspoken critic of doping and rogue doctors for many years. Asked about what teams can do to avoid scandals, De Maeseneer told the CSC Web site, "The right food, the right drink, the right treatment; this is the 'doping' of our team. This is the work of our team. We don't need doping. It takes a lot of work and preparation, but medically, it's the safest way to do it."

> **"It's difficult for us to explain to the general public that we're working with a big professional team, and we say we're clean, but no one believes us. It's a little sad ..."**

He agreed that teams were at the center of cycling's credibility problem. "It's difficult for us to explain to the general public that we're working with a big professional team, and we say we're clean, but no one believes us. It's a little sad," he said. "Who believes you when you're working in the Tour de France, that it is so hard, so big, with so much publicity—who believes you that you can do it clean? There are always one or two guys who do stupid things, but they get caught. So we have to live with it."

Just as the T-Mobile sponsors endorsed their confidence in the German team's ability to race clean, so the California-based Computer Sciences Corporation announced two weeks before the 2007 Tour that it was supporting the team's antidoping efforts and reaffirmed its title sponsorship for at least one more season.

"Needless to say, we are deeply disappointed by Bjarne Riis's recent admission of past doping," said Henrik Bo Pedersen, the CSC official overseeing the sponsorship. "While we remain steadfast in our condemnation of doping, we accept Bjarne's apologies and believe that his candor—and his commitment to cleaning up the sport—represents a potential turning point for cycling. We have therefore concluded that we will continue our sponsorship.

"An important factor in our decision is Team CSC's groundbreaking antidoping program, which has become a model for clean sports in general.

Bjarne has been instrumental in establishing the program, and we believe his continued leadership in Team CSC and the sport is critical to ongoing efforts to clean up cycling. Indeed, we strongly encourage all of the ProTour teams to implement antidoping programs similar to the one in place at Team CSC."

Because Riis wanted his team's antidoping program to be an example for the other team managers, he recused himself from following the 2007 Tour. He met with the CSC staff and the nine riders on the eve of the race at their accommodations, the Selsdon Park Hotel, in south London.

"Bjarne was there and explained his decision to us," related Voigt, the team's senior rider. "He said, 'I don't have enough energy to support you. I don't want to be a distraction.' It will protect us a little so we can concentrate on racing our bikes."

And "race our bikes" is what everyone wanted to focus on.

3

The Road to the Tour

*Getting to the start of the Tour de France can
sometimes seem as tough as the race itself.*

The preseason list of events posted on the modest Barloworld team's Web site included an asterisk next to the Tour de France indicating "participation to be confirmed." The South African-sponsored, British-registered, Italian-run Pro Continental squad advanced toward that goal in May by winning the Tour of Picardy, an event also run by Tour de France organizer ASO.

By rights, the 21st and final team selected for the Tour should have been the UCI ProTour squad Unibet.com, but a season-long dispute with ASO had sidelined Swedish-based Unibet from every ASO race in 2007. The team's title sponsor is an online betting company, and ASO claimed that a French law banned non-French Internet betting firms from its races. So Barloworld's performance in Picardy pushed it to the front of wild card candidates.

Ironically, it was a Tour veteran, South African sprinter Robbie Hunter, who gave Barloworld a chance to earn the Tour's final slot—by winning the opening stage of the three-day Picardy race and then holding the lead all the way to the finish.

Hunter, 30, spent the first eight years of his career competing for big league teams Lampre, Mapei, Rabobank, and Phonak, and riding the Tour five times. "I've always played different roles," he said. "Last year, I was trying to get Floyd [Landis] into Paris in yellow, so I didn't take part in the sprints," he recalled of his duty with Phonak. Although the Paris part of the mission was accomplished, Landis's positive testosterone test ruined Phonak's celebrations and caused its title sponsor to pull the plug. Hunter was left scrambling for a new team. He accepted a late offer from Barloworld, a team established in 2003 with a long-term goal of riding the Tour de France. That goal was achieved earlier than expected when ASO confirmed the squad's wild card spot a month before the London start.

Barloworld is a multinational company headquartered in Johannesburg. It represents and manages leading brands in 23 countries and distributes products and services in more than 100 countries. It has 23,000 employees and annual revenues of $3 billion. The cycling team's budget is less than $5 million—a lot of money, to be sure, but a pittance in comparison with the sport's big hitters, which boast annual budgets of $12 million or more.

Money doesn't always buy wins, though. For ASO, the team's strength in helping Hunter win and defend the yellow jersey was just as important as his overall Picardy performance. Impressively, Barloworld put six riders in the winning break of 26 during stage 1. Besides the experienced Hunter and his former Phonak teammate Fabrizio Guidi, the team was represented in the break by Italians Enrico Degano and Giosue Bonomi, Russian Alexander Efimkin, and Welsh rookie Geraint Thomas. "Now the goal is clear," Hunter said on winning that stage. "Control the race and keep the yellow jersey to prove our team's strength."

The plan worked. ASO liked what it saw, and Barloworld hurriedly put together its Tour lineup, led by Hunter accompanied by a host of young riders ready to put the team's red and white jerseys into the attacks. "I've got a lot of faith in this team," said veteran Italian team manager Claudio Corti, who had participated in the Tour 15 times as a rider and team official. "When I was in the team car following Gianni Bugno [in the early 1990s] we were racing to win overall. During the Saeco team years, we had [sprinter] Mario Cipollini as team leader and so focused on doing well in the opening ten days. Finally, there was the experience with [climber] Gilberto Simoni, who won stages but was never an overall contender. This year is different because we haven't set ourselves impossible objectives but we are determined to be in the action. We know we'll have to take on the race and that is what we aim to do every day."

Besides Hunter, the Colombian climber Félix Cardénas was the only other Barloworld rider to have competed in the Tour; in his only appearance, in 2001, he won the first Pyrenean stage at Ax-les-Thermes, just hanging on to win after a long-distance break, finishing 15 seconds ahead of a fast-charging Lance Armstrong.

Perhaps the most promising young rider on the team was Cardénas's compatriot, Juan Mauricio Soler, who came to Barloworld after a rookie season with the small Italian team Acqua & Sapone.

Soler was only 12 years old when he traveled with his parents from their hometown of Ramiriqui, more than 7,000 feet above sea level in the Andes, to nearby Duitama. It was 1995, the year that the world road cycling championships came to Colombia. Watching Italian climber Marco Pantani doing battle on the mountainous Duitama circuit with Spanish stars Miguel Induráin and Abraham Olano made a deep impression on the preteen Soler. He soon acquired a racing bike and fell in love with cycling even though the only road from his village descended 20km—and the only way home was back up the same 20km climb. That ride made Soler comfortable with climbing.

He wasn't an overnight success as a racer. He competed regionally as a junior for two years and as an amateur for three more years. At age 21, in October 2004, he finished seventh overall in the weeklong Clasico RCN, which earned him a spot on the Orbitel team for 2005. The highlight of that season was the Tour of Colombia, in which Soler finished sixth overall—and, significantly, finished up the two-week race in grand style. In the final three days, he was second on a mountain stage in a four-man breakaway and fourth in an uphill 20km time trial. He won the final stage in a solo move on a hilly circuit in Bogotá.

That performance, combined with placing sixth in his national elite championship, encouraged Soler to seek a place on a European team. Like many Colombians, he went to Italy, and in his first pro season of 2006 raced for Pro Continental team Acqua & Sapone. His most significant rides came at the four-day Circuit de Lorraine in France, where he won the mountain stage through the Vosges in a two-minute solo break to take the overall win; and at the five-day Tour of Burgos in Spain, where he placed second to overall winner Iban Mayo on the stage with a summit finish—finishing 20 seconds ahead of riders like Alberto Contador—and placed seventh overall.

Soler signed a better contract for 2007 with Barloworld. "Mauricio is a true professional who found in our team the perfect conditions to demonstrate his skills," said team manager Corti, who was delighted that his Colombian climber had an immediate success. Soler broke away with Liquigas star Danilo di Luca on the closing climb of the Milan-Turin classic in early March and helped the pair stay clear, with di Luca taking the win ahead of Soler.

To clinch his place on Barloworld's Tour de France squad, the Colombian was the team's top finisher (22nd) at the five-day Ster Elektrotoer race in the Netherlands. Next stop for the lanky Colombian was the Tour. "The Tour is going to be a voyage of discovery for me," Soler said. "I can still remember when I was a boy and I listened to the race on the radio in Colombia every afternoon. I've got to learn a lot but I also hope to show myself, so that one day I can be in the thick of the action."

Getting selected for the Tour on a small team like Barloworld, which has to choose 9 from a roster of only 17 riders, is much easier than the situation on a ProTour squad that has a 30-strong roster. Just ask Mark Cavendish, the rookie British sprinter who was shoehorned into T-Mobile's Tour team at the last minute. How he obtained that precious final slot on his team is instructive.

Cavendish first came to the cycling world's attention when he won a gold medal at age 19 in the 2005 world track championships in Los Angeles, winning the Madison race with senior British teammate Rob Hayles. He followed that up a year later with a gold medal for his native Isle of Man—an island in the Irish Sea halfway between Liverpool and Dublin—in the track scratch race at the Commonwealth Games in Australia.

With the speed he acquired from track racing, Cavendish spent two seasons with the small German team Sparkasse, which was a feeder to the ProTour T-Mobile squad. The Manxman almost began his 2007 rookie season with a victory. "I was good enough to win the first stage of [the Étoile de] Bessèges," he told *VeloNews*. "But I had to work for the team there, so unfortunately I was second [to the Italian Angelo Furlan]. Obviously if I'd won that, people would have opened their eyes quicker."

Cavendish's nascent season hit a setback when he picked up a stomach virus at Bessèges in the south of France. "There's been a big bug that swept through the peloton this year. I was one of the first people to get it," he said. "I went home [in mid-February] and didn't recover from it properly. I tried to get back too quickly because I wanted to be fit for the [April] classics, and I got sick again. Then I started again, and I got sick big style. I was in bed for two weeks. I was, like, sweating, really cold, swapping ends on the toilet for two weeks. That ended my classics season."

Only two weeks after his return to training, Cavendish was given a free-lance role by T-Mobile at Belgium's classic Schelde Grand Prix—and he took full advantage of it. The rapid 197km race, which featured several sections on cobblestones, came down to a field sprint, which Cavendish took in an exciting tussle with veteran Aussie sprinter Robbie McEwen, the owner of 11 stage wins at the Tour de France. With the T-Mobile squad leading him out for the first time in a major race, the young Brit came from behind to beat McEwen by half a bike length.

"I knew I could do it," Cavendish said right after the finish. "It's my first professional win, but I was by far the fastest amateur in the last two or three years. I grew up respecting Robbie and I just hope that I can be the next Robbie McEwen."

After his breakthrough win, Cavendish was given team support whenever a field-sprinting opportunity opened up. The result was two stage wins at the Four Days of Dunkirk in France, two stage wins at the Tour of Catalonia in Spain, and one more at the Ster Elektrotoer in the Netherlands. Six wins in a nine-week period in his rookie year were enough for T-Mobile management to put Cavendish on its long list for the Tour de France.

Asked a few weeks before the Tour whether Cavendish would be selected, team manager Bob Stapleton said, "We're really struggling with that. He's a really young guy. Is it the right thing to do? Will he really benefit from the experience? And how do we set practical limits? He would have no realistic chance of finishing, for sure, so does the ability to ride five, six, or seven stages make sense or not? Just to give him a feel for where he would really have to be in the future, I think we're open to that, and this is a good year for us in that there's not a superhigh expectation [on the team]."

At the same time, Cavendish said, "Of course I'd love to ride it in London, but at the end of the day I'm [fine with] whatever's best for the team . . . whatever gets T-Mobile noticed most, that's what I'm happy with."

To prepare himself for the possible challenge of the Tour, Cavendish moved to Pistoia, Italy, and trained on the steep climbs under a hot Tuscan sun. That prepared him for the rigors of Spain's Tour of Catalonia, much of which takes place in the mountains of the Pyrénées. It was his first ProTour race.

So how did he get through the tough stages? "It was hard," he admitted. "I did suffer a lot. To say that I'd concentrated on training in the mountains the weeks before, and I was one of the worst climbers there, puts in perspective, you know, how much I am a pure sprinter. So it was just a case of being mentally strong.

> **"I did suffer a lot. To say that I'd concentrated on training in the mountains the weeks before, and I was one of the worst climbers there, puts in perspective . . ."**

"There was one day when I was 100K on my own. We were going up to Andorra. I went out the back and I just had to dig in and try to make it. I caught the *gruppetto* on the last climb actually, but I was just smashing myself. I think, mentally, it was the hardest day I've ever had on a bike. I think I impressed a lot of people there by getting through it."

After surviving that stage, Cavendish had another mountaintop finish to tackle the very next day, this time in an individual time trial. "I'd say I had to push myself as hard as some of the fastest people, you know, just to try and make the time limit," he said. "It's always going to be hard for me doing uphill time trials, but at the end of the day it's just about survival for me. I'm an out-and-out sprinter."

The young man's grit greatly impressed his teammates and directeurs sportifs, particularly on the stage following the time trial. "I was actually dropped that day. We went 3K and then directly up a 26K category 1 climb and I was in the *gruppetto*. But we just chased and chased, and didn't give up. And after we got back on it came down to the sprint. It was just about survival in the mountains and whether I'm tired, whether I'm fresh, I've always got the speed at the end and the tactical nous to be there."

He also had the full support of his teammates to lead him out for the stage win. "I had a great team there," he stated. "Selfless. Selfless team. There's a young lad comes on and there's riders like Mick Rogers and Bernhard Eisel working for me. You know all those riders there are preparing for the Tour de France and they're risking themselves to get me to the front at the finish. That makes me more proud than the actual win.

"The last two races, Dunkirk and Catalonia, I got more satisfaction, more pride out of the fact that the team had got faith in me than I had from the actual win. Brilliant."

Respect from his colleagues and confidence in his abilities are crucial in the development of a young rider on a new team. "I'm not going to be modest," Cavendish said. "I always knew I was going to be good. I just wanted the opportunity to prove it."

Cavendish also knew he couldn't do it alone. He had great support from coaches and teammates throughout his career. And he feels tremendously secure with his pro team of choice, T-Mobile. "I know I've got a brilliant team behind me," he said. "I love every rider on the team. I love every staff person on this team. I think it's the best place for a young rider to come into. It's been brilliant. Bob [Stapleton] is brilliant. I'd love to stay here for a long while. Get the wins."

And could he get one at the Tour? "People say to me, 'what race do you want to win next?' and I say, 'The next one with a finish line.' If I'm there at the finish, I want to be first across it. That's how it is."

Besides rookie sprinter Cavendish, the T-Mobile team was planning to debut two other young riders at the Tour, Markus Burghardt and Linus Gerdemann, both German, both age 24, and both in their third pro seasons. Of the two, Gerdemann had the more interesting story. A strong climber who can also time-trial, Gerdemann created waves from a young age. He turned pro in 2005 under Team CSC boss Bjarne Riis, who had tapped him as a potential Tour winner and signed him to a two-year deal. In his very first pro race, Gerdemann wore the leader's jersey at the Four Days of Dunkirk, finishing fifth overall; in his second race, he placed third at the Tour of Bavaria; and then, in his third race, he won stage 7 of the Tour of Switzerland.

That was quite a start to his career. But at the end of the season Gerdemann signed a contract that would take him to T-Mobile when his contract ended with CSC a year later. The proclamation 12 months in advance infuriated Riis, who released him from his contract. This wasn't the first time Gerdemann had left a program on bad terms. During his time with the German national amateur team he was labeled "uncoachable" by Peter Weibel, who refused to take him to the 2004 world under-23 championships, even though Gerdemann was the German national champion.

Had Gerdemann ridden that world championship in Verona, Italy, he would have faced his Dutch equivalent, Thomas Dekker, who won two silver medals there. He's another young man who was about to start the Tour for the first time. Just as Gerdemann has been tapped as the next Jan Ullrich, many believe that Dekker has the potential to become the first Dutch rider to win the Tour since Joop Zoetemelk in 1980. That hope has gained momentum since he won the weeklong Tirreno-Adriatico stage race in 2006. Dekker was supposed to make his Tour debut that summer but illness intervened. Perhaps that was just as well, because a year later he came into the Tour with stronger results to boost his confidence.

At May's demanding Tour de Romandie he placed second on the hardest mountain stage and won the final day's time trial, to take the overall victory ahead of three seasoned grand tour contenders, Team Astana's Paolo Savoldelli and Andrey Kashechkin, and Predictor-Lotto's Cadel Evans. Then, two weeks before the Tour, he took a stage win at the Tour of Switzerland, on the Crans-Montana summit where Laurent Fignon won a stage of the 1984 Tour de France on his way to overall victory.

Those performances fueled the media hype surrounding the 22-year-old's Tour debut. Dekker, however, tried to remain realistic. "After all, I've been plagued by a lingering hip injury the entire spring season," he said at a prerace press conference. "In hindsight, I sometimes wonder how I was able to win both the classification in Romandie as well as that stage in Switzerland. At the Tour, I want to support my team captains [Denis Menchov and Michael Rasmussen] as best I can, and when possible capture a nice prize. I was able to quickly get over missing the Tour last year. My body simply said no. That is frustrating, but I knew I could not venture anything. That makes it easier to accept."

While Dekker was a shoo-in to ride the Tour, the Discovery Channel's Russian hope, Vladimir Gusev, 25, had to battle all year to make his team's Tour lineup. But riding lots of races suits him. While most of today's top professionals ride fewer races and focus on specific goals, Gusev is an anomaly. He's a workaholic.

Rumors of Gusev's old-fashioned approach of racing from February to October began to circulate at the end of his rookie year with Team CSC in

2004. At age 21, he had ridden the spring classics (8th at Ghent-Wevelgem, 20th at Paris-Roubaix), finished the Vuelta a España (in 93rd overall), and ridden the world's and the fall classics (79th at Paris-Tours and 19th at the Tour of Lombardy).

CSC press liaison Bryan Nygaard recalled that Gusev always wanted another race. "The day after Lombardy," Nygaard said, "he planned to ride the Herbiers time trial in west France. It wasn't a race that the team was going to, so he had to get there under his own steam. Well, Gusev had a friend waiting with a car at the Lombardy finish to drive him through the night to France."

After the 1,200km journey, Gusev kitted up and finished the hilly 48km time trial in second place, just ten seconds behind Belgian specialist Bert Roesems.

Gusev started his second pro season with another second place, at the GP de l'Ouverture in Marseille on February 1. He again ended his season in late October at the time trial in Les Herbiers, placing third behind world hour record holder Ondrej Sosenka and world time trial champion Michael Rogers. In between, Gusev was remarkably consistent at the UCI ProTour classics, with top-20 finishes at the Tour of Flanders, Ghent-Wevelgem, Paris-Roubaix, Hamburg, Paris-Tours, and the Tour of Lombardy. Those results attracted Discovery team manager Bruyneel, who enticed Gusev from CSC with a big contract offer. "I think he can be a contender almost everywhere," Bruyneel said. "He's good in the hills and is a strong time trialist."

The Americans on the team soon nicknamed their mop-haired Russian "Goose," and the 5-foot-10, 160-pound Gusev took wing in his new colors. After a spring campaign that included fourth place at Paris-Roubaix (later retracted because of the infamous train-crossing disqualification incident), he took his first pro win, the overall title at the Tour of Saxony, a low-key five-day German stage race. In August 2006, he won the opening 12km time trial at the Tour of Germany (placing fourth overall) and came in 23rd at the Vuelta, after riding support for teammates Tom Danielson and Jani Brajkovic.

Gusev's 2007 season again began in February, before he raced most of the spring classics, finishing an excellent fifth at the Tour of Flanders ("my favorite event") and 17th at Paris-Roubaix, before he began his bid to race La Grande Boucle. By winning the Tour of Belgium, Gusev sent a strong message to team boss Bruyneel that he was more than ready to start his first Tour de France.

The young Russian won the five-day Belgian race with his all-around skills: He was one of only three team members to make it into the 30-strong stage 1 group that split the race open in the fierce crosswinds by the North Sea coast; in stage 3 he won the flat 16.7km time trial by 18 seconds over Quick Step's Belgian prospect Sébastien Rosseler; and he showed great climbing skills to defend his leader's black jersey in the Ardennes with the help of

American teammate Danielson, another Discovery rider seeking to make his Tour debut.

Gusev's victory at the Tour of Belgium eventually hinged on stage 4, and in particular the hill 12km from the finish, the Côte de la Redoute, famed for its strategic role in the annual Liège-Bastogne-Liège classic. While Rabobank's Dutch rookie, Robert Gesink, dashed clear on the steep climb to win for the first time as a pro (he wasn't a danger on GC), Gusev and Danielson controlled an attack by Predictor-Lotto's Leif Hoste, while defending champion Maarten Tjallingii (Skil-Shimano) was happy just to follow and claim second overall this time.

Despite that victory, Gusev still had not been selected for Discovery's Tour team. He clinched the last spot at the Tour of Switzerland, where he won the prestigious mountain stage, finishing atop the mighty Grimsel pass; he did so in his own style by outlasting a group of riders who had been on the attack all day, to finish two minutes ahead of runner-up Chris Horner of Predictor-Lotto.

Gusev comes from the medieval city of Novgorod and, like many Russian riders, lives near Bergamo, Italy. He spends most of the year on the road, seeking success in yet one more race. The next one would be the Tour de France.

4

Preparing for Battle

Sprinters and climbers will do anything to win a stage of the Tour, which can be as big a thrill as winning the Tour itself.

Ultimately the Tour de France is a battle for the yellow jersey, but true fans get just as excited about the daredevils who contest the pack sprints or the climbers who do battle in the high mountains. A boring flat stage in the opening week of the Tour can come to life in its dying seconds when a Tom Boonen or a Robbie McEwen bursts out of the throng to claim victory. Just as engaging can be a late charge to a summit finish by an Iban Mayo, eating into a big lead that an opportunist like Michael Rasmussen has created on a long-distance break over multiple mountains.

What makes the Tour different from every other bike race is that the whole world is watching. A great performance that might be a one-liner in a lesser event can bring an athlete instant recognition at the Tour, where a thousand reporters representing every conceivable publication, Web site, radio station, and television network make winners into instant heroes (or villains).

Nothing grabs more headlines than high-speed crashes, which are a fixture on any highlights reel from the Tour. Most of the pileups occur on the early, flatter stages when the peloton of almost 200 riders is racing flat out in the final kilometers. That's why there are few professions as dangerous and intense as that of Tour de France sprinter. For the men who covet stage wins and the Tour's green points jersey, positioning, accelerating, and weaving through the field while hammering along at 65kph in front of thousands of screaming fans is all part of the job.

At the 2006 Tour, Norwegian strongman Thor Hushovd, while defending the yellow jersey in the hectic finish in Strasbourg, was struck midsprint on the right arm by a fan brandishing a large green cardboard sign advertising the sponsor of the sprints, PMU. After crossing the line, the blond-haired Viking collapsed onto the road, blood spurting from a deep gash. Tour officials banned the green hand-shaped signs from the final kilometers of subsequent stages, but they could do nothing to change the intensity of the Tour's sprint finishes, where horrendous crashes are almost inevitable.

One of the worst came on the opening stage of the 1994 Tour in the northern French town of Armentières. A gendarme standing in front of the crowd barriers in the final 200 meters foolishly leaned out to take a photograph of the approaching sprinters with a point-and-shoot camera. Not appreciating their great speed, he didn't pull back in time, and Belgian sprinter Wilfried Nelissen collided with him violently. Nelissen was knocked unconscious, while his bike bounced across the road, causing French speedster Laurent Jalabert to fall face-first, breaking his jaw and losing most of his front teeth.

Jalabert needed months of rehabilitation and dentistry. He was so shocked by the crash that he gave up sprinting as his specialty (he won the green jersey in 1992) and converted into a GC contender and climber, winning the KOM title in 2001 and 2002.

Crashes have never deterred Belgium's superstar sprinter, Tom Boonen, who negotiates the chaotic field sprints with calm authority. He practically grew up on a bike, learning superb bike-handling skills on the narrow cobblestone roads of Flanders. After dominating his peers through the junior and under-23 ranks, Boonen quickly adapted to the increased tempo and longer distances of pro racing, earning a third-place finish at Paris-Roubaix at age 21 in his rookie season.

Two years later, in his Tour debut in 2004, Boonen won his first stage at the end of the first week and then took the prestigious final stage on the Champs-Élysées. He won two more stages in the first week of the 2005 Tour, but after multiple crashes he quit the race in the Alps, not starting stage 12. That was a huge disappointment for a young man who had scored a sensational classics double at that spring's Tour of Flanders and Paris-Roubaix classics. But Boonen's star kept climbing when he won the world road championship at the end of the same season.

With the rainbow jersey on his back and heavy expectations on his shoulders, Boonen was supposed to give his Quick Step-Innergetic team many more stage wins, and perhaps the green jersey, at the 2006 Tour de France. But Boonen did neither. He spent four days in the yellow jersey, but he came up short in every field sprint and left the Tour after stage 15. Among his reasons for leaving were "sickness, heat, difficulty breathing, and bad hotels."

Asked about his love-hate relationship with the Tour, Boonen smiled and said, "The Tour has given me more than I have taken from it. I've won four stages, I've had the green jersey for two weeks, I've worn the yellow jersey for four days, so that's not so bad on three Tours. But I've had some bad luck also, just like every rider. It's a race like every other, and if you have bad luck or injuries because of a crash, that's it. I like the Tour but maybe I dislike it a little because it is so hard. In any case it's a very nice way to get to know yourself and where your limit is."

Looking back at his disappointing 2006 performance before the 2007 Tour, Boonen told *VeloNews,* "Last year, for sure, I trained wrong. From the first day it went bad; I started to think about it and everything went the wrong way. I was a little too skinny last year. I lost my speed, and then I got sick.

"I worked too hard, that was the problem. I did too much work in the mountains. I was trying to get the condition as high as possible. It was okay, I was very good, but because I did so much work my speed went a little bit down. It cost me 1 to 3 percent in the sprint, and that's the difference between winning and losing. In my case it was losing. It wasn't so hard to realize that afterward.

"This year I am going to the Tour with a different attitude, no pressure. I will try the first week; if I still feel good, I will ride the second week; and then we'll see about the third week. I like the Tour de France. I don't hate the Tour. Everyone keeps asking me about the green jersey. It's a lot easier when I don't think about it."

A couple of days before the Tour started in London, he said, "I feel relaxed now—better than last year. I think I'm fresher. The very, very good sensations in the legs aren't there yet, but I know from the past that my best sprints I always did when I was feeling bad, so I hope it will the same this year."

For the second year in a row Milram's Italian sprint maestro, Alessandro Petacchi, wouldn't be a factor in the Tour's mass sprints. In 2006, he was recovering from a broken kneecap; a year later he was left off Milram's team because he was caught up in a possible suspension after he tested over the permitted limit for Salbutamol, a drug contained in an asthma spray he had permission to use. "I must have given myself one too many sprays and it showed up positive," Petacchi said. But sitting out the Tour was one penalty for his mistake.

Boonen didn't foresee Petacchi's absence having a profound effect on the mass sprints. "The teams of Quick Step and Milram have always been able to work together pretty perfectly," Boonen said. "We're trying to get the same goals. During the preparation of the sprint it was always nice to work together with them. They have the team here right now that is able to do it, and I'm sure they will work for [Erik] Zabel. Maybe the motivation is a little less, but they would be stupid not to. The sprints won't be harder or less hard. It's just one less sprinter to compete with."

Asked about his main objective for the Tour, Boonen played it coy, initially saying, "My main objective is to ride my bike and have a nice time here," before finally admitting, "Of course, to win a stage is the first objective." But given his less than perfect race in 2006, it looked like it would take more than a stage win to make Boonen's 2007 Tour a success. The green jersey, which he wore in 2005 before abandoning, would be a nice addition to his wardrobe.

Though Boonen, the handsome "crown prince" of Belgium, is regarded as the most powerful Tour sprinter, he would again face fierce competition. McEwen, Predictor-Lotto's confident Australian, a three-time green jersey winner, is regarded as the fastest in the final 150 meters, particularly if the finish is uphill. Crédit Agricole's Norwegian star Thor Hushovd, the 2005 points champion, is best when the sprint is a bit chaotic. Germany's consistent old veteran, Erik Zabel, has lost much of his punch since he won the points title six times from 1996 to 2001. And Rabobank's Spaniard Oscar Freire is the craftiest.

Asked about the accuracy of that assessment, Freire laughed and said, "Ah, it depends on the moment. Sometimes maybe I am the fastest. Sometimes maybe I am the strongest—also McEwen, also Boonen. I think we are a little bit different riders. McEwen is always in good position, and he fights to take the position, and he does very well. Boonen has a strong team, he's very smart, and he's also young. He takes a lot of risks because sometimes when you have a lot of pressure, you are very nervous. And when you are young you can do it, but we'll see the next few years, because it's not easy to do the same thing every year. The problem is, he's a good rider, he wins many races, but the Belgian people want the most important victories. It's not easy to be in that situation."

At the 2006 Tour, Freire won stages 5 and 9 before he was forced to abandon due to illness. Heading into the 2007 Tour, a run for the green jersey seemed to be a natural direction for Freire, but perhaps less so for his Rabobank team. "The *maillot vert* is important for me, but last year I was good, and maybe it was not the first goal for the team," he said. "When you are in the Tour and you are thinking of the green jersey, and the team says it's better to be calm and wait and try to win one or two stages and then we'll see, you lose a little morale. This year I would like to be there for the green jersey."

Team priorities are the same reason Freire doesn't have a lead-out train built around his finishing kick. Instead, the Spaniard is known for finding the finish line without the help of teammates. He admits it would be nice to have a train built for him, à la Mario Cipollini and Alessandro Petacchi, but acknowledged that's not Rabobank's primary goal. With riders like Denis Menchov and Michael Rasmussen looking to race for the final podium in the overall and KOM competitions, Freire had to accept being just another star on a stacked squad.

"I think every year it's more difficult to have the train," Freire said. "If you see Milan-San Remo for example, only one team has the train, which was Milram. But they don't have a team for the Tour de France, for the general classification.

We have a different team. We go to the Tour with one rider to do the overall, one rider to do win the mountains jersey, and I think we have different objectives. You have to do different things in the Tour. I would like to have a team for me like I do at the world championships [a title that Freire has won three times]."

Freire's biggest problem over the years has been not being able to race because of injury. The hardest part, he said, was never knowing how long a given injury might take to heal. "Sometimes I would think, if I had a broken arm or something, it's one month's rest and then you are back again. But my problem was different. It was the back, and I never knew if it would be good in one month, two months, or one year," Freire said. "I think all my problems were related with my back. When I was younger, I never had problems. But I think the small problems began in my back and became bigger problems. Now I am good, but I have to take care of my back, because maybe one day I'll wake up and it will be bad. I have to pay attention to it."

Freire has scored big victories despite his often unusual, lingering injuries. Just before this Tour, he had recovered from a crash at the Tour of Switzerland, but he was again plagued by saddle issues like those that forced him off the bike at the tail end of the 2005 season. This time, Freire said, his current pain stemmed from a cyst on the opposite side.

"Once again I have a problem," Freire told *VeloNews.* "I'm very worried. We'll see what will happen. I don't have a lot of time for recovery."

He explained that he had recently switched saddles, which might have led to his condition. After two days of training, he felt pain under the sit bone, the bottom part of the pelvic girdle, known as the ischial tuberosity. Freire had since swapped back to his previous saddle. The cyst, he said, was under his skin, making treatment difficult. "It's the worst place," he said. "If it's outside the skin, maybe it's good, you can treat it, but under the skin you can only treat it with cream."

The injury couldn't have come at a worse time—days before he was due for battle with Boonen, McEwen, and company in the biggest race of the year.

Courage in times of adversity is common among sprinters. Bravery of a different kind is required by the men who shine in the Tour's mountain stages. The opportunists who break free from the peloton need endurance of both mind and body to sustain breakaways of several hours in duration, while the pure climbers, those riders with the best power-to-weight ratios, often wait for the end of a stage to make breathtaking accelerations in their quest for stage wins or the polka-dot jersey of King of the Mountains.

Then there are riders like Fränk Schleck, who achieve success through perseverance, which demands its own type of courage.

At his first Tour in 2006, the lanky Schleck won the stage to L'Alpe d'Huez after a thrilling duel with Italian prodigy Damiano Cunego up the infamous alpine climb, to carve his name into the history books. For the levelheaded Luxembourger, such a success merely confirmed that his career was on the right track.

"I always want to stay the same," said the modest Schleck, who races for CSC. "I just come from a normal family that was bitten by the passion of cycling. I had a hard time to make it as a professional, and I think you should never forget where you are coming from, so I believe and I hope that nothing has changed personally in my life. Of course, for cycling, for the media, a lot of things have changed. But I think that's the price you pay, and I really appreciate it, too."

"I had a hard time to make it as a professional, and I think you should never forget where you are coming from, so I believe and I hope that nothing has changed personally in my life."

While cycling has always been a struggle for Schleck—at one point he reverted to amateur status before being given a chance by CSC boss Bjarne Riis to prove his worth—winning seems to have come easier to a natural climber like Rasmussen.

At the 2005 Tour, the skinny Dane took enough time in a breakaway on the first mountain stage through the Vosges to take the King of the Mountains jersey and also become a GC threat (before he imploded during the final time trial). With Denis Menchov riding as Rabobank's protected leader in 2006, Rasmussen, known as "Chicken" for his likeness to a character on a Danish children's program, instead said he would focus on winning stages and trying to take the KOM jersey for a second consecutive year. He succeeded at both tasks, winning stage 16 in a mainly solo effort over four of the longest climbs in the Alps. Despite badly fracturing his femur in a fall at an Italian race in October 2006, even fearing it might end his professional career, Rasmussen was ready to shoot for a third KOM jersey at the Tour.

Like Rasmussen, Mayo is a pure climber—long, lean, and sinewy. A winner at L'Alpe d'Huez in 2003, Mayo won the Tour warm-up, the Dauphiné Libéré, in 2004, as he broke the course record for the 21km climb up Mont Ventoux. But at the Tour he lost time after a crash on cobbled roads and again in the Pyrénées, causing many to speculate he had peaked too early. The disappointment in front of his Spanish fans was too much to bear, and a dejected Mayo abandoned the race. The Basque rider came into the 2006 Tour as an outside favorite once more after winning a climbing stage of the Dauphiné, but he again quit in despair, this time on stage 11.

For 2007 Mayo was returning to the Tour with a new team, Saunier Duval-Prodir, after a seven-year run with Euskaltel-Euskadi. Whether this switch was the spark he needed to regain his confidence remained to be seen. Did he think he could find the form he had when he was battling with Armstrong?

"When I was going blow-to-blow with Armstrong, it's something that's kind of bittersweet for me," Mayo told *VeloNews*. "I look fondly at those moments, but I've also been frustrated that I haven't been able to regain my footing and return to those heights. I had a horrible year in 2005 and I thought I had returned last year after winning a stage at the Dauphiné, but once again I disappointed at the Tour. You can only make excuses for so long, but the truth is I just didn't feel good when I was on the bike."

Asked how he coped with the disappointments, Mayo said, "You take some blows and sometimes they're hard to accept. When things don't go as well as you hoped, sometimes it's easy to get down and feel sorry for yourself. I have to look at myself in a different way and I have to take things in the best possible way. After I abandoned at the 2004 Tour, it was a major blow. I didn't like anything at all that was happening to me and my morale hit an all-time low. It was hard to keep going. I think that's why this change [to Saunier Duval] is positive for me, because if things kept going like they were, I am not sure I could have continued."

Commenting on the change of teams, Mayo added, "I was an integral part of Euskaltel for a long time. They counted on me a lot, but they also put a lot of pressure on me. I felt a huge weight on top of me that sometimes was too much for me to support. I started to have discussions [with Saunier Duval-Prodir] last year about coming over here. They are confident in me and support me. There is more than one captain on this team with broader ambitions. And the ambiance is much more relaxed."

Mayo was hoping that all the changes would mean a better experience at the Tour de France. "The priority is simply to regain my footing in the Tour," he said. "Since 2003, the Tour has been nothing but disappointment for me. The most important thing is to set realistic goals, to try to win a stage maybe, but we have to aspire for the maximum. If things are going well, who knows what can happen? The Tour is always hard and I will always have the handicap of the time trial. I'd like to do well in the overall, but I would prefer to win a stage. If I could decide between being in the top 10 and winning a stage, I would take the stage victory."

The same could probably be said for most of the climbers. Short of finishing on the podium in Paris or taking the King of the Mountains title, there's nothing like the thrill of winning a stage of the Tour. That was a feeling that Mayo, Rasmussen, Schleck, Freire, McEwen, and Boonen were all hoping to have at least one more time.

5

Confident (and Contentious) Contenders

The Discovery, Astana, and Caisse d'Épargne
teams held the key to the 2007 Tour de France.

Besides signing Ivan Basso in the winter of 2006, Discovery Channel team boss Johan Bruyneel also recruited three other riders who appeared on the Operación Puerto blacklist. All three had been members of the Liberty Seguros team run by Manolo Saíz, the ambitious Spanish coach who previously managed the powerful ONCE team that Bruyneel raced for between 1992 and 1998. The influential Saíz was one of the strongest proponents of the UCI ProTour, the league of 20 elite teams whose charter includes a strong antidoping code of ethics, and yet Saíz was caught red-handed meeting with the Puerto ringleader Eufemiano Fuentes in May 2006, exchanging a briefcase containing almost $80,000 in cash for a cold bag containing drugs and what was believed to be frozen blood.

The three riders Bruyneel signed were Spanish climber Alberto Contador, Australian sprinter Allan Davis, and Portuguese all-rounder Sergio Paulinho, all of whom were barred from starting the 2006 Tour de France for Astana (the Kazakh sponsor that replaced Liberty Seguros midseason that year). Unlike Basso, the other Discovery recruits were eventually cleared of Puerto charges by their respective national cycling federations. So when Contador was asked in an interview with *VeloNews* in February 2007 how he felt about what happened in the Puerto affair, he replied, "I never had any problem with that. I am looking forward because there's nothing that can change what happened. It seems that the Puerto business was more something that was played out in the media and in the end they weren't able to prove anything against . . . the riders."

As for joining Discovery for the fifth season of his pro career, Contador said, "I always had interest in this team and this team was always looking at me since the first year I became a professional. This team has a great structure, successful history, and there's room for me here to grow."

Within a month of that interview, Contador took a superb victory in the weeklong French stage race, Paris-Nice. He was the first Spanish rider to win the prestigious event since Miguel Induráin in 1989 and 1990, and many observers were impressed enough to say that Contador could be the first Iberian to win the Tour de France since Induráin's five-year sweep in the mid-1990s.

An explosive climber with improving time trial skills, Contador had a setback in 2004 when he suffered a brain aneurysm during the Tour of Asturias in northern Spain. He later underwent surgery to treat what doctors called a genetic condition. Contador came back to win five races in 2005 (including a mountaintop stage of the Tour de Romandie, and the hilly 9.3km time trial at the Tour of the Basque Country); and two more in 2006 (another summit finish in Romandie, plus a mountain stage at the Tour of Switzerland).

"I didn't really realize what a big talent he was until he came to our training camp [in January 2007]," observed the Discovery team's Levi Leipheimer. "After you see someone ride and do a few accelerations and big efforts, that's someone who makes a big impression on [you]. I think he's someone who will someday win a grand tour."

Sensing Contador's great potential, Discovery made him the team leader for Paris-Nice. Going into the final stage he trailed the overall race leader Davide Rebellin by six seconds, a deficit he would try to overcome on the two punchy 8km-long climbs in the finale. After seven Discovery riders led the way over the day's first big mountain, Americans Leipheimer and Tom Danielson set a blistering pace up the penultimate climb to La Turbie and then unleashed Contador with about 5km to go on the Col d'Eze.

"We acted like [Contador] was already the [race] leader," Leipheimer said. "Tom hit it hard at the bottom of Col d'Eze, then I took it a kilometer, and then [Yaroslav] Popovych really capped it off. I was lucky enough to be there to see Contador take off and then I listened on the radio to the time differences; that was awesome."

Rebellin's face was twisted in pain as Contador danced away. No one could follow the Spanish phenomenon, and he held a 37-second gap over the summit with 16km to go, having completed the famous Eze climb at record speed. Rebellin couldn't find any allies, and Contador held his form on the long descent to Nice to turn his six-second deficit into a 26-second winning margin.

"This is the biggest win of my career," Contador gushed. "I came here with the idea of winning and, even though it took a while, I'm very happy to have been able to win."

That victory took on greater significance when Discovery's expected Tour de France leader, Basso, left the team in May because of his Puerto connections. With the Italian out, Leipheimer was tagged as the team leader, with Contador as his first lieutenant.

Reacting to Basso's departure, Leipheimer said, "I was preparing to race a good Tour and now we are just one less guy. For me nothing's changed. I've always focused on doing a good Tour and visualized placing very high. I'll go there to try to win because if you don't try to win you can never win."

Regardless, the Californian had already demonstrated the characteristics of a Tour champion. His time trialing had stepped up a notch in 2007 as proved by his TT stage wins at the Tours of California and Georgia, and his climbing ability in the high mountains had already been proven in his outstanding overall victories at the 2006 Dauphiné Libéré and 2005 Tour of Germany.

As if to confirm his uphill strength, Leipheimer made quick work of two-time Giro d'Italia winner Gilberto Simoni and the rest of the peloton on the 20 percent pitches of Brasstown Bald, the grueling summit finish at the 2007 Tour de Georgia. It was on that stage where Leipheimer demonstrated another key element of Tour champions—ruthlessness.

On the morning of the Brasstown stage, teammate Danielson felt good about his chances of winning atop Georgia's highest peak for the third year in succession. Team director Bruyneel first wanted Leipheimer and Danielson to ensure that the team's race leader, Jani Brajkovic, made it safely to the finishing climb before they tried to take the stage win.

"If Jani's okay, then I get to go for the stage win," Danielson said as he rolled up to the stage start. "It's important to be a good teammate. I think we'll be able to control it as we have such a good team, so I should be able to go for the stage win."

As the lead group neared the final, murderously steep 5km of Brasstown, a Danielson three-peat looked likely. Simoni was setting tempo, followed by Leipheimer and Danielson. Behind, Brajkovic was marking CSC's Christian Vande Velde, who sat second in GC.

Then Leipheimer attacked.

"I thought I would try to hit [Simoni] hard first, and if that didn't work then Tom would follow," Leipheimer said afterward. "Fortunately, I felt great, and I had the legs to keep going. And Tom was gracious enough to let me win Brasstown Bald this year."

But when he stormed across the line, looking almost furious for the win, Leipheimer's body language said something else. With both hands pointing at his chest, the message was clear: I'm the man.

When asked by *VeloNews* about his motivation for the 2007 Tour as the leader of a team he first raced for in 2000 and 2001 before five seasons on

European teams, Leipheimer said, "I am motivated by the fact that I am back on Discovery Channel with staff like Johan and Dirk [Demol] and riders like George [Hincapie]. It feels like a homecoming and I am very comfortable in this setting. This entire team is special. The directors, mechanics, soigneurs, et cetera . . . are very close, like a family, and there is not the tension you see with other teams."

Leipheimer hoped that getting better support than he had at the Gerolsteiner and Rabobank teams, combined with his third year of training under California-based Italian sports doctor Massimo Testa, would help him ride his best-ever Tour.

"I improve and grow every year," he said, "physically and mentally. Max Testa not only gives me superior training, but he is always preaching the importance of being confident, especially in the time trials. I did a lot of work with Trek and [aerodynamicist] Steve Hed in the wind tunnel [last winter], changing my position on the bike and, with Max, in my time trial training, and it has really shown. I always try to improve and reach higher, and this year my goal is to finish on the podium and win a stage at the Tour."

Leipheimer's position as the Discovery leader was reinforced at the team's prerace news conference held at the Excel Centre, a sprawling steel-and-glass expo complex in the Docklands area of east London, two days before the prologue. Leipheimer was the only Discovery rider who attended. Asked about his form, he said, "I think I am coming into this Tour a little fresher, and a little off my best form. Last year, I was too good too early. This year, I've tried to push that back because the end of the Tour this year is so difficult."

Leipheimer added that although he'd be the team's main GC contender, Discovery would ride with more options than it did in the Lance Armstrong era. "We're not set up like when Lance was here. I am not Lance Armstrong. There are other riders on the team. We are going to see a lot of Discovery jerseys in the attacks and the breakaways," Leipheimer said, citing Contador, Hincapie, Popovych, and Vladimir Gusev as likely stage winners.

Both Leipheimer and team director Bruyneel said their most dangerous rival was the Astana team's threefold threat of Alexander Vinokourov, Andreas Klöden, and Andrey Kashechkin. "Most of the peloton will be watching Astana. We have to keep an eye on Vinokourov, but also Klöden, who in my opinion is just as much a favorite as Vinokourov," Leipheimer said. "We cannot give them any time anywhere, that's for sure."

Bruyneel then questioned the efficacy of having three riders at a team's disposition. "Astana is the strongest team on paper with three strong leaders—but is that a good thing? I don't know," he said. "It's been proven in the past that hasn't been the best strategy. When you have three potential winners, maybe it's an advantage this year. I expect it to be a very open race."

— ◉ —

While the Discovery team's press conference was relatively low-key, Astana's, which followed immediately, was like something out of a bad movie. Vinokourov kept his paparazzi-blocking sunglasses on as the team strolled into one of the Excel's huge conference rooms enveloped by photographers. Klöden sulked in his chair on the stage wrapped in a turtleneck sweater and a heavy jacket, his team baseball cap pulled low over his eyes. Germany's Tour favorite refused to speak to the German media that had grilled him for months following admissions of doping by his former Telekom teammates.

In between the riders sat Astana team manager Marc Biver, an intense 55-year-old Luxembourger who once managed the Swiss branch of the world's largest sports marketing company, IMG. He opened the tense press conference with a 10-minute tirade about how the team had been persecuted by the media and how they wouldn't answer any more questions about doping. With his shiny bald scalp and piercing blue eyes magnified by thick glasses, Biver had the look of a villain out of a James Bond movie.

"We've had a bad week and we've suffered through a media persecution of the team," an angry Biver said. "There's been no respect for our team and no respect for our riders."

But the press didn't play along, and Vinokourov was hammered over his association with the notorious Dr. Michele Ferrari. London *Sunday Times* sportswriter Paul Kimmage, a former racer who exposed doping in pro cycling in his 1990 book, *A Rough Ride,* confronted Vinokourov directly: "I think it's disgusting that you're working with him, and I'll be disgusted if you win this Tour. Does it not affect you at all that many people in this room are disgusted by what you're doing?"

Vinokourov barely reacted to the abusive question. His answer was spoken in his usual subdued tone. "Ferrari has not done anything illegal," the Kazakh said. "He was never condemned in Italy. He is my trainer, not my doctor. Why do you think that 'trainer' means doping? I have done my work and have nothing to reproach myself for."

As for Klöden, the poker faced German finally muttered, "I prefer to speak about sport, about the Tour. I will not respond to these questions."

Biver said the team had "nothing to do with the former structure of Manolo Saíz," referring to the Liberty Seguros team owner who was at the center of the Puerto doping scandal. He concluded, "Our main objective is to win the Tour. We have a good balance of young and experienced riders on the team. We have a good ambiance on our team now and we want to focus on the Tour."

Though Vinokourov's status as race favorite increased after he won the time trial stage of the 2007 Dauphiné Libéré, all the doping innuendo began to derail the Astana train in the six weeks that led up to the Tour. And after years of riding support for both Klöden and Jan Ullrich at T-Mobile—combined with the disappointment of not starting in 2006—the 33-year-old Vinokourov couldn't hide his bitter desperation to win the Tour. "It's now or never," he said.

— ◎ —

Commenting on the possibility that Vinokourov and Leipheimer would be the Tour's main contenders, T-Mobile team manager Bob Stapleton said, "They are both good bets. They're both winning personalities. Discovery hasn't done great lately but they've got strong players. I think Contador will be outstanding. That's a guy in the mountains who's able to make a difference. He'll be a real aid to Levi. And Popovych is pretty strong. Maybe they're a hope to rival Team Astana. We at T-Mobile need some things to happen tactically to help us, so maybe we can exploit the clash of the Titans."

Also hoping to take advantage of the likely Astana-Discovery clash was the Spanish team, Caisse d'Épargne, whose passionate team director, Eusebio Unzué, had a front row seat at the Tour's biggest battles in the 1990s. The affable Unzué from Spain's Navarre region helped guide Pedro Delgado and Miguel Induráin to a total of six Tour victories in what were his country's golden years at the Tour. Now 52, Unzué is well into his third decade behind the wheel at Spain's most consistent and successful team, Caisse d'Épargne, the successor of the formidable Banesto and Reynolds formations.

In the lead-up to the 2007 Tour, Unzué said he didn't get nostalgic for the Induráin years because his team was a perennial contender. "We were always promoting candidates for victory," he said, "which is never easy, especially when you're up against a phenomenon like Lance Armstrong. Now that Armstrong is enjoying his retirement, the rest of us can once again have dreams of victory. We believe that with Valverde, we have such a candidate."

The Spanish official had no hesitation in naming Alejandro Valverde as his team leader, despite also having the 2006 Tour runner-up, Oscar Pereiro, on his team. "Oscar hasn't been able to enjoy his second place because of the uncertainty [over Floyd Landis's USADA hearing]," said Unzué. "Even if we are awarded the victory, it's a hollow victory because we're all a little discredited. The only medicine is to race again."

Pereiro remained stoic about the possibility of being named the 2006 Tour winner should Landis be found guilty of doping. "The people are treating me in Spain as if I won the Tour de France," he said. "That's very nice. I've been trying to take advantage of the situation and enjoy it to the maximum rather than be bitter or upset."

As for the 2007 Tour, Pereiro, 31, said he was content to race alongside Valverde, who is four years younger. "Alejandro is a rider with a lot of promise and I think he can go far in the Tour," Pereiro said. "I have a lot more experience with the Tour [and] I think it's better for Alejandro that I am by his side. I can teach him when he can be tranquil, when he should take risks."

Valverde had been touted as a Tour favorite ever since he outsprinted Armstrong to win the Courchevel mountain stage of the 2005 Tour. But the young Spaniard had to pull out of that debut Tour with a knee injury, and in 2006 he crashed out with a broken collarbone after just three stages.

"Alejandro has learned from both of those experiences," said Unzué. "He has been able to assimilate the pressure of the Tour, from the media, from the team, from the other riders. The stress and the pressure of the Tour are totally different."

Just *how* different the Caisse d'Épargne boys were to find out 24 hours before the 2007 Tour started in London. Back in the Excel Centre, where the Astana team stars had been grilled the day before, Valverde and Pereiro faced a hostile press looking for answers on their alleged involvement in Operación Puerto.

Despite a request from team director Unzué that journalists only ask queries about sport, one German journalist directly challenged Valverde to comment on a document from the Puerto files that allegedly made references to "Piti," a code name that some said was the name of Valverde's dog and could link him to the Spanish doping scandal. When Valverde stoically refused, journalists yelled out, "Answer the question! It's a press conference!" Another journalist stood up and asked, "Why not answer such important questions in a press conference?"

> **"We are tired of all the accusations. What are the proofs? First, you have to have proof. We are at the end of our patience."**

Valverde finally said, "We are tired of all the accusations. What are the proofs? First, you have to have proof. We are at the end of our patience."

"I don't understand why they keep asking the same questions," said Pereiro. "The moment that we have something official, we can respond. We cannot be denying rumors every day. Tomorrow they might say I have four children; do I have to prove that I don't? I would like to remind people that before being cyclists, we are human beings."

Both riders admitted that the intense media scrutiny had been unsettling. "It's difficult with this situation," added Pereiro. "It gets old to hear the same questions over and over again. I'm a rider who can make a good Tour de France, [but] it's hard to concentrate when it's the same questions every day, every day, every day. Maybe we have an advantage over the other riders because we received the same questions for a long time, and now it won't be a distraction for us."

Things finally calmed down and there were a few questions about the race. Pereiro said he was satisfied that he would start last in the next day's prologue despite not having the honor of wearing the number 1 start bib. Tour officials refused to issue the number 1 bib, which traditionally belongs to the defending champion, because the Landis case remained unresolved. Instead, the numbering this year would begin with 11.

Despite the distractions, Pereiro said he was ready to "fight for victory," while Valverde said he would just focus on making it to Paris. "The last week of this Tour is the hardest," he said. "The most important thing for me is to arrive in Paris. If it's in a good place, even better."

Both of the Spanish stars picked Vinokourov and his powerful Astana line-up as their biggest rivals at the Tour, and cited Leipheimer, Denis Menchov, Cadel Evans, and Carlos Sastre as additional challengers.

— ◉ —

Sastre, Evans, and Menchov were respectively the fourth, fifth, and sixth finishers at the 2006 Tour, and all were looking to climb higher in 2007.

The 32-year-old Sastre joined Team CSC in 2002. Over the years, he had quietly developed into one of the most reliable riders in the peloton. He finished on the podium at the 2005 Vuelta a España, a race that came in the middle of a remarkable streak of riding and finishing five consecutive grand tours, from the 2005 Tour through the 2006 Vuelta.

How far could Sastre go in this Tour?

In 2006 he pulled within 12 seconds of the yellow jersey, Pereiro, on the final mountain stage to Morzine but faded to fourth overall after losing too much time in the last time trial.

"Carlos is a pure climber," CSC team manager Riis said about his reliable leader a few weeks before the 2007 Tour, "but among the climbers, he's the best in the time trial. He's underappreciated by everyone. He's always there, he's always serious, he's always working hard. He's been so close; maybe one day he can win the big one."

Sastre is not one to tout his own chances. When asked about them at the CSC team's prerace news conference in London, he said, "I have respect for all of [the favorites], and as soon as we start the race we'll know who's good and who's not good."

Sastre didn't deny that he hoped to one of the "good" ones. Nor did his teammate Fränk Schleck, the 27-year-old Luxembourger who on his Tour debut in 2006 won the prestigious L'Alpe d'Huez stage on his way to 11th overall. "We know Carlos is in great shape," Schleck said in London. "I will give him 100 percent. I will sacrifice myself for him."

The other CSC team members were similarly supportive. Stuart O'Grady, who won the 2007 Paris-Roubaix classic, said, "Working for Carlos is easy. He's the easiest guy in the peloton to ride for."

Riis too had said he was throwing his weight behind the shoulders of the humble Spanish climber, while hoping that Schleck would also be prominent. "Fränk is still learning, and he will go for the podium with Carlos. He deserves that," said Riis.

Sastre didn't have an easy spring in 2007, however. In March, a hurricane blast of wind knocked the little Spaniard off of his bike during the Tour of Murcia. Wracked with back pain, he was forced to take a ten-day rest right in the middle of an important training and racing period. "I had to make some changes to my schedule and I wasn't at my best at País Vasco," said Sastre, referring to the Tour of the Basque Country. "I felt better at Romandie [in early May] and hopefully I will be . . . ready in time for the Tour."

While Sastre could boast that he had ridden 15 grand tours, including four top-10 finishes at the Tour de France, Evans had ridden just one Giro d'Italia and two Tours in his six years as a pro. That comparative lack of experience led the Predictor-Lotto's Australian climber to take a conservative view of his chances in the 2007 Tour.

"I'd like to improve on my fifth place," he told *VeloNews* in his buildup to the race. "I'd like to go one step at a time at the Tour. To improve on last year's Tour, that's the main thing for me this year. At this point, I'm 30 years old; I've still got a few good Tours ahead of me. That's going to be my ambition for a few years."

Evans then spoke about his performance at the 2006 race. "I was dead after the Tour," he recalled. "That means I rode a good Tour in my book. If you're not dead after the Tour, and you're a GC rider, that means you didn't ride a good one. I gave everything I had. I'm happy with my Tour. Everything I had in the legs went onto the result sheet."

He then revealed that he "was tired before the [2006] Tour." As a result, he had made radical changes to his training program and race schedule in preparation for 2007. "This year I'm pushing everything back and racing later," he said. "There are always plenty of races after the Tour that I'm asked to go to. If I do have energy left over it won't go to waste.

"[Predictor team manager] Marc Sergeant is a smart guy—he sees that every year I'm making refinements and the results are getting better. He understands that I'm also going for results outside of the Tour. I don't do so many races, but nearly every race I do is for a result. I think he's happy I'm doing what I'm doing."

With a later start to the season, Evans wasn't as competitive as he normally is for the hillier spring classics like Liège-Bastogne-Liège. "This year hasn't come so good for April," he admitted, "but I'm not stressed about it because my training is more geared for the Tour."

That later preparation seemed to be paying off when Evans showed excellent form in both the time trials and climbing stages in the high Alps at mid-June's Dauphiné Libéré to place second overall, only 14 seconds down on French veteran Christophe Moreau. "Moreau was exceptionally strong; he's unbeatable this week," said Evans during the race. "I came here to prepare for the Tour. Circumstances gave me a chance to win so I couldn't pass that up. The real objective is to be ready for July."

Evans has trained under Italian coach Aldo Sassi of the Mapei Sports Science Center near Milan ever since he raced for the former Mapei team in 2002. A new focus for 2007 was Evans's position on the time trial bike, even though time trialing was already one of his strengths. "I need to gain in the flat time trials, and [the Tour time trials] are fairly flat this year. That's something we're on. We're also working on the bikes," said Evans, who was concerned about lowering his back to improve aerodynamic positioning. "I can't seem to get lower. My knees hit my chest, so I can't improve there."

Evans may not be perfect in any one of the disciplines required of a Tour winner, but he's not weak either. He is among the best climbers, can hold his own in a time trial, and can win sprints from small groups. Perhaps the Aussie's biggest strength is his ability to recover day after day in long stage races.

In addition, Evans has never been involved in a doping scandal, which has added to his reputation as a natural athlete. When asked if racing against men suspected of doping bothered him, he replied, "I try not to think about it. It makes an already psychologically difficult task even more difficult."

While Evans seemed to be Australia's best hope for the Tour podium, his countryman Michael Rogers of T-Mobile had his own ambitions. Three years younger than Evans, he has time on his side. "My goal is to win the Tour in the next three or four years," Rogers said in early 2007.

Nicknamed "Dodger" and called Mick by his friends, Rogers has long been expected by fans down under to become the first Aussie to win the Tour. But that notion has been changed by Evans, who equaled Australia's best-ever Tour finish of fifth in 2006, tying the mark set by Phil Anderson in 1982 and 1985. Rogers laughed at any suggestion that he has some sort of rivalry with Evans.

"I want to win the Tour. I don't care if I am the first Aussie to win it or not," Rogers said. "I know I still have a lot to learn in the Tour. It's such a hard race. If another Aussie wins it before me and I win it later, that would be fine with me."

In four Tour starts, Rogers had made steady progress capped by his top-10 finish in 2006, when he worked for then T-Mobile team leader Andreas Klöden. But going into the 2007 Tour Rogers still lacked a little spark in the high mountains. Already an established time-trialist (he won three straight world TT titles), Rogers said he had taken the necessary steps to improve in the decisive climbs, which he partly confirmed by taking second place in the major mountain stage at May's Tour of Catalonia, in which he also placed second overall.

"I think Catalunya got his motivation back," said T-Mobile team manager Stapleton. "He was very demotivated earlier. He didn't do well in [the Tour of] California, he didn't do well in Pays Basque, and he really felt that the playing field wasn't level. But he's done good work, he's come up a lot in form, and we've pulled out all the stops in terms of supporting him on equipment."

T-Mobile had selected a Tour team that would lend support to Rogers, but he wouldn't have the entire team at his disposal. "Things will be different for us this year at the Tour. Rogers was tenth last year and I think that's realistic again for him this year," said T-Mobile directeur sportif Valerio Piva, who added that the German team would also shoot for stage wins, either in break-aways or sprints. "That's a big change for our team when we always would shoot for the [overall] win."

Aiming for less could deliver more for Rogers. After all, no one expected him to replace former team leader Jan Ullrich—or would want him to. "I know I have big shoes to fill, but I think this team will do better than people expect," Rogers said tentatively. "The team offered me a chance to be the leader for the Tour. I am ready for the challenge."

At 29, Denis Menchov can no longer be considered a racer for the future—as he was when he won the Tour de l'Avenir (the young riders' Tour de France) in 2001, and took the Tour's white jersey for the best young rider in 2003. He has consistently been tipped as the first Russian who could win the Tour, but inconsistency has held him back. The biggest result of his career remains his second place at the 2005 Vuelta a España, which was later up-graded to first when Spanish climber Roberto Heras tested positive for EPO after the closing time trial. Then, at the 2006 Tour, Menchov won the decisive mountain stage in the Pyrénées but faded in the final week to finish sixth. It was still his best Tour, but his gradual drop from contender to also-ran was not what Menchov had envisioned.

"I had confidence that I could make a good Tour," he told *VeloNews*. "The Vuelta gave me the confidence that I could do well in a three-week tour. At the same time, the difference is big between the Tour and the Vuelta, and I tried not to forget this. The level at the Tour is higher; the hours of work are longer, too. At the Tour the stages are 200km, 220km; at the Vuelta, 150km, 170km—so that's an extra hour to hour and a half racing each day. What's sure is that I have to improve my resistance."

In 2006, Menchov's resistance started to falter on the first alpine stage to L'Alpe d'Huez. Until then, he had enjoyed the firm support of his Rabobank teammates Michael Boogerd and Michael Rasmussen, and the Russian wasn't surprised when Rasmussen attacked the next day to win the stage and take over the best climber's polka-dot jersey.

Asked whether he was concerned about his teammates pursuing their personal goals at the 2007 Tour, Menchov replied, "I am satisfied with the support I am receiving from the team. They support me a lot already, but until the moment comes that I can clearly demonstrate that I am a candidate to win the Tour, I cannot expect the team to completely sacrifice all interests for me. Once I demonstrate that, then the team can take its decision.

"I still believe that a team like this can have riders who have their own interests, either in the GC or the overall, like Michael Boogerd or Michael Rasmussen; we can still be a competitive team and I can still count on enough support. Once I demonstrate that I can win the Tour, maybe some things can change."

Menchov could probably rely on the aging Dutch rider, Boogerd, who was riding his final Tour, and also on Boogerd's youthful countryman, Thomas Dekker, who was making his Tour debut. But what about Rasmussen, the 33-year-old Danish climber, who was the Tour's two-time defending King of the Mountains champion? In 2005, Rasmussen challenged for the yellow jersey and held third place overall until he had a disastrous final time trial and dropped to seventh. Would he shoot for the yellow jersey again in 2007?

Asked about his relationship on the Rabobank team with the ambitious Rasmussen, Menchov said, "I think we are good together. We can each look for our own results and not step on each other's toes. He wants to win the big mountain stages and chase the climber's jersey—that only helps me in the GC—and it's good for the team. Our interests are different, but the team benefits."

At the team's press conference in London, Rasmussen said his objectives remained the same as they were in 2006: a support role for Menchov and, if the situation presented itself, a mountain stage win that might lead to KOM glory. "It doesn't have to be one thing or another, and I think last year was a good example of that," Rasmussen said. "I rode in the service of Menchov for the whole Tour, and took just one day off and got away with the stage win and the jersey, so it was pretty good. Last year showed me that it's not too late to change objectives after the Alps. It's possible to get away with something important even when you're having one or two good days here."

Rasmussen indicated that he was returning to the Tour in good form, no small feat considering he had broken his left femur in a crash at an Italian one-day race, the Giro dell'Emilia, in October 2006. "My condition is pretty much the same as it was last year," the Dane said. "Hopefully the results will be the same also. My leg injury is still there; it's not going away from one day to the other, but it's not really bothering me on the bike. I'm feeling good. I'm ready to get a number on my back and get this show on the road."

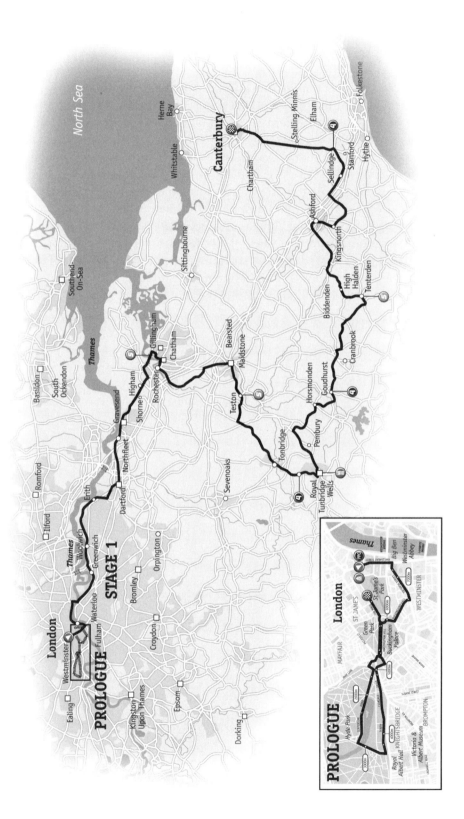

6

Le Tour's Brilliant Send-Off

An estimated 4 million fans watch London's spectacular opening ceremonies and grand départ.

"I hope this is a Tour where we can focus on the racing," said former 7-Eleven team member Dag-Otto Lauritzen, a deeply tanned Norwegian who provides commentary for his national television broadcast at the Tour de France. He was speaking in the shadow of the triple arches of London's Admiralty Arch building, which separates Trafalgar Square, where the 2007 Tour's team presentation ceremonies had been held the previous evening, and the Mall, where the prologue time trial had just finished.

Lauritzen won a mountain stage of the 1987 Tour, the last year the Tour started in a city as huge as London. The start in Berlin had been confined to its western sector, which was still surrounded by the Berlin Wall. "The crowds there were massive," he recalled.

Lauritzen remembers a time when stories about doping rarely broke into public awareness. He said he would much rather be interviewing racers for their daring deeds—including his countryman Thor Hushovd—than reporting on yet another drug scandal. He spoke for the majority of the Tour's 5,000-strong entourage, especially the racers, that had come to London to give the 94th Tour de France a memorable send-off.

Symbolically, there was a clear separation between the Excel Centre, where the confrontational team news conferences had been held during the week, and Trafalgar Square in the heart of London, where the British traditionally gather to celebrate victories in sports and wars, and to party every New Year's Eve.

The official shuttle from the Excel Centre in the Docklands area of east London to the city center took only 35 minutes but traversed centuries of history. The first part was on a double-decker bus via bridges and underpasses to the ritzy high-rise apartment blocks and riverside cafés of Canary Wharf. Then came a rapid boat ride—spectacular in the evening sunshine of Friday, July 6—along the meandering Thames. Zipping over the windblown white-caps, the flashy catamaran passed vibrant new neighborhoods and sparkling glass edifices in the financial district before reaching the city's famed skyline.

After docking at Charing Cross, it was a short walk past pubs, including the Sherlock Holmes, where drinkers spilled out onto the traffic-free streets, to the epicenter of the Tour's *grand départ*. Tens of thousands filled Trafalgar Square, squeezed between St. Martins-in-the-Fields church, Admiralty Arch, and the other grand buildings constructed in another age from Portland-quarried limestone. Dancers and BMXers warmed up the cosmopolitan crowd before the welcoming speeches by the mayors of London and Paris, Ken Livingston and Bertrand Delanoé, who are both ardent bicycle-use campaigners. For the next two hours or so, the fans applauded the 21 teams of racers as they rode up the ramp, painted like a highway, onto a concert stage erected in front of the National Portrait Galley. Riders were interviewed by cycling commentator Hugh Porter and a British network newscaster Katie Derham, with close-ups being relayed to the spectators on giant television screens. After the interviews, each team rode on a short loop down Whitehall and back through Admiralty Arch to the team buses on the Mall. The crowd reserved its biggest cheers for stars like Alexander Vinokourov, as well as the popular Australian and British riders.

When the team presentations were finished, London-born soul singer Lemar performed his version of Queen's "Bicycle Race" and kept the spectators humming as they dispersed into the night, strolling past St. Paul's Cathedral, capped by its ancient dome; filling the pubs, restaurants, and nightclubs; climbing aboard the London Eye, the 443-foot-high observation wheel that looks down on the 2,000-year-old city; or taking taxis, buses, and trains to their homes and hotels around the metropolis.

People had come from all over the British Isles, as well as many parts of Europe and North America, to witness this historic weekend in a country where cycling has deep roots. The chain-driven safety bicycle was invented here, and the winner of the first documented bike race (in Paris in 1868) was an Englishman, James Moore, who was born in Bury St. Edmunds, northeast of London, and lived his later life in the Hampstead suburb of north London.

Coincidentally, one of the men expected to do well in the London prologue, Bradley Wiggins of Cofidis, grew up in the same part of town. He first rode a bike in Hyde Park, where half of the prologue course was located, and he trained in London before his string of individual pursuit gold medals at the Junior World's (1998), World Track Championships (2003), and Olympic Games (2004).

Wiggins hadn't been able to transfer his talent to the road until 2007, when he won the opening time trials at the Four Days of Dunkirk and the Dauphiné Libéré. Asked about his prologue chances by his local paper, the *Hampstead and Highgate Express*, Wiggins said, "Some people are touting me as one of the favorites. But six months ago a lot of people didn't give me a look, and even I didn't, because I hadn't seen any evidence I was capable of doing it. Now I have made that transition . . . I have shown I can do on the road what I did on the track. It's reassuring and it helps me to relax more now."

Another home country favorite at the team presentations, and also favored for the prologue, was David Millar of Saunier Duval-Prodir. The Spanish team gave the Scot a chance to return to elite cycling in July 2006 after his two-year ban for EPO use, which he had confessed to after being interrogated by French police. Millar almost won the 2003 Tour prologue in Paris, losing to Aussie Brad McGee by a split second after the Scot's chain derailed. McGee wasn't back for the 2007 Tour because of knee surgery, but Millar was in London as a favorite.

Millar and Wiggins were only two of five Brits among the 189 starters, the highest number to wear the Union Jack on their jersey since the 1978 Tour. The other three home riders were veteran Charlie Wegelius of Liquigas and rookies Mark Cavendish of T-Mobile and Geraint Thomas of Barloworld. Strangely, none of the five was born in England. Wiggins started his life in Belgium, Millar in Malta, Wegelius in Finland, Cavendish on the Isle of Man, and Thomas in Wales. But all five have raced for Great Britain, and all five were thrilled to be participating in the Tour's first-ever start in Britain (the 1998 *grand départ* was in Dublin, Ireland; the first British Tour stage was held on a circuit course at Plymouth in southwest England in 1974, and two other stages were held in southeast England—Dover to Brighton and Portsmouth—in 1994).

In 1974, there were only two Brits in the race, veteran sprinters Barry Hoban and Michael Wright; they finished respectively ninth and nineteenth in a field sprint at the Plymouth stage won by Dutchman Henk Poppe, though Hoban did score his seventh career win (out of eight) later in that Tour.

Twenty years later, there were again two Brits on the start line, both of whom made headlines. Chris Boardman won the 1994 prologue in Lille on a 7.2km circuit course that featured some cobblestones and half a dozen turns, which didn't stop the Englishman from setting a record prologue speed of 55.152kph and beating runner-up Miguel Induráin, the three-time defending champion, by a massive 15 seconds. Boardman lost the yellow jersey before the race reached Britain for the two road stages (won by Spaniard Francisco Cabello and Italian Nicola Minali), but the first day back in France saw the yellow jersey taken by the other Brit in the race, Sean Yates, who raced for the U.S. team, Motorola.

When the Tour returned to the British Isles in 1998 for the prologue in Dublin, Boardman won again, this time averaging 54.193kph. The two road stages in Ireland ended in bunch sprints (won by Belgian Tom Steels and Czech Jan Svorada), but Boardman crashed out of the race just before the stage 2 finish in Cork and lost the yellow jersey.

Would there be another yellow jersey for the Brits this time, perhaps in the prologue?

Other prerace favorites for the prologue were Team CSC's Fabian Cancellara, the 2004 prologue winner and reigning world time trial champion, and his teammate Stuart O'Grady; the Discovery Channel team's George Hincapie, Vladimir Gusev, and Levi Leipheimer; T-Mobile's Michael Rogers, the former world TT champ; and Astana's Vinokourov and Andreas Klöden.

While all these riders were on their way to Friday night's team presentations, many of their chief mechanics were still working on their prologue bikes at hotels near the Excel Center and others in the capital's southeast suburbs. Teams were scrambling because of an 11th-hour "clarification" of an equipment regulation that affected the riders' time trial positions.

The problem was a poorly written rule that governs hand position when aerodynamic extensions are used on time trial bikes. At the preceding Dauphiné Libéré and Tour of Switzerland, teams were free to interpret what was within the boundaries for positioning when using the high-hands position that Floyd Landis pioneered in 2006. At both races, some riders were allowed to use the position and others were not. What was allowed seemingly came down to how the riders achieved the position. If riders had more than two points of contact—if their wrists touched the bar extensions in addition to their hands and forearms—then the position was not allowed; if only the hands and forearms touched, it was acceptable.

In London, UCI officials reassessed the rule and clarified it. After photos and e-mails were exchanged between the officials at the Tour and Jean Wauthier, the UCI technical commission's adviser, it was decided that both the aero extensions and the riders' forearms must remain parallel to the ground. No matter what shape extension was used, riders were prohibited from using an upright time trial bar position.

Despite this explanation, the rule remained unclear. Cancellara's CSC was hard hit as many of its riders were trying out the new upright position. Not wanting to take unnecessary risks, all then changed back to a traditional position. American Christian Vande Velde had already been forced to modify his position at the Dauphiné.

"They made me change on the line; that was nice," said Vande Velde sarcastically. "It's been a joke. They said because I could, maybe, touch my arm here [at the wrist], which I would never do, that it was illegal. Levi [Leipheimer] was doing his [equipment check] the same time and his was okay but mine wasn't. [Apparently] it's because he has a different kind of bar, but he has the same hand placement as mine."

Apart from the last-minute position change, many of the riders were up in arms because they had specifically changed to a bullhorn bar and clip-on extensions to use the new position. Had they known the upright position was illegal, they would not have replaced their sleeker one-piece aerobars.

"The other bar was much better," said Vande Velde. "It's stiffer, lighter, and more aerodynamic. This setup is what you would buy at a bike shop."

The UCI made Vande Velde's teammate Cancellara switch from the upright position as well, right before starting the Tour of Switzerland closing time trial. "[They made me change] half an hour before the start," he said. "It was the only position that I trained and raced on until that day. It's like for a [soccer] player to change from a round ball to a square one."

On the eve of the London prologue, the position of Discovery rider Gusev's bike had to be changed because it was still illegal, as Discovery mechanics interpreted the rule. "Before, the rule was that the extensions could not be higher than the top of the saddle," said Salvatore Miceli, the Italian marketing manager of FSA, a company that manufactures aerobars. "This is what I understood, but it seems at the stage races, it depends on the judge attending the race."

Even though Discovery's Leipheimer got by with his upright time trial position at the Dauphiné, the team wasn't taking any chances at the Tour. Team mechanics had a special set of custom extensions built and sent to London by the team's American tech guru, Steve Hed, but at 4:45 Friday afternoon they decided not to risk using them.

Discovery team director Johan Bruyneel said the rule appeared to have been drawn up arbitrarily. "The new rules for the time trial do not seem to have been developed with much thought. Levi's position is not dangerous or a major deviation from the usual position used by many riders," Bruyneel observed. "It only draws attention because he is smaller and more compact than most, but the position is not drastic. There has been no clear explanation as to why he cannot use this position and this is what bothers me the most. He spent a lot of time in the wind tunnel finding a position that is fast and safe, and now he has to change. Rules like this are being made by people who do not understand the correct application. These types of decisions limit the advancement of the sport."

Bruyneel later added that he was trying to accommodate any possible interpretation of the rule by the officials. "I just think it's stupid if you make a rule and at the end nobody knows anymore what it's about," he said.

Ben Coats, Trek's liaison to the Discovery team, observed that UCI officials in London seemed to allow Leipheimer's position, but if other teams sent a complaint to the UCI technical commission, it would be evaluated and he could be disqualified.

While some team mechanics were still dealing with the UCI's clarification of equipment regulations late Friday afternoon, others were still building special bikes for the prologue. With dinnertime rapidly approaching, T-Mobile's Rogers was conferring with his team's mechanics next to a half-built aluminum time trial bike. Across the parking lot, Saunier Duval mechanics were tidying up the team truck, where all of the bikes, including Millar's, were snugly packed away and ready for the next day's ride into the heart of London.

The common bond between the T-Mobile and Saunier Duval teams was that each had equipped its time trial star with a third TT bike specially built for Saturday's prologue. The course was said to have only one corner that required braking, so these riders had refined their regular positions for maximum aerodynamics and maximum rear-wheel traction.

Saunier Duval mechanics were kind enough to show off the custom-painted Scott Plasma, supplied by Scott USA, although it had already been packed away in the truck. While the frame was said to be identical to his long-course and backup time trial bikes, the cockpit of the special prologue machine had a few modifications for the city streets, which were expected to be bumpy.

Millar's bike had aero extensions that were longer than the ones used for a traditional time trial. His mechanics had also fixed small homemade stops at the ends of the bars to keep his hands from slipping off. Below, at the crankset, Millar's bike had a chain watcher affixed to his braze-on derailleur mount; he didn't want his chain unshipping, as it did in 2003, when he rode for Cofidis.

Before the Tour, it was said that T-Mobile's Australian leader, Rogers, had spent less time honing his time trial strength in favor of improving his climbing ability in the high mountains. But with the effort his mechanics were making in the last hours before the prologue, he still had the aspiration, and the confidence, to shoot for a TT success.

The mechanics were working on a Giant aluminum bike made specifically for Rogers and the London course. They were tight-lipped as to how it was different, but the major changes presumably pertained to the bike geometry. "It's a special bike for the prologue," said one mechanic. "I can't tell you any more."

The rumor floating around the pits was that Rogers had tested some of his competitors' bikes prior to the start of the Tour and found at least one that was faster. This new bike supposedly mirrored the geometry of the fastest one. Visually comparing Rogers's backup Giant TCR Advanced carbon fiber machine and the new bike, it looked as though the new one had slightly shorter chainstays.

Whether the prologue specials would make a difference was something everyone would have to wait to see. But clearly riders like Leipheimer who had to change the hand positions they had used all year (the American had won time trials at the Tours of California and Georgia, and finished second in the Dauphiné prologue) would start in London with some doubts that the modified bike would be as fast as it could be.

When outgoing race director Jean-Marie Leblanc chose London as the starting point of the 2007 Tour, he didn't know that his decision would be both prescient and fortuitous. It was prescient because London is a city enjoying a twenty-first-century renaissance, with an influx of immigrants from every continent that has given new life to this proud capital and could give new life to the Tour. It was fortuitous because pro cycling, and the Tour in particular, was in need of renewal as it sought to put its ongoing doping problems in the rearview mirror.

London had already delivered the finest team presentations in recent history. And now came the prologue on a course that was even more spectacular than the one the French had chosen to kick off the centennial Tour in 2003. That circuit in Paris was impressive, starting at the foot of the Eiffel Tower, looping over the Seine, past the Place de la Concorde, and back along the Left Bank to a finish by Les Invalides. But London's would pass a much longer string of historic sights, starting outside the Old War Office Building in Whitehall, near the prime minister's residence on Downing Street. It would then pass Big Ben, the Houses of Parliament, Westminster Abbey, Buckingham Palace, go through the Wellington Arch, around Hyde Park and its lake, the Serpentine, and return via Constitution Hill to finish on the Mall, the regal avenue linking the Palace with Admiralty Arch.

Despite London's sporting weekend, which included the finals of the Wimbledon tennis tournament and Formula One's British Grand Prix, an estimated million-plus spectators lined the prologue course, a good proportion of them picnicking in Hyde Park and St. James' Park, watching the action on the 18 big-screen TVs set around the course.

The prologue's success was greatly appreciated by pre-Tour favorite Vinokourov, who was trying to forget the media furor over his controversial Italian *preparatore,* Dr. Michele Ferrari. "I was surprised by the crowd massed all along the course," Vinokourov said. "This is the best publicity that cycling could have at this moment."

Standing on the Mall, London's most regal avenue, at 6:15 p.m. on that Saturday evening, July 7, nobody would have taken this for a sport riddled with scandal. Right then, when Tour prologue favorite Fabian Cancellara came powering toward the finish line on the Mall, cycling seemed more vibrant than ever.

The sleek Swiss time trial machine, wearing a long-sleeved, rainbow-striped skin suit of world champion, sped between fans packed six deep behind the barriers. Above him, blown by a fresh westerly breeze, dozens of huge Union Jacks flew from gold-crown-topped flagpoles. At his back, late evening sunlight magically lit the gilt-covered angel atop the Victoria Memorial outside Buckingham Palace. And to his right, beyond the shade-dappled lawns of St. James Park, the London Eye poked over the treetops like a giant bicycle wheel. A symbol, perhaps, of a renaissance for both London and cycling.

In these monumental surroundings, it was only fitting that a world champion would win. Cancellara took the prologue by the third-widest margin (13 seconds) in the third-fastest average speed (53.660 kph) in Tour history to take the coveted yellow jersey.

It was a remarkable ride on a course that wasn't as straightforward as it looked. CSC's Stuart O'Grady had set the fastest halfway time (5:04) in the first half of the field when his right pedal clipped a plastic-covered hay bale, "It just threw my foot into the back wheel and threw me completely off balance," said the winner of Paris-Roubaix, who crashed over his handlebars. "And that was that. I took a bit of a blow to the knee—it's a bit inflamed. But it'll be all right."

His teammate Cancellara was smooth and fast from start to finish. Even though his margin of victory was a shock, what may have been more significant for this Tour was the fact that Klöden finished second. The reclusive German—who barely spoke at the Astana team news conference—had never done well in Tour prologues. Perhaps he knew that his legs would be talking for him this time. But his prologue performance sent a warning to all potential rivals, including teammate Vinokourov, that he, Andreas Klöden, two-time Tour podium finisher and best friend of the disgraced Jan Ullrich, was capable of becoming the second German to win the Tour, 10 years after Ullrich.

When Cadel Evans, one of his probable challengers, was told that Klöden beat him by 23 seconds, the normally reticent Australian exclaimed, "Oh shit!" And then added, "I wouldn't say that's good [for me]. It concerns me. That's really quite impressive."

Equally astonished was U.S. champ George Hincapie, who finished in an excellent third place in the prologue, but 23 seconds slower than Cancellara (and 10 seconds behind Klöden). Hincapie, who lost last year's prologue by less than a second to Thor Hushovd (who was not 100 percent fit and came in 28th this year), couldn't believe he had been beaten by such a huge margin in such a short distance (7.9km). "It was very, very amazing," said the Discovery Channel rider. "I went as hard as I could and couldn't go much faster. We had a strong headwind on the way out, and on the way back it was 55×11 or 12 the whole way. I was disappointed with my result but I'm pleased with my effort. There was one corner where I screwed up but it was not significant at the end of the day."

Wiggins, who finished fourth on the same second as Hincapie, was equally shocked. "What's that, 23 seconds?" he reportedly asked his team personnel as he warmed down. "Well, what can you do? It's not as if it was only one second. I gave it everything. I didn't brake at all throughout and I could not have gone any faster. I said I wouldn't let the crowd get to me, but once I was out there it was amazing and it gave me a real lift."

Cancellara, who has two identical Cervélo P3s, used the same one he rode to convincing victories at the opening and closing time trials of June's Tour of Switzerland. And just as at the September 2006 world's, the Swiss was at a higher level than the opposition—the other prologue favorite, Millar, was 33 seconds back in 13th place. Cancellara's effort was similar to Britain's prologue speed record holder Boardman with his 15-second margin at the 1994 Tour, and Belgian Freddy Maertens, who beat Spanish prologue specialist Jesús Manzaneque by 17 seconds in 1976.

At 6 feet 3 and 171 pounds, Cancellara is built for time trialing. His long legs enable him to turn long 177.5mm cranks, and years of training under the controversial Italian sports trainer Dr. Luigi Cecchini helped him learn the high-cadence pedaling style that Lance Armstrong perfected with Ferrari. And just as Armstrong eventually dropped his Italian guru, so Cancellara has reluctantly stopped working with Cecchini as part of the CSC team's policy of distancing its riders from any semblance of doping.

"It's not easy to find someone with a lot of experience to train me like Cecchini," Cancellara said. "He had 30 years of experience. But I'm on the best team in the world. If I was on a bad team I wouldn't be here."

When he won in the 2004 Tour prologue in Liège, Belgium, ahead of Lance Armstrong, Cancellara was a promising, ambitious, yet largely unknown racer riding for the Fassa Bortolo team. He left when the Italian *squadra* folded at the end of 2005, and joined CSC. More mature but still ambitious, Cancellara roared into the 2007 prologue determined to erase the disappointment of being left off CSC's nine-man Tour team a year earlier.

"It was a big difference when I won in Liège. No one knew me and no one expected me to win," he said. "This time was different. Everyone called me the favorite and I had all the pressure. To win in London in the world champion's jersey on 07-07-07, that makes it even better.

"We can race now with less pressure. I trained to be strong for the entire Tour, not just in the prologue. I can maybe win another stage in the time trial, but I will also be helping the team and helping Carlos Sastre."

While the Swiss rider brought CSC the yellow jersey (much to the liking of team boss Bjarne Riis, who greeted Cancellara at the team bus before voluntarily leaving the Tour so his recent confession of EPO use in 1996 wouldn't be a distraction), his teammates Sastre and Fränk Schleck began their Tour campaigns with awful rides. Sastre, who just missed the final podium in the 2006 Tour, was 92nd (42 seconds behind Klöden) and Schleck 95th (another second back). The team played down the poor performances by its two leaders, but the lost time would probably prove costly later in the Tour.

As Evans said about his own 23-second loss to Klöden, "People say that's not so much once we reach the mountains, but in my first Tour I was eighth, just 25 seconds off fifth place. That's a big difference."

And in a Tour as wide-open as this one, a half minute could be the difference between winning and losing the title. That's why it was worth noting the gaps that Klöden created over the other prerace favorites: 17 seconds on teammate Vinokourov; 22 seconds on Discovery's Alberto Contador; 23 seconds on Evans; 24 seconds on Michael Rogers and Oscar Pereiro; 27 seconds on Leipheimer and Rabobank's Denis Menchov; and 30 seconds on Caisse d'Épargne's Alejandro Valverde.

Leipheimer didn't blame the last-minute changes to his time trial position for what he admitted was a mediocre ride in comparison to the second place he took in the Dauphiné prologue only three weeks earlier. "I was a little blown," he said. "It's not my best time trial, but I'm coming into this Tour very fresh. I didn't expect to be at my best. I had some sensations that I am very fresh, so we'll see how the race goes."

Teamwise, Discovery Channel (with Contador and Leipheimer) was not far behind Astana (with Klöden and Vinokourov) and Caisse d'Épargne (with Pereiro and Valverde). These three pairings, perhaps with CSC's Sastre and Schleck, and climbers Evans, Iban Mayo, and Michael Rasmussen, looked like the ones that would decide this Tour when it reached the Alps and Pyrénées.

In its prerace forecast, the French sports newspaper *L'Équipe* made Vinokourov its three-star Tour favorite, followed by Klöden, Schleck, and

French national champion Christophe Moreau with two stars, and Menchov, Sastre, Evans, Valverde, Discovery's Yaroslav Popovych, and Caisse d'Épargne's Vladimir Karpets as its one-star favorites. These predictions either proved how open this 94th Tour was going to be, or they simply lacked insight: how could a publication that is regarded as Europe's premier inside source for cycling ignore Discovery's coleaders, Contador and Leipheimer, and former top 10 finishers Mayo, Pereiro, Rasmussen, and Rogers?

After the challenging prologue, the race favorites could look forward to letting the sprinters fight it out in four of five stages. Just as a race without an overwhelming favorite was promising to reveal new winners in the mountains, so the dynamic of the bunch sprints was unpredictable after dominant Giro d'Italia stage winner Alessandro Petacchi was barred from the start—pulled from the Tour when the Italian cycling federation recommended a one-year suspension after one of his drug tests from the Giro came back over the legal limit for his prescribed asthma medication, Salbutamol.

In Petacchi's absence, defending green jersey Robbie McEwen was ready to extend his list of 11 Tour stage wins, while perennial rival Tom Boonen was eager to forget his blank run at the 2006 Tour. Their respective Predictor-Lotto and Quick Step-Innergetic teams dominated the opening road stage, but the finish at Canterbury was far from predictable.

Stage 1's 203km trek from London was watched by an estimated 2.4 million spectators. The thick crowds, combined with narrow winding roads past the hop fields and country pubs through the rolling hills of the so-called Garden of England, proved to be a major factor in the outcome, keeping the riders on all-day alert and eventually contributing to crashes that would affect the stage's outcome.

The fans stood five and six deep on the streets of London, with the race starting from the Mall and weaving a touristy route over the Thames bridges and past the Tower of London to Tower Bridge, where the peloton stopped between hundreds of yellow-shirted club cyclists and a military band, before the Tour's official ribbon was cut and the race departed to the east.

The day would roughly follow the walk taken by Charles Dickens's autobiographical character David Copperfield from London, via Canterbury, to Dover—where the Tour entourage would cross the English Channel to France. Copperfield was a young boy when he made the long journey after escaping from forced labor in a London factory. His walk was complicated by robbers and beggars in the small villages and towns he traversed.

The back roads through the Kent countryside, with its half-timbered houses and stone castles, haven't changed much since Dickens's times. The rolling English roads perfectly suited a solo effort by Britain's Millar, who broke clear of the pack exiting the London suburbs. By the time he was caught by four chasers after 48km, he had a 5:35 lead.

When the Quick Step and Predictor-Lotto teams took up the chase after CSC's long effort, the gap quickly dropped to two minutes, with Millar falling back to the peloton. Only one of the breakaways, Frenchman Stéphane Augé of Cofidis, stayed clear till the last of three category 4 climbs, while Saunier Duval pulled Millar for several kilometers and set him up for second place on the Farthing Common hill, which earned him the day's polka-dot jersey.

While the Saunier Duval men were pulling the pack through the twisting country lanes, there was a small pileup on a left turn just about 22km from the finish. Half a dozen riders fell and caused a score more to stop. Among the fallen was McEwen.

"The fall itself was just on a small road," reported the 35-year-old Aussie sprinter. "They were braking in front of me and almost stopping. I also went hard on the brakes. I almost stopped, but whoever was behind me wasn't paying attention and just ran straight into the back of me. It flipped me over the handlebars. I actually tried to keep flipping over to land on my feet or land on my back, but my hand was the first thing to hit the ground and then my knee.

"The first thing I thought was I'd broken my wrist because it wouldn't move and it was very sore. I also thought I'd broken my rib [as] I couldn't breathe." After the stage, McEwen grimaced while cradling and icing his right wrist, and following the postrace doping control he went to the hospital for an x-ray and an examination.

While McEwen's Italian teammate Dario Cioni helped his leader get back on his feet and began pacing him up the road, one of his potential rivals, T-Mobile's rapid Brit, Mark Cavendish, was also in trouble. "I was coming up the final climb and hit a spectator at the side of the road and came off my bike," Cavendish said. "By the time I'd had a bike change I was too far behind."

The fiery Cavendish was furious that he had lost a once-in-a-lifetime chance to win a Tour stage in his homeland, and after finishing the stage 2:45 back, he sped past the stragglers slowly heading to the team compound, dropped his bike with a team worker, and stormed onto his team bus with his mouth clenched tight in anger.

Cavendish had only frustration after his crash. That was in sharp contrast to the remarkable recovery made by McEwen, who was gradually being paced back to the fast-moving pack led by Boonen's Quick Step train. "I didn't think he was going to come back once Quick Step started riding," said teammate Evans. "And the next second I see Robbie flying past."

Four Predictor riders pulled McEwen for 15km, and two lead-out men, Leif Hoste of Belgium and Californian Fred Rodriguez, were waiting to take McEwen through to the front. That proved a challenge on a looping 3km run-in around Canterbury's thousand-year-old city walls that included three roundabouts and a curving uphill haul to the line.

Before the final kilometer. Rodriguez lost McEwen's wheel, as did Hoste, on a tricky chicane. The three-time U.S. champ said, "It was a chaotic finish. At first I panicked a little, saying to Leif, 'Go, go, go, go! We have to make it back on.'

"And then we make the last corner, we're in about 20th position, I look up and there was nobody really leading it out. We were all coasting for a little bit, and I think it was Barloworld's [Enrico Degano and Robbie Hunter] who went first. But at that point the speed was so slow that it was just a sacrifice to get it up to speed."

"I tried to get a gap," explained Hunter, "but unfortunately the guys came after me straightaway. It happens."

"I knew the sprint was difficult," said McEwen, who was still moving up the line. "It was uphill and there was a bend to the left and you could only see the finish with about 160 meters to go. For me, it was a finish similar to [the stage I won at] St. Quentin last year. With the speeds low like they were today toward the finish, that's good for me, because I have good acceleration. I saw the board of 200 meters and that's when I started to move. I came out of the wheels and out into the wind at 150 and that was the perfect moment, and I was strong enough to hold everybody off."

Rodriguez added that the slowing and subsequent acceleration "put Robbie in a perfect position for an explosive sprint that nobody else in the peloton could even imagine doing. He had so much adrenaline coming back from crashing. . . . He was just on fire."

The burst by the injured McEwen was so fast that Boonen sat up and conceded second place to a still sprinting Hushovd. "During the sprint itself, nothing was hurting except my muscles, which is normal," said McEwen. "But 100 meters after the finish everything started to hurt again. But it's worth that pain to win a stage at the Tour de France."

The cocksure Aussie rider admitted, though, that he was nervous to see his x-ray results. "It was a great day for me," he concluded. "But now I'm starting to get a bit worried for the rest of the Tour."

For GC riders like his teammate Evans, the challenge was simple survival. "Just getting through the first week safely is like winning a race," Evans said, as he rolled down to the team buses before the ride through the Channel Tunnel to France. "It was a bit hairy today. I was surprised there weren't more crashes. It was a beautiful race, lots of people, but too many people, too many traffic islands and roads like this," he said, pointing at cracks along the centerline of the road where he was riding. "It's quite dangerous racing at 60kph on stuff like that."

Accidents aside, what was most gratifying about the Tour's spectacular English start was that all the action was about racing, not doping. With an astonishing four million watching its *grand départ*, the Tour proved to be as impregnable as ever. Its popularity was still growing, despite the plague of doping stories that threatened to drag it down.

But would it be the same story on the upcoming days through Belgium and into France?

PROLOGUE: LONDON–LONDON TIME TRIAL

1. Fabian Cancellara (Swi), CSC, 7.9km in 8:50 (53.7kph)
2. Andreas Klöden (G), Astana, at 0:13
3. **George Hincapie (USA), Discovery Channel, at 0:23**
4. Bradley Wiggins (GB), Cofidis, at 0:23
5. Vladimir Gusev (Rus), Discovery Channel, at 0:25
6. Vladimir Karpets (Rus), Caisse d'Épargne, at 0:26
7. Alexander Vinokourov (Kz), Astana, at 0:30
8. Thomas Dekker (Nl), Rabobank, at 0:31
9. Manuel Quinziato (I), Liquigas, at 0:32
10. Benoît Vaugrenard (F), Française des Jeux, at 0:32

STAGE 1: LONDON–CANTERBURY

1. Robbie McEwen (Aus), Predictor-Lotto, 4:39:01
2. Thor Hushovd (N), Crédit Agricole, same time
3. Tom Boonen (B), Quick Step-Innergetic, s.t.
4. Sébastien Chavanel (F), Française des Jeux, s.t.
5. Romain Feillu (F), Agributel, s.t.
6. Robert Förster (G), Gerolsteiner, s.t.
7. Oscar Freire Gomez (Sp), Rabobank, s.t.
8. Marcus Burghardt (G), T-Mobile, s.t.
9. Francisco Ventoso (Sp), Saunier Duval-Prodir, s.t.
10. Tomas Vaitkus (Ltu), Discovery Channel, s.t.

GENERAL CLASSIFICATION AFTER STAGE 1

1. Fabian Cancellara (Swi), CSC, 4:47:51
2. Andréas Klöden (G), Astana, 00:00:13
3. David Millar (GB), Saunier Duval, 00:00:21
4. **George Hincapie (USA), Discovery Channel**, 00:00:23
5. Bradley Wiggins (GB), Cofidis, 00:00:23
6. Vladimir Gusev (Rus), Discovery Channel, 00:00:25
7. Vladimir Karpets (Rus), Caisse d'Épargne, 00:00:26
8. Thor Hushovd (N), Crédit Agricole, 00:00:29
9. Alexander Vinokourov (Kz), Astana, 00:00:30
10. Thomas Dekker (Nl), Rabobank, 00:00:31

CHRISTIAN VANDE VELDE | JULY 7

Fatherhood and, oh yeah, that bike race, too.

The pre-*everything* is finally over.

As of Friday evening, there had been little biking, a ton of bus riding, two press conferences, health controls, team presentations, sponsors . . . enough! So today getting ready for the race was a nice change.

But before we go into any of these bike-related things, I have something much bigger in my life than the Tour de France: I became a father last week. Leah gave birth to Uma last Wednesday night. Both girls are great and I am more than proud of my wife and the fact that I am now a *father*!

So, the last week was a bit crazy at home and not your typical week of prep for the Tour. I wouldn't trade the experience for anything in the world. Missing my daughter during the first month of her life is not easy, but the opp' to ride the Tour with the team that we have, and of course the fact that I don't have a choice, helped me get on the plane.

Fast-forward to Saturday night and I am on the bus and—surprise, surprise—on the way back to the hotel. The mood is now calm after everyone freaked out watching our teammate Fabian Cancellara smoke the entire peloton.

It was insane. I am still in shock as to how fast he went. We all were expecting him to win, but like *that*? Damn! I think that I spent as much energy watching him as I did racing. Truly, I am in awe.

I started my '07 Tour campaign pretty poorly. I felt okay but I wasn't so sharp, mostly on the mental side. But I am happy to be done with today and to get on with the race tomorrow.

Fabian will be in yellow tomorrow and, of course, that means we will be on the front protecting him. I don't know why. He's *obviously* strong enough to ride for himself.

The front isn't always the best way to start the Tour, but on the roads that we will race on tomorrow, it could be a blessing in disguise. We will waste some energy to be sure, but maybe we will also stay out of trouble.

See you on the front tomorrow morning.   ⊗

RIDER DIARY

SIMON GERRANS | JULY 7

What a rush!

What a way to kick off the 2007 Tour! The prologue in London was nothing but an enormous rush. There's no feeling like rolling down the start ramp to the roar of a million spectators. Hearing the crowds shout "GO! GO! GO!" rather than the usual "Allez! Allez! Allez!" was really cool and I'm sure is going to give the English speakers in the bunch an extra motivation.

It was a huge relief to finally get the race under way, as the past few days of the whole prerace protocol of medical checkups and interviews really drags on. Pressure just seems to build and build.

I was wrapped to get selected for Ag2r's Tour de France team. I was the ninth rider selected and I only got the final nod earlier in the week.

Following such a successful Tour in 2006 and also having Christophe Moreau, the recently crowned French champion, as team leader, Ag2r is going to be under a lot of pressure for results. Our number one objective for the Tour is to have Moreau standing on the podium come Paris. Following his recent wins at the Dauphiné and the French championships, everybody on the team believes it is achievable.

Our Ag2r Prévoyance team consists of Christophe Moreau (La Grande), Stéphane Goubert (Gouby), Martin Elminger, Ludovic Turpin (Ludo), Sylvain Calzati (Calzate), Cyril Dessel, John Gadret, Jose-Luis Arrieta (Arrie), and, of course, myself.

My role on the team is simple: I take care of basic domestic duties, fetch food and drinks for everyone, and do my best to make sure Moreau doesn't have any wind in his face for the first week of the Tour. Then if everything goes to plan, my teammates and I will be riding to defend his place on GC through the mountains and the final few days into Paris.

Personally, I am really hoping to go for a stage win. During the Tour's transfer stages between the Alps and the Pyrénées and then in the final few days before Paris, where it's an advantage for the team to have someone in the breakaway, I'm hoping to go for it.   ⊗

RIDER DIARY

SIMON GERRANS | JULY 8

You can't see the race for the fans.

The crowds!! I have never seen so many people anywhere in my life, let alone at a bike race. By the time we'd finished the stage in Canterbury my ears were nearly ringing. Spectators literally lined the road for the whole 203km. One of the trickiest parts of the stage was trying to find an empty bit of roadside for a toilet break.

Robbie McEwen really impressed me today. After seeing him crash with around 20km to go I thought there's no way he'd be back up there for the sprint. The bunch was sitting on at over 60kph and with 8km to go, Robbie and his teammates were still 18 seconds behind the bunch. Then at 3km to go he shot past me, back in 120th position, and then at 200 meters to go he shot past whoever was on the front to win the stage.

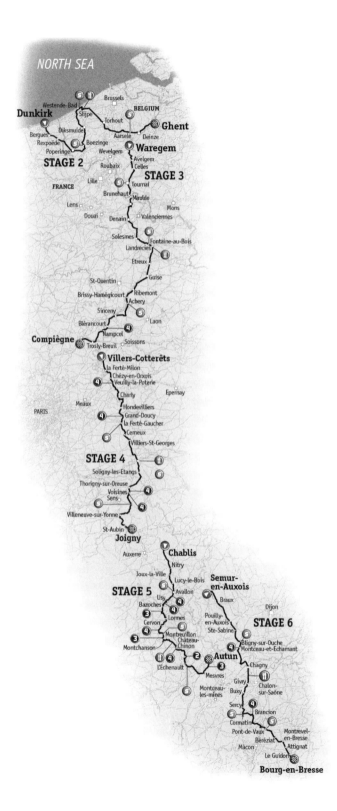

NORTH SEA

Westende-Bad
Dunkirk
Bergues · Diksmuide · Slijpe · Torhout
Rexpoëde · Boezinge · Aarsele
Poperinge · Wevelgem
Brussels
BELGIUM
Ghent
Deinze
STAGE 2
FRANCE
Avelgem
Celles
Roubaix
Lille
Tournai
Brunehaut
Maulde
Lens · Douai · Denain · Valenciennes
Mons
Solesmes · Fontaine-au-Bois
Landrecies
Etreux
St-Quentin · Guise
Brissy-Hamégicourt · Ribemont
Achery
Sinceny
Blérancourt · Laon
Nampcel
Trosly-Breuil · Soissons
Compiègne
Villers-Cotterêts
la Ferté-Milon
Chézy-en-Orxois
Veuilly-la-Poterie
Charly
Epernay
Meaux · Hondevilliers
Grand-Doucy
la Ferté-Gaucher
Cerneux
Villiers-St-Georges
PARIS
STAGE 4
Soligny-les-Étangs
Thorigny-sur-Oreuse
Voisines
Sens
Villeneuve-sur-Yonne
St-Aubin
Joigny
Chablis
Auxerre
Nitry
Semur-en-Auxois
Joux-la-Ville · Lucy-le-Bois
STAGE 5 · Avallon
Usy · Braux
Bazoches · Dijon
Cervon · Lormes
Pouilly-en-Auxois
Ste-Sabine
STAGE 6
Montchanson · Montreuillon · Château-Chinon
Bligny-sur-Ouche
Montceau-et-Échamant
L'Échenault · Autun · Chagny
Mesvres
Montceau-les-mines · Givry · Chalon-sur-Saône
Buxy
Sercy
Brancion
Cormatin
Pont-de-Vaux · Bréziat
Mâcon · Attignat
Le Guidon
Bourg-en-Bresse

STAGE 3
Waregem

7

Daily Drama on the Road to the Alps

Spectacular crashes and sprints can't budge Cancellara from the lead.

Throughout an opening week of scary pileups, marathon break-aways, and chaotic sprints, Fabian Cancellara spent almost 1,200km of racing in the yellow jersey—the first prologue winner to hold the lead for a week since German Didi Thurau did so in the 1977 Tour. Cancellara's leadership put unspoken pressure on his CSC team, though GC hopefuls Carlos Sastre and Fränk Schleck kept a fairly low profile. But the other six men on the Danish squad spent every stage except one riding tempo at the head of the peloton. The one exception was the hilliest day before the Alps, stage 5, when CSC felt the Swiss colossus would lose the lead because of the stage's menu of one category 2, three category 3, and four category 4 climbs. But the team workers were fully engaged at the start of the week.

"To set the record straight, I am not here for the GC," said CSC's U.S. national time trial champion Dave Zabriskie. "I don't know why people haven't realized that. If I soft-pedal for the last few kilometers to save my legs to help Carlos Sastre later in the mountains, that's because I am here to work for the team."

And once the sprinters' teams took up the chase behind the breakaways near the end of the flat stages, Zabriskie was allowed to look for a sweet spot near the back of the peloton, or even ride into the finish at his own pace. That's why he finished stage 1 in Canterbury almost three minutes back.

Besides helping Sastre, the Utah native was doing his fair share of work to keep Cancellara safely in yellow. "We'll keep [the jersey] as long as we can," he said. "We're happy with how [things] have gone."

Despite the effort by his teammates, Cancellara was just as exposed to the risks of the nervous opening stages as anyone, as he would find out on the first stage on the Continent.

Following the overnight English Channel crossing, many of the riders were concerned about July 9's flat run across the fields of Flanders to the city of Ghent. A brisk west wind, which brought in squally showers earlier in the day, was blowing off the choppy waters of the North Sea at the Dunkirk start. "A huge chance of rain, a lot of crosswind, it's going to be a really nervous and fast stage," said stage 1 winner Robbie McEwen, a Belgium resident who knew that members of his big fan club would be out in force.

His Predictor-Lotto teammate Fred Rodriguez confirmed, "It's going to be more than nervous trying to get to the finish today without any kind of problem." He didn't know how true his prediction would turn out to be by the end of the day.

The echelons that form in crosswinds on these flat, straight roads in spring classics like Ghent-Wevelgem didn't materialize. Instead, a break of three riders—Agritubel's Cédric Hervé, Euskaltel's Ruben Perez, and Milram's Marcel Sieberg—went up the road, and the CSC squad kept their lead to a maximum of 5:45. The Belgian rains picked up during the final hour as the peloton approached Ghent, but again the wet conditions kept would-be aggressors in check.

There weren't quite so many people watching as in England, but there were still walls of fans lining the whole of the S-shape course, with the crowds particularly thick in towns that host the popular Belgian kermesse races every year, including Diksmunde, Westende, Gistel, Koolskamp, Tielt, and Deinze. The fanatical cycling supporters, who did not worry about getting wet, dearly wanted a Belgian sprinter to win the day, especially as the finish line was on the highway right outside Ghent's indoor velodrome, site of the city's annual six-day race, where the Flemish fans flock every November. Perhaps a six-day expert like Erik Zabel would win on this damp day in July.

"In the final [hour] it started raining," said Predictor rider Chris Horner. "We had the crosswinds, you couldn't see, you couldn't brake . . . dangerous scenario. Then it dried up before the finish and I thought, 'Oh man, this is great. We're going to go into the finish nice and safe.'"

It was dry on the fast run-in to Ghent, where hazards like tram rails and traffic islands make the roads dangerous even without wet conditions.

By now, CSC had given way to the Belgian teams of star sprinters McEwen and Tom Boonen that were pulling the pack at a steady 60kph. "The tactic was not to bring back the break too quick, to really wait until the final kilometers," said Quick Step-Innergetic rider Sébastien Rosseler, one of Boonen's teammates. "We didn't want to start working too soon, like we did on Sunday [in England]."

The Quick Step plan worked perfectly because the three leaders, after a 148km-long breakaway, were caught just inside the 3km-to-go marker, where a right turn took the fast-moving, 188-strong peloton onto the Rooigemlaan. All the top sprinters were near the front: Boonen was following his lead-out train; Milram's Zabel was craftily sitting on Boonen's wheel; McEwen was moving up about 20 riders back, looking for his second win in two days; Crédit Agricole's Thor Hushovd was behind his pilot fish, Julian Dean; Liquigas's Filippo Pozzato was on the wheels of two colleagues; T-Mobile had a couple of lead-out men for Mark Cavendish and Bernhard Eisel; Lampre-Fondital's Daniele Bennati and Danilo Napolitano were both well placed; and Barloworld's Robbie Hunter was planning to make a late effort after his previous day's mistake.

With 2.5km to go, the crowd lining the barriers was particularly thick because of a giant television screen placed at the last turn. Then, right in front of them, and from the overhead aspect of a helicopter camera on the big screen, the fans witnessed a giant crash. Suddenly bikes and riders were bouncing between the barriers like tennis balls, while those from behind (including race leader Cancellara) landed atop the pile of humanity that soon blocked the street.

Zabel later admitted to Belgian reporters that he was the catalyst of the pileup. "The preparations for the sprint were very nervous and the road wasn't that wide. Then, just after it narrowed a bit, I touched the wheel of Boonen, who was right in front of me. The blow knocked me off my seat and my foot came out. I was just able to regain my balance and I didn't really know what was going on behind me."

What was happening behind Zabel was chaos. The rider on his wheel, Liquigas lead-out rider Manuel Quinziato, couldn't avoid falling. "The Milram rider caused me to lose my balance," said the Italian. "I really hit the ground very hard with my head as my helmet was pretty much smashed on the back. The worst was that once I was down I slid more than a meter, pushed by the mass of riders who fell behind me."

Trying to avoid the carnage, Discovery's best sprinter, Tomas Vaitkus, veered to the right at full speed, crashed hard, and caught his right thumb in the barriers, fracturing it in five places. He would be the only rider not to start the next day, but there were plenty of riders who'd be nursing cuts, bruises, and strained tendons.

Only 25 riders escaped the pileup, including Zabel, who regained his balance and focus to take fifth place in the uphill sprint to the line. Sprinters who had fallen or been stopped included Bennati, Cavendish, Hushovd, and Napolitano.

The finish was competently controlled by the Quick Step team, which had five riders in the group that escaped the crash, including lead-out man

Rosseler. "We let two Milram riders [Alberto Ongarato and Enrico Poitschke] go by us," Rosseler said, "but when I saw three riders from T-Mobile go to the front I took their wheel. I started the sprint . . . and when I sat up there were still three Quick Step riders on my wheel. And with three Quick Steps only 450 meters from the line, that's a good start for the victory!"

After Rosseler, his Dutch teammate Steven de Jongh took it to inside 200 meters, leaving his Belgian colleague Gert Steegmans—who was the lead-out man for McEwen in 2006—to give Boonen the final kick uphill to the finish. Except that Boonen couldn't come past Steegmans and was a wheel behind his teammate at the line.

Boonen, a surprised smile on his face, pointed across at Steegmans and then extended his left arm to tap his victorious teammate on the back. Both men were mobbed by Belgian reporters, who were as thrilled as the fans to get a 1-2 finish for the home team, several bike lengths clear of third-place Pozzato.

Steegmans said his first words to Boonen were, "You let me win, right?" He said his team leader didn't reply. "I think he gifted the stage," Steegmans added. "If that's true, then it's the most beautiful gift he could give me. Incredible."

Boonen, who clearly would have liked to end his Tour stage-win drought, didn't deny that was the case, but one of Steegmans's former teammates, multi-Tour stage winner Tom Steels, later commented, "Rosseler's hard work allowed Steegmans to start his effort a little later than usual. And, over 150 meters, my old teammate is certainly capable of holding off the best sprinters in the world. I think . . . the strongest man won."

While the Belgians were celebrating, the pileup victims began rolling in slowly, all being given the same time as the leaders, since the crash occurred within the final 3km. The UCI extended the "no time loss" limit from 1km to 3km after a similar wreck happened on the Angers stage of the 2004 Tour. Because of the new rule, most of the remaining 160 riders stuck behind the mass pileup stood astride their bikes and watched the finishing sprint on the big TV screen where they'd stopped—an almost comical scene.

Rodriguez, the last of the injured men to ride in, almost nine minutes after the leaders, wasn't laughing as he held his left arm to his chest as if his collarbone were broken. "It was a crazy finish, tight roads, a lot of fans, the peloton was flying—if there was a crash, I knew that would be the place. It was completely crazy," said the Predictor rider, who a year earlier had a tita- nium brace inserted in his shoulder after he fractured his left clavicle for the fifth time in his career on stage 3 of the 2006 Tour. "That titanium rod saved my shoulder," he said.

Rodriguez's friend George Hincapie, who also fell heavily, rolled through with a gash to his right knee, visibly shaken. The Discovery rider said, "I was in the top 25, and I just ran into the big group of [fallen] riders. My knee landed directly on the pavement and I kind of dragged it. I couldn't move it at first, but once I got back on the bike and started pedaling, it just got better."

His teammate, Vaitkus, was pushed to the line by his Spanish colleague Egoi Martinez. Holding his right arm to his torso, Vaitkus was in tears. The violent impact that occurred when he hit the crowd barrier left his brake cable housing stripped bare. The young Lithuanian knew that his Tour debut had ended after only three days.

Thankful he hadn't suffered a similar fate, race favorite Alexander Vinokourov made the sign of the cross as he reached the finish. Race leader Cancellara pedaled to the line with only his right hand on the bars. The grimace on his face spoke of the pain in his left wrist, but it wasn't broken.

"I felt bad right after the crash because of the cold and the tension at that moment," said Cancellara. "It was a difficult day for everyone. But in two days there have been only two attacks—that's different from earlier years. That tells me something has changed and everyone knows there's a long way to go."

Whether Cancellara would hold on to the yellow jersey was doubtful because his overall lead on the top sprinter, Boonen, was down to 26 seconds, a margin that could be wiped out with sprint time bonuses the next day.

There was an air of expectation among the fans lining a 300-meter stretch of cobblestones straddling the 1km-to-go archway in Compiègne. Some were watching the final kilometers of stage 3 on a big-screen TV set up in the cobblestone courtyard of the eighteenth-century palace where King Louis XVI of France first met his future wife, Marie Antoinette. Other spectators were already squeezed between the palace's northern sidewall and the crowd barriers. They were ready to watch the racers make a sharp right onto the first section of the big cottage-loaf cobbles along a narrow street leading to a left turn into the 1km finish straight.

The fans didn't know what they'd see. Some argued that the current four-man breakaway would make it to the finish, while others were sure there'd be a field sprint. Clearly the outcome of this longest stage of the Tour (236.5km) would be touch and go.

Before the day's start in Waregem—known as Belgium's city of the horse because of its annual horse race, the Waregem Koerse—there was a feeling that this wouldn't be a normal day at the Tour. A score of riders were still nursing wounds from the mass pileup in Ghent. The injured—including a strapped-up Rodriguez—weren't looking forward to this marathon stage, especially since they'd be riding into a strong headwind on their way south into

France. Indeed, when race director Christian Prudhomme waved the start flag from the sunroof of his red Skoda number 1 car—which is usually a signal for instant attacks—the pack continued at the same snail's pace it'd been maintaining in the neutral zone.

There was still no acceleration from the field when Frenchmen Martin Ladagnous of Française des Jeux and Nicolas Vogondy of Agritubel broke clear after 6km. They effortlessly gained 11 minutes in 20km and rode into the wind for most of the day on the small chainring. The pack even slowed to walking pace—with the yellow, green, white, and polka-dot jerseys leading the way—to honor outgoing race director Jean-Marie Leblanc in his hometown of Fontaine-au-Bois, 105km from the finish.

The hardworking CSC team kept the two leaders within five minutes, but Ladagnous and Vogondy picked up the pace when they were joined by Belgian Frederik Willems of Liquigas and Stéphane Augé of Cofidis on the day's only category 4 climb, 35km from the finish. This gave new momentum to the breakaways, who reached the final 20km with a 2:15 buffer.

The four were still 22 seconds ahead when they sped downhill into Compiègne with 2km remaining through the streets of the historic city. The peloton was in one long line, with the sprinters' lead-out men using their energy to help close the gap rather than preparing their teammates for a third field sprint in three days.

Meanwhile, Cancellara was slowly moving up the line, smoothly accelerating from one lead-out man to the next. "I knew it was very important to be in a good position before the difficult section with one kilometer and a hundred meters to go," he said.

Cancellara was in eighth position in the peloton when he reached the "difficult section"—the right turn onto the chunky cobblestones, followed after 100 meters by a left turn onto a further 200 meters of *pavé*. The Swiss moved past T-Mobile's Bernhard Eisel on the first section of cobbles, then powered past Barloworld's Robbie Hunter on the outside of the left turn, almost scraping the metal barrier. Then, right outside Compiègne's grandiose palace, where the annual Paris-Roubaix classic starts, Cancellara continued his charge in the style that won him the fabled cobblestone classic in 2006.

Before the *pavé* ended, he had passed the first five in the line: Quick Step lead-out riders Sébastien Rosseler and Steven de Jongh, T-Mobile's Marcus Burghardt, Barloworld's Paolo Longo, and Lampre-Fondital's Alessandro Ballan. They all hesitated when Cancellara continued his effort, and he was 10 meters clear when he left the cobbles to pursue the four breakaways still 100 meters ahead of him.

Hunter summed up the thinking of all of the sprinters as they watched the yellow jersey go away. "I just didn't see the point of going with him," said the South African, "because I saw two Quick Step guys in front of me, and I really thought from what they did the day before [setting up the stage win for Steegmans] that they'd pull it back and set up the sprint for Tom [Boonen].

"I saw Steven de Jongh turn around, Rosseler was right there. There was one guy between them . . . so there were at least three guys in front of me and there was about 700 meters to go. And I thought, no, it's a perfect position to beat Tom. Steven turned around and he started going, and by that time I thought that Tom was in the right position. They started going, Steven swung off, eventually Rosseler pulled off, and there was still 400 meters to go—which was way too long [for a sprint]."

By that point, Cancellara had overtaken three of the breakaways, with only Ladagnous trying to stay on his wheel. Nobody could believe what the race leader was doing. The Swiss was racing just as hard as he did to win the London prologue,

> **By that point, Cancellara had overtaken three of the breakaways, with only Ledagnous trying to stay on his wheel. Nobody could believe what the race leader was doing.**

except he had the fastest sprinters in the world pursuing him. And he came out on top, to win the stage and a 20-second bonus that bolstered his overall lead to 33 seconds on runner-up Andreas Klöden, and 46 seconds on Boonen.

Zabel was the strongest of the sprinters, but he was still a length behind when he threw his bike at the line to take second place, with a fast-finishing Danilo Napolitano in third, Boonen fourth, and Hunter fifth.

No wonder Cancellara said, "That was the hardest kilometer of my life." Such final-kilometer explosions are so rarely successful that Cancellara's was only the fifth one in the past 20 years. The only comparable athletic feats in recent Tour history came from Brad McGee in his stage win at Avranches in 2002, Viatcheslav Ekimov at Mâcon in 1991, Jelle Nijdam at Wasquehal in 1989, and Steve Bauer at Machecoul in 1988.

"It was extraordinary that Cancellara did this with the yellow jersey," said a clearly impressed Zabel, the team Milram veteran who had just failed to catch the man they call Spartacus.

It's not often that Tom Boonen is satisfied with fourth place in a sprint finish at the Tour, especially in Compiègne, near the start of his beloved Paris-Roubaix, which he won in 2005. But the Quick Step leader was more than pleased after padding his lead in the battle for the green points jersey.

"I was left without my train today," Boonen said after stage 3, "because I had to spend [Matteo] Tosatto, Rosseler, and Steegmans in the final kilometers to shut down the breakaway. In the final sprint, I wanted to be on McEwen's wheel, and I was waiting for him to start his sprint, but he waited too long. By the time I did start my sprint, it was too late to try to catch Cancellara. I was able to finish ahead of McEwen, so I am satisfied."

Boonen began the stage with a one-point lead over archrival McEwen but saw his lead move to 80-74 by finishing three places ahead of the Aussie. McEwen was livid at the line and said that Hunter barged his line and forced him to restart his sprint, allowing Boonen to come around him. "There's no story to talk about, mate," McEwen stewed.

Before the stage, McEwen said he was feeling better after falling hard on the stage into Canterbury. "The stiffness is going away and I hope to be better in the coming days," he said. "The green jersey comes with winning stages. Right now the priority is to win stages."

Winning stages was everyone's priority on the next day's stage from Villers-Cotterêts to Joigny, when the day's four-man, 153km breakaway never gained more than four minutes. The lead was restricted partly because of a sudden acceleration by Pozzato's Liquigas team after 63km. Creating a fast-moving echelon, all nine green team riders went to the front and split the race into three groups. It was a bold move that caught out sprinters Hushovd, Freire, and Bennati, who were all struggling in the back group until the peloton regrouped in the town of Ferté-Gaucher.

"We did it for maybe 10Ks," said Liquigas's British veteran Charlie Wegelius. "There was a slight crosswind, but maybe the road was too wide. Maybe if we'd done it 10Ks later it could have worked. It's worth trying those things, I think, because it keeps everyone on their toes."

The sprint into Joigny started a few kilometers out, on a fast, curving road alongside the Yonne River. None of the lead-out trains were effective, partly because of a headwind, and there was a free-for-all in the final kilometer through the town. T-Mobile's Cavendish, who was recovering from the crashes he suffered on stages 1 and 2, opened up the throttle with 500 meters to go, but on the other side of the road, Hushovd had quietly worked his way forward on the wheel of Kiwi teammate Dean. The Norwegian sprung off Dean's wheel with 250 meters to go to hold off a fast-charging Hunter, who crossed in second, thumping a fist on his bars in frustration, with Freire in third.

The win was Hushovd's first victory of any kind since he took a stage of the Vuelta a España 10 months earlier—a long and dry period for a sprinter of his caliber.

Maybe it's the long winter nights in his native Norway or perhaps it's because he's the peloton's only practicing Buddhist, but Hushovd is one of the most patient riders in the peloton. He never lost faith during almost a year of bad luck and crashes, and he showed supreme calm before launching his winning sprint in Joigny.

"This is a very big win for me," Hushovd said. "I prepared very well for the spring classics [this year], but I got sick right before Milan-San Remo and I wasn't able to race the entire April classics season. I raced the Giro d'Italia to regain my strength and I came to the Tour in good form. It's a relief."

The victory was Hushovd's fifth Tour stage win, and it made up for a frustrating spring that tested his patience. Two second places at the Giro bolstered his confidence, and a hard week of racing at the Dauphiné Libéré put the finishing touches on his Tour form. "I felt confident when I started the Tour. I knew that I had done my job before arriving," he said. "In my head I knew I would win a stage this year. I was sure that my form wasn't too bad. The first sprint I was second, so that was good. I had two hard days, and now I have won here, and I hope the work I did last winter pays off for the rest of this Tour."

Hushovd was coming off two spectacular Tours. In 2005, he became the first Norwegian to win the green jersey, which came without winning a stage, and in 2006 he won the prologue and the final stage on the Champs Élysées. A nasty scar on his upper right arm is a souvenir from stage 1 a year earlier when he collided with a placard held by a fan leaning over the barriers that left him gushing blood on the finish line.

"This scar reminds me of trying to overcome difficulties," Hushovd said. "I've had some problems with my health, and I'm finally finding my strength. The prologue was too hard for me [this year] and I wasn't too disappointed. I was angry after crashing [in stage 2] because I lost 30 points to McEwen and Boonen in the race for the green jersey. I was very angry, but after dinner I calmed down and decided I needed to look ahead and be patient."

Patience doesn't seem to be a virtue of the fiery Hunter, a rider still in search of a stage win after racing the Tour five times. Angry at coming in second at Joigny, he went straight to his Barloworld team bus for a quick shower. He sat on the steps of the bus and chatted with a couple of reporters as he put on fresh socks and sneakers.

"Obviously I'm a little disappointed," he said, though the look on his hard, freckled face indicated a deeper frustration. "I was fighting to get on the right wheel over the last 500 meters, and I had to go a long way 'round on the right-hand side in the wind. I put in a bit of an effort there, then by the time Thor went he had a bit of a gap, about 10 meters, on me . . . and I ran out of distance in the end."

Hunter said he didn't have the luxury of a lead-out man like New Zealand national champion Dean, who did a phenomenal job preparing the sprint for

Hushovd. "The majority of our team are climbers, so they're not much help in the sprints," said the blond South African. "Geraint [Thomas] is a young guy, and [Enrico] Degano's a sprinter. But I can't ask for more; they're doing what they can."

For the GC riders, stage 4 represented another day closer to their first big rendezvous in the mountains. "The last two days have been pretty easy," said Discovery leader Levi Leipheimer. "So I think everybody's legs feel good. This Tour is wide-open. Nobody knows what's going to happen, so a stage like tomorrow could definitely be dangerous."

— ⊙ —

Twenty-four hours later, Leipheimer was feeling stressed after finishing the ferocious stage 5 through the forested hills of the Morvan into Autun. But his voice was calm and his bright blue eyes squinted in the evening sunlight as he slowly pedaled toward the black Discovery Channel team bus. "I've been telling myself not to take any risks," Leipheimer said to *VeloNews*, reflecting what other prerace favorites were doing in the opening week. "Sometimes that means being a little bit far back, but I think it's worth it."

The American was so careful the first week that some journalists were calling him the invisible man. At stage starts he'd stay in the team bus until the last moment, only appearing when the media and fans had tired of waiting.

Top favorite Vinokourov also avoided the autograph hunters and television crews. Each day, he rode from his bus to the start behind two of his sky-blue-clad Astana teammates, while two others rode sweep-up. At each stage finish, he was protected by Lance Armstrong's former Belgian bodyguard, Serge Borlée.

Vino wanted to arrive at the mountains in perfect shape, both mentally and physically. But his plan came apart on a long, fast downhill just moments before the strung-out peloton sped through the village of Fontaine-la-Mère, 26km from the finish of stage 5. "We were doing 70km an hour when he went down," said Saunier Duval's David Millar.

Vinokourov said he didn't know exactly how he crashed. "Perhaps it was the chain jumping off that made me lose my balance," he told his journalist friend Philippe Le Gars of *L'Équipe*. "I saw myself falling, but the only thing you think about then is getting back on your bike as quick as possible."

That wasn't so simple. The blond Kazakh was in deep pain. In falling, his body must have twisted and skidded along the pavement because he gashed the front of both knees and scraped his hip and backside, along with his right arm.

On getting up from the crash, Vino clenched both hands and threw his arms up in anger, perhaps thinking his last chance of winning the Tour was trickling away with the blood oozing down his legs.

Even before directeur sportif Mario Kummer could hit the radio panic button, Astana's Toni Colom, who was riding slightly behind Vino, had already screeched to a halt, dumped his bicycle on the road, and started fixing the chain on his team leader's bike. Five other Astana riders made U-turns and came back to help. Within a minute, with their leader tucked in behind, they were tearing along in team time trial formation in a desperate attempt to bridge to the peloton. Only Vino's first lieutenants, Klöden and Andrey Kashechkin, were left in the bunch.

The one-minute gap barely changed in the 10km before reaching the day's eighth and final climb because the pack was flying. Liquigas's Wegelius and CSC's Christian Vande Velde were leading a chase after Cofidis team leader Sylvain Chavanel and Française des Jeux's Philippe Gilbert, who were clinging to a 1:40 lead after being at the front for more than three and a half hours over the most difficult terrain of the week. Liquigas, which wanted to set up the stage win for Pozzato, had instigated the chase with another half dozen teams when the break had a 14:50 lead, while CSC was only joining in when it saw a chance to keep Cancellara in the yellow jersey.

CSC team director Kim Andersen testily rejected suggestions that his riders ramped up the speed about the same time Vinokourov crashed. "Stop that BS. We were not at the front when he crashed; it was Liquigas. Our riders didn't even know he crashed. And no one waited when [Carlos] Sastre crashed," Andersen said, referring to Sastre's crash about 5km before Vinokourov's. "The whole team was waiting for Carlos. We only had two riders at the front."

Even so, two was enough with the Liquigas riders to pull the 80-strong pack up to Gilbert and Chavanel partway up the category 3 climb to the Croix de la Libération. By this point, all of Vinokourov's troops had peeled off. "We rode as hard as we could," said Colom. "But eventually Vino had to go it alone."

Gritting his teeth, the injured warrior charged up the hill between lines of screaming fans, picking his way past pockets of riders shed by the peloton. His team car drove ahead to clear the way and give him some illicit draft, although any benefit was negated by the chaos of the narrow climb, as more riders dropped back from the fast-moving pack. Vinokourov was 50 seconds back cresting the climb.

There were several crashes and near-crashes on the tricky 6km descent. The attacking Yaroslav Popovych of Discovery and counterattacking Cancellara overshot a sharp left turn on the zigzagging drop through a forest to the ancient city walls of Autun. "I locked up once," said Millar. "It was a technical descent, we were doing 100 percent, so it's obviously going to be a bit hairy."

Popovych's Spanish teammate Benjamin Noval, who had finished his day's work, was cruising down the hill to the finish when an inattentive Bouygues Telecom car suddenly braked and Noval smashed into its rear window. He shredded his right arm and said later that he had "stitches all over, in my arms hand, chin, some 25 to 30 stitches in all." The injuries would take more than a week to heal, but Noval wasn't planning to give up, knowing that he would be needed to help his roommate Alberto Contador.

Meanwhile, on a twisting roller-coaster route through the medieval town, Bouygues Telecom's Spanish rider Xavier Florencio attacked with Millar, hoping to surprise the few sprinters left in the 74-strong group. "I was obviously trying to win the stage; that's why I attacked," said Millar. "I actually thought from the race plan that there were two corners into the finish, and I thought it was flat, so when I came 'round the corner and there was this big fucking hill I thought, Oh, no."

Millar sat up and was quickly overtaken by the stretched-out pack, with the Italians Bennati and Pozzato leading the charge. "With 250 meters left, I had to decide whether to brake or go," said Pozzato, "I decided to go. I liked that it was an uphill finish."

The Liquigas leader held on to win, with Rabobank's Freire kicking through into second and Bennati in third.

"Good win, big win, he deserved that," said Pozzato's teammate, Wegelius. "There are so many times you work for nothing, when you don't get a result, so it's nice to work hard and get a win."

By the time the wounded Vinokourov arrived at the head of an 18-strong group, 80 seconds had ticked by on the clock above the finish line. He used the back of his right glove to wipe away sweat and tears from his reddened face, while T-Mobile's Bernhard Eisel extended his right arm to give the Kazakh a consolatory pat on the back.

"That was the real Tour de France today," exclaimed Millar. Leipheimer agreed. "It was hard, it was really hard, especially the last climb, the downhill and all the turns," Leipheimer said. "The last 5K, I was on the limit."

Leipheimer was surprised that on this demanding run-in at the end of a 26km chase, Vinokourov crossed the line only 1:20 back. "When he crashed there was a long way to go, and we were full gas," Leipheimer said. "I don't know how he lost only 1:20. That's really very impressive. I would have expected him to lose a couple of minutes at least."

The drama of Vino's heroic ride was compounded by the earlier crash of his teammate Klöden. The German somersaulted over the handlebars when a rider braked in front of him going up the day's highest climb, the category 2

Haut-Folin, and he fell on his back. X-rays later showed a fissure of the coccyx, but the team thought the injury was a possible hangover from a crash that put Klöden out of the 2005 Tour.

"I think that too much bad luck has hit me and the team," Vinokourov said later. "When things don't go right, they don't go at all. You can do everything you can to prepare yourself perfectly for the Tour and in a second it all falls apart. It's infuriating because I crash so rarely."

Later that night, at a hospital in Beaune, each of Vinokourov's knees required 15 stitches. He got more stitches in his right elbow and the ends of the fingers on his right hand. He didn't get back to his hotel until after midnight. It had been a long day.

Injuries were on the minds of many others after a traumatic opening week. The sprinters had come off particularly badly. McEwen had been trying to contest the sprints, despite the pain still bugging him from his stage 1 fall in England. "I'm suffering like a dog. My neck's really stiff, I have a bump on my head, and I'm getting pins and needles in my right hand from the neck," he said before stage 5. The rugged Aussie added that he might have broken something, but he didn't want to know, and so hadn't had his spine scanned. In 2004, after a bad first week crash, McEwen rode for two weeks with two fractured vertebrae, which were only identified in post-Tour x-rays.

Also struggling was T-Mobile's Cavendish, who was still trying to recover from his two tumbles in the first two days. The Brit was hoping that stage 6, the last one before hitting the Alps, might give him a chance to finally contest a field sprint.

As for Freire, he had finished top three in Ghent and Autun, but the cyst on his backside that threatened his participation in the Tour was still a problem. "I have to speak with the doctor, because the problem is not getting better," he said. "I don't want to go to the hospital. If I keep going, maybe I will end up in the hospital. I've been through this before and I don't want to lose the rest of the season."

The riders' physical injuries and problems suggested that stage 6 would see a gentle pace. No team wanted to threaten the race favorites' chances for recovery before the Alps, but there was still a race to contest on a scenic route through the Burgundy hills, past *grand cru* vineyards, and across the Saône River valley to Bourg-en-Bresse.

Among those eager to get up the road was Cofidis's Bradley Wiggins, who said before the Tour, "I want to be part of the race throughout, instead of being part of the prologue and then being anonymous for three weeks." He would get his wish.

Wiggins attacked as soon as the flag dropped. "There were five of us at the start," Wiggins said. "Then I pulled a big turn and looked around and I was on me own. I thought, Bloody 'ell, what am I supposed to do, sit up? It's the Tour de France, and I thought I had to continue."

With a headwind discouraging a significant chase, and after just 2km of the 199.5km stage, Wiggins had become the first solo breakaway. "Someone had to do it, it just ended up falling on me," he said. "I thought there might be a counterattack, but there wasn't. I started getting 10 minutes, 15 minutes, so I thought, there you go. What are you supposed to do?"

> **"Then I pulled a big turn and looked around and I was on me own. I thought, Bloody 'ell, what am I supposed to do, sit up? It's the Tour de France, and I thought I had to continue."**

Talk before the stage was that one of the Tour's five riders from the United Kingdom might do something special to mark the fortieth anniversary of the tragic July 13 at the 1967 Tour, when the best-ever British cyclist, Tom Simpson, died on the upper slopes of Mont Ventoux.

Simpson was the first non-European to wear the yellow jersey (in the 1962 Tour), and his palmarès included four one-day classics: Milan-San Remo, the Tour of Flanders, Bordeaux-Paris, and the Tour of Lombardy. He became a true legend of the sport when he won the world championship in 1965. He dearly wanted to win the Tour in 1967, even though he didn't have the team to support him because of the national team format (1968 would be the final year that the Tour was contested by national teams).

The 1967 season began well for Simpson when he won Paris-Nice, and in return for the help his young teammate Eddy Merckx gave him there, Simpson rode for the Belgian in the spring classics. Merckx was still too young to ride the Tour, and in the absence of five-time winner Jacques Anquetil—who rode his final Tour in 1966—the big favorite was Anquetil's perennial French rival, Raymond Poulidor.

But things went sour for Pou-Pou, whose France national team colleague Roger Pingeon took the yellow jersey on stage 5. Three days later, Poulidor crashed and had huge mechanical problems on the finishing climb to the Ballon d'Alsace. He lost more than 10 minutes and ceded team leadership to Pingeon, the eventual Tour winner.

That stage was won by a third French team rider, defending Tour champion Lucien Aimar, while Simpson finished 19 seconds back, and 1:14 ahead of Pingeon, to jump up the GC. The Alps, however, weren't kind to Simpson.

The Tour took its toll on the wiry Englishman, who was having stomach problems and had lost weight.

Making things worse was the stifling weather in Provence. But Simpson was still in the top 10 overall, and he said he was going to try something over the Ventoux on stage 13. Temperatures were already in the 90s that morning and headed to the triple digits.

There was no live TV back then, just occasional updates via Radio Tour. On the early slopes of the Ventoux Simpson was reported to be in the front group, which split halfway up the 21km climb. Simpson was then riding in the first chase group with Aimar, who would later say that the stubborn Brit kept on accelerating, trying to bridge back to the leaders.

Then, as Radio Tour focused on the battle up front between Spanish climber Julio Jimenez, Pingeon, Poulidor, and Dutch star Jan Janssen (who would win the stage), there was no more news of Simpson. The story only emerged later that evening, when race directors Jacques Goddet and Félix Lévitan went to the pressroom to report that Simpson had collapsed and died 2km from the summit of Mont Ventoux.

They said a couple of amphetamine ampules were found in his back pocket. But that was no surprise. There were no antidoping controls in 1967 and no rules against using drugs. Stimulants, including amphetamines, had been in vogue since they were used by the military in World War II.

Simpson has since been condemned for being a "doper." He paid the ultimate price for the errors of the time, but he was no more culpable than any other racer of the 1960s. He is remembered fondly by his contemporaries, and on this July 13, 2007, Simpson's two daughters, now in their 40s, were making a pilgrimage to the Tom Simpson Memorial to honor their father at the place where he died, 400km south of where a young compatriot was in the middle of a 191km solo break.

"I didn't know anything about [the Simpson anniversary], actually," Wiggins said later. But his countryman, Millar, most definitely did. At the start in Semur-en-Auxois, he said, "It's an important day that deserves to be remembered more than it is being. He was our greatest rider, and it's a tragedy that he's not here today."

Asked if a stage should have been held on Mont Ventoux to memorialize Simpson, Millar answered, "I think it would have been pertinent to have done that. We have to remember the past, not forget it, if we want to create a better future for cycling. We definitely have to remember Tommy."

Wiggins's lead reached a maximum of 17:20 after 50km alone, but it gradually dwindled, and when the gap was 1:44 with 20km still to ride, he wondered if he still had a shot at the win. "At 10K to go, I thought it might happen," he said. "I was still doing 45K an hour, but I knew they'd be doing

50, 52 in that headwind." The swarm of voracious sprinters' teams eventually reeled in Wiggins with 8.5km remaining, and the peloton went streaming past. He'd finish 3:42 behind them.

The finale was as hectic as all the others that week. Boonen, who discounted theories that he had lost his touch, noted, "The guy who finds the room to do his sprint is the one who wins all week."

One who didn't find the room was British rookie Cavendish, who had another frustrating what-might-have-been experience. His Austrian teammate Bernard Eisel was in good position with a few hundred meters to go, thinking that Cavendish was on his wheel. But Cavendish wasn't there. Moments before, in the hectic jockeying for position, he had bumped into Boonen. "I was on Boonen's wheel," said Cavendish. "Bernhard came up, so I went on his wheel to get the lead-out, but Boonen swerved right—just with the bunch, it wasn't his fault—and his rear [derailleur] went in my front wheel."

The big Belgian's rear derailleur didn't treat Cavendish's front wheel too gently. Five spokes were ripped out of the deep-dish rim, and after the race T-Mobile mechanics marveled at the destroyed wheel, which flopped loosely around the hub. Amazingly, Cavendish had managed to keep his bike upright and pedaled slowly to the line, finishing third from last, two minutes down.

The accident was costly for Cavendish, who was on target to get his best result of the week, certainly better than the tenth place he took at Joigny. "I was on the perfect wheel with Boonen, and Bernhard coming up," he confirmed. "But all I could do . . . was laugh."

Up where Cavendish should have been, Hunter, Zabel, Boonen, and Freire were fighting out the stage victory. "With 250 meters to go I saw an opening on the right," Boonen said. "I braked, moved across, and then went again." The Quick Step leader burst clear to win by a clear bike length over Freire and Zabel. It was his first Tour stage win since he took stage 3 at Tours in 2005. "Today I found new lungs," he said. "I hope they stay for a few weeks."

But the day's runner-up, Freire, was unlikely to stay around even for a few days. The Rabobank sprinter said he might not make it out of the Alps for fear that his cyst might become worse and he would need another surgery. He voiced frustration: "I'm feeling better every day but the problem is getting worse. Twice in second place is frustrating. It was not an easy sprint today. Everyone had a lot of power. In the finale, I was going to Boonen, but he changed his course twice, so I backed off a little. Boonen was good in the end."

That was it for the sprinters, most of whom would go into survival mode until after the Alps. The spotlight was about to return to the GC men, headed by Astana's Klöden, who despite his injured sit bone was still in second overall, a week after his brilliant London prologue. The time gaps to the other main favorites all remained the same—except for the unlucky Vinokourov, who sat in 81st overall, 1:37 behind his teammate.

The two Astana men had no real problems riding in the slow-moving pack to Bourg. The mountains would pose a vastly more difficult challenge. How they would fare against the likes of Cadel Evans, Alejandro Valverde, and Leipheimer would soon become known.

It seemed likely that climbers like Michael Rasmussen, the two-time defending King of the Mountains champion, would go on the attack. When asked what was going to happen on stage 7 over the first category 1 climb of the Tour, the Col de la Colombière, Rasmussen said, "Even though you might get over the climb with 20, 30 seconds, it's a long way down the other side and you have to pedal on that descent, so I think there will be 15, 20 guys sprinting for it in Le Grand Bornand. My favorite for that type of finish would be Valverde."

Speculation is cheap. But in this Tour, it seemed, nothing was predictable.

STAGE 2: DUNKIRK–GHENT

1. Gert Steegmans (B), Quick Step-Innergetic, 3:48:22
2. Tom Boonen (B), Quick Step-Innergetic, s.t.
3. Filippo Pozzato (I), Liquigas, s.t.
4. Robert Hunter (RsA), Barloworld, s.t.
5. Romain Feillu (F), Agritubel, s.t.
6. Robbie McEwen (Aus), Predictor-Lotto, s.t.
7. Erik Zabel (G), Milram, s.t.
8. Heinrich Haussler (G), Gerolsteiner, s.t.
9. Oscar Freire Gomez (Sp), Rabobank, s.t.
10. Sébastien Chavanel (F), Française des Jeux, s.t.

STAGE 3: WAREGEM–COMPIÈGNE

1. Fabian Cancellara (Swi), CSC, 6:36:15
2. Erik Zabel (G), Milram, s.t.
3. Danilo Napolitano (I), Lampre-Fondital, s.t.
4. Tom Boonen (B), Quick Step-Innergetic, s.t.
5. Robert Hunter (RsA), Barloworld, s.t.
6. Robert Förster (G), Gerolsteiner, s.t.
7. Robbie McEwen (Aus), Predictor-Lotto, s.t.
8. Bernhard Eisel (A), T-Mobile, s.t.
9. Mark Cavendish (GB), T-Mobile, s.t.
10. Heinrich Haussler (G), Gerolsteiner, s.t.

STAGE 4: VILLERS-COTTERÊTS–JOIGNY

1. Thor Hushovd (N), Crédit Agricole, 4:37:47
2. Robert Hunter (RsA), Barloworld, s.t.
3. Oscar Freire Gomez (Sp), Rabobank, s.t.

4. Erik Zabel (G), Milram, s.t.
5. Danilo Napolitano (I), Lampre-Fondital, s.t.
6. Gert Steegmans (B), Quick Step-Innergetic, s.t.
7. Robert Förster (G), Gerolsteiner, s.t.
8. Tom Boonen (B), Quick Step-Innergetic, s.t.
9. Sébastien Chavanel (F), Française des Jeux, s.t.
10. Mark Cavendish (GB), T-Mobile, s.t.

STAGE 5: CHABLIS–AUTUN

1. Filippo Pozzato (I), Liquigas, 4:39:01
2. Oscar Freire Gomez (Sp), Rabobank, s.t.
3. Daniele Bennati (I), Lampre-Fondital, s.t.
4. Kim Kirchen (Lux), T-Mobile, s.t.
5. Erik Zabel (G), Milram, s.t.
6. **George Hincapie (USA), Discovery Channel, s.t.**
7. Cristian Moreni (I), Cofidis, s.t.
8. Stefan Schumacher (G), Gerolsteiner, s.t.
9. Bram Tankink (Nl), Quickstep-Innergetic, s.t.
10. Jérôme Pineau (F), Bouygues Telecom, s.t.

STAGE 6: SEMUR-EN-AUXOIS–BOURG-EN-BRESSE

1. Tom Boonen (B), Quick Step-Innergetic, 5:20:59
2. Oscar Freire Gomez (Sp), Rabobank, s.t.
3. Erik Zabel (G), Milram, s.t.
4. Sébastien Chavanel (F), Française des Jeux, s.t.
5. Thor Hushovd (N), Crédit Agricole, s.t.
6. Daniele Bennati (I), Lampre-Fondital, s.t.
7. Robert Förster (G), Gerolsteiner, s.t.
8. Robert Hunter (RsA), Barloworld, s.t.
9. Romain Feillu (F), Agritubel, s.t.
10. Murilo Fisher (Brz), Liquigas, s.t.

GENERAL CLASSIFICATION AFTER STAGE 6

1. Fabian Cancellara (Swi), CSC, 5:49:55
2. Andréas Klöden (G), Astana, at 00:33
3. Filippo Pozzato (I), Liquigas, at 00:35
4. David Millar (Gb), Saunier Duval-Prodir, at 00:41
5. Oscar Freire Gomez (Sp), Rabobank, at 00:43
6. **George Hincapie (USA), Discovery Channel, at 00:43**
7. Vladimir Gusev (Rus), Discovery Channel, at 00:45
8. Vladimir Karpets (Rus), Caisse d'Épargne, at 00:46
9. Erik Zabel (G), Milram, at 00:48
10. Mikel Astarloza (Sp), Euskaltel-Euskadi, at 00:49

CHRISTIAN VANDE VELDE | JULY 9

Crash, bang, oooomph!

Day 2 is over and done with and apart from four of us hitting the deck thus far, all is well.

Stuey [Stuart O'Grady] went down in the prologue, Kurt [Kurt-Asle Arvesen] went down trying to protect Carlos's wheel [Carlos Sastre], Fränk [Fränk Schleck] went down in the rain while trying to navigate through a roundabout, and then Fabian went down in the big crash near the finish.

We were talking at breakfast this morning and commiserating for the poor guys he landed on. Fabian went over the top like Walter Payton into the end zone, landing his big 86 kilo Swiss cheese ass on top of all of those tiny little men.

The Swiss bear was down but not out; he came back loud as ever, turning up Shakira full blast during dinner. And to make it worse, he tries to sing along.

The rest of us were behind the crash and we were all relieved. The suffering was over and done with and within the last 3km, so all was good.

The day ended up perfect for the fans as well, with Gert Steegmans kicking Tom Boonen to the curb. They both seemed happy, but something tells me Gert was happier than Tomke. But Tom has techno-pop songs named after him, so he doesn't even have to win anymore.

We have controlled the race without spending too much energy and will continue to do so until we reach the point of no return. In other words, we won't destroy the team to defend the jersey for one more day.

Today we can expect 235km of wind and most likely rain. I will be on the front line at the start, as usual.   ⊗

CHRISTIAN VANDE VELDE | JULY 10

Yeah, we meant to do that.

Well spank me and call me Patrice.

Fabian the bear is a bad man and when you have other bad men working for the most badass of the bad, then sometimes you get *genius*. But that's still pretty rare.

Most times you work with all of the good intentions in the world and still come up short. Then, when you least expect it, when your pants are down and you're scrambling just to stay alive, you win *anyway*! In those moments you come off looking like we did today . . . like we meant to do it.

Jens [Voigt] was laughing the other day, commenting on how the first three guys who had to work on the first stage would be team captains on any other team. Jens, Stuey, and Dave Z [David Zabriskie] had to work first and God bless anyone trying to get away with *those* guys pulling behind them.

But honestly, right now I am still in shock. We all are.

Jens and I looked at each other after the stage and just shook our heads in disbelief.

The guys all just had a couple glasses of champagne in celebration of the bear.

Hopefully it won't be our last.   ⊗

CHRISTIAN VANDE VELDE | JULY 12

1,000km in the bag

Which came first, the chicken or the egg?

What is better? Being physically or mentally exhausted?

This is a serious question. Is it better to have tired legs from riding at the front all day for a week or because you haven't slept in a week, sitting bolt upright every time you dream that you are riding into the back of the guy ahead and your brakes aren't working?

Personally I like the situation we are currently in, dictating the race, rather than having its terms handed to us by other teams. Really, it sucks having no impact on the race whatsoever and suffering at the back of the pack while getting from point A to B.

Being on the front hurts, but sitting on the wheel is kinda like an annoying pain that kills you mentally. You start to think that you are the only guy in the field hurting. After a while, your self-esteem takes a knock when you begin to wonder how it's possible that those guys on the front—including some you never even heard of—are breaking your legs like this.

These things add up and before you know it you are docile and lack the confidence to attack or to even think of attacking. Unless, of course, you have the amazing mentality of a person like Jens, who yells things at himself like, "I am the great Jens Freakin' Voigt! These poofters on X team can't break you! They are nothing!" (He learned his English from the Australians; cut him some slack.)

Unfortunately we don't think the same way. Well, come to think of it, maybe that is fortunate after all.

Anyway, the whole point of this is that a little work never hurt anyone. (I hope I don't eat these words in the mountains.) ⊗

RIDER DIARY

SIMON GERRANS I JULY 9

To the front, to the back

Today's stage was really nervous. The wind was blowing a gale and changing direction a lot. I think every directeur sportif was screaming in his race radio to every rider to stay at the front, which created a fast tempo and a lot of pushing and shoving. In situations like this you seem to spend five minutes busting your ass to get to the front of the group, only to stay there for 20 seconds before you get swamped from behind. Then you start the whole process over again. ⊗

RIDER DIARY

SIMON GERRANS I JULY 10

Long and boring,
and did I mention long?

Six hours and 36 minutes in the saddle! Today was long and boring. Two blokes got away after 6km of racing, so with 230km of headwind to the finish the bunch was willing to let them go. The two guys up the road stayed at around 10 minutes all day. When the bunch slowed down, they slowed down . . . ⊗

RIDER DIARY

SIMON GERRANS | JULY 12

Hero time! Ah, no, wait a sec . . .

I felt like we were racing across sand dunes today. The roads were dead slow and consistently up and down.

We had our first real bit of excitement in the Ag2r camp. Moreau punctured at the base of a category 4 climb. I was right beside Christophe when he flatted, so stopped with him to give him my wheel. Big mistake! By the time I had my wheel out and ready to put into Christophe's bike, the team car had arrived and the mechanic was there to do the same thing. I left him to do his job and went and put my own wheel back in my own bike. By the time I got going Christophe had already taken off and joined two teammates who had slowed down to tow him back to the group, leaving poor old me to find my way back by myself. Twenty minutes later under the close eye of a motorbike commissaire, I had clawed my way back to the comfort of the peloton.

Vino hit the deck hard with around 25km to go, which looked like it really hurt. Nearly all his teammates sat up to help him get back on. He finished a little over a minute down, looking seriously knocked around.   ⊗

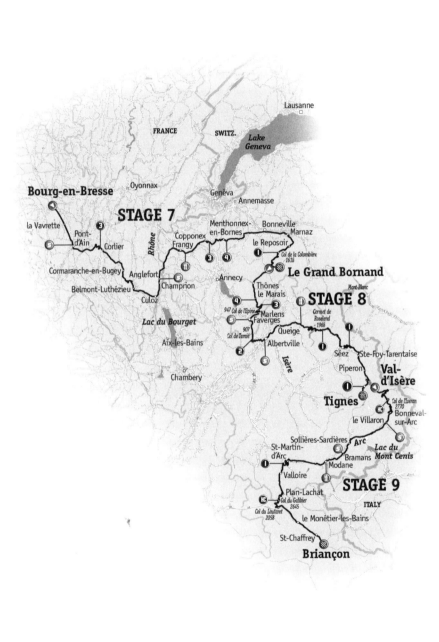

Bourg-en-Bresse

la Vavrette

STAGE 7

Pont-d'Ain

Corlier

Cormaranche-en-Bugey

Belmont-Luthézieu

Anglefort

Champrion

Culoz

Rhône

Copponex

Frangy

Menthonnex-en-Bornes

Bonneville

Marnaz

le Reposoir

Col de la Colombière
1618

Le Grand Bornand

Annecy

Thônes

le Marais

STAGE 8

Mont-Blanc

947 Col de l'Épine

Marlens

Faverges

Cornet de Roselend
1968

Lac du Bourget

907 Col de Tamié

Queige

Albertville

Isère

Aix-les-Bains

Chambery

Séez

Ste-Foy-Tarentaise

Piperon

Val-d'Isère

Tignes

Col de l'Iseran
2770

Bonneval-sur-Arc

le Villaron

Sollières-Sardières

Arc

Lac du Mont Cenis

St-Martin-d'Arc

Bramans

Modane

STAGE 9

Valloire

ITALY

Plan-Lachat

Col du Galibier
2645

Col du Lautaret
2058

le Monêtier-les-Bains

St-Chaffrey

Briançon

FRANCE

SWITZ.

Lake Geneva

Lausanne

Oyonnax

Genèva

Annemasse

8

Still Wide-Open

Rasmussen grabs yellow in the Alps, but the main favorites remain clustered behind the Danish climber.

Ever since the route of the 94th Tour de France was announced in October 2006, people had speculated about the total impact of an opening week with no team time trial or long individual time trial, and only six flat stages before the high mountains. Most experts believed this unconventional setup would lead to a more open race. They were right.

Going into stage 7, almost half the field was sitting within two minutes of the leader, so if any one of those 78 riders made a decent attack, solo or otherwise, they had a good chance of taking over the yellow jersey.

This uncertainty affected the overall classification and also determined individual team strategies. Whereas in recent years teams had a good idea who their strongest players were by the end of the first week, they were still having to hedge their bets.

Take the case of Discovery Channel, which was using very different tactics from those in the past. This wasn't the Lance Armstrong era, when protecting a single leader meant that eight riders worked hard for him every day. That strategy only worked if the leader could virtually guarantee he'd win or be on the podium. Armstrong delivered.

In 2006, without an Armstrong, Discovery went with four potential leaders, waiting until the first time trial to see who would emerge as the strongest. That tactic didn't work because the team riders didn't know whether to shoot for stage wins or help one of the potential leaders—none of whom emerged. Team manager Johan Bruyneel didn't want to repeat that flawed policy in 2007, so he invested in two riders he thought could fill the void. He recruited proven Tour top-10 finisher Levi Leipheimer from Gerolsteiner and the youthful prospect

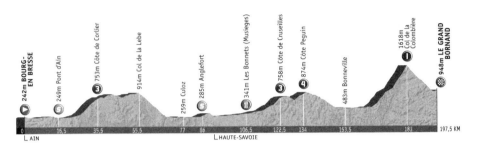

STAGE 7: BOURG-EN-BRESSE–LE GRAND BORNAND

Alberto Contador from the troubled Astana/Liberty Seguros squad. He also signed Ivan Basso—but that's another story.

For the Tour, the seasoned Leipheimer was Bruyneel's leader on paper, while the unproven but potentially brilliant Contador would also be protected. "Levi is our life insurance," Bruyneel said, "Alberto is our joker."

A comment by one of Bruyneel's directeurs sportifs, Sean Yates, reflected the team views. "Yes," he said, "Contador is a great climber, but you can't count on him [for the GC]. And we know that Levi's got his limitations, but we also know that anything can happen in a bike race. But to get a podium in Paris is the ultimate for us. That would be a major achievement and that's possible."

In the first week, Discovery did not have to work at the front, and individual riders had tried to go with breaks every day to take the pressure off their teammates. But all the stages had ended in mass finishes, and Discovery's only potential sprinter, Tomas Vaitkus, was eliminated in the Ghent pileup on stage 2. Even so, because of their strong prologue rides, Discovery had four riders in the top 25 at week's end: George Hincapie (sixth), Vladimir Gusev (seventh), Contador (14th), and Leipheimer (22nd). They were all within 30 seconds of the virtual *maillot jaune*, second-place Andreas Klöden, because race leader Fabian Cancellara would almost certainly fall back on the first mountain climb.

That climb, the category 1 Col de la Colombière, was waiting at the end of the 197.5km stage 7 from Bourg-en-Bresse to Le Grand Bornand, where the Tour entered the Alps. Teams planning to have a GC presence needed to get a rider in the day's early breakaway. Hincapie made it into the first serious move after 24km of racing on flat roads, along with two other potentially dangerous riders, Iñigo Landaluze of Euskaltel and Stefan Schumacher of Gerolsteiner. The attack was quickly closed down by rival teams.

Discovery put another rider, Egoï Martinez, into the next breakaway, shortly after Rabobank's Michael Rasmussen took the KOM sprint on the category 3 Côte de Corlier as the race entered the deeply dissected limestone ridges of the Jura. Other big teams represented in the initial seven-rider attack were T-Mobile (with Tour rookie Linus Gerdemann) and Astana (former Giro d'Italia winner Paolo

Savoldelli), while latecomers to the break included Euskaltel (Landaluze again), Saunier Duval (the 2006 Tour's most aggressive rider, David de la Fuente), Caisse d'Épargne (Ivan Gutierrez), and Rabobank (Juan Antonio Flecha).

Having a man up front allowed Martinez's eight Discovery teammates, and those of the other 12 teams represented in the eventual 15-man break, to have an easy time on the next 120km of lumpy roads through the Jura before reaching the base of the Colombière. Neither Evans's Predictor team nor the CSC squad of Carlos Sastre had riders in the break, so they were stuck with doing most of the pace making for the next three hours. Their efforts were enough to close the break's lead from an 8:30 maximum to 4:20 by the start of the decisive climb, with 32km to go, but that type of effort begins to make a difference in a team's strength as the Tour takes its toll.

It was instructive to see yellow jersey Cancellara pulling like crazy for CSC on the flat roads along the Arve River valley leading to the base of the Colombière, just as then race leader Sergei Gontchar did for T-Mobile on the first mountain stage in 2006. Cancellara's impressive effort helped his team leaders Sastre and Fränk Schleck somewhat, but it was more of a "farewell to yellow" gesture by the Swiss, which he confirmed by waving good-bye to the French TV camera just after a spectator sign saying, *Bonjour à la Montagne* ("Welcome to the Mountains").

As the hero of the opening week disappeared from view, it was hoped—in vain—that the Tour's first difficult climb would break the stalemate of stages 1 to 6. Rabobank set a steady tempo, followed by Caisse d'Épargne on the steeper second half of the 16km climb, and the first rider in the break was still three minutes clear on the 5,320 foot summit. Following a 14km descent, the deficit for the 36-rider group at the finish was 3:38.

While the top names were still biding their time, two other riders were making outstanding rides over the Colombière: T-Mobile's Gerdemann and Barloworld's Juan Mauricio Solei.

After riders in the break made initial accelerations on the early slopes, winding up a steep valley next to a fast-flowing creek, Gerdemann answered a more decisive attack by Crédit Agricole's Dmitry Fofonov. They emerged from the valley together, and Gerdemann immediately jumped away from the young Kazakh.

It was a bold move by the 24-year-old German, but he managed to ride the remaining 22km alone, while holding off strong solo pursuits by Landaluze and de la Fuente. Gerdemann was 18 seconds clear of Landaluze over the summit and took a brilliant stage win 40 seconds ahead of his Spanish pursuer, to also take over the yellow jersey. "It's a dream . . . unbelievable," he said.

The victory didn't come easy though. "I had such bad cramps that I was beyond my [limit]," Gerdemann said. "I was so tired on the final climb. When I was nearing the summit, I was waiting for the 500-meter sign. At the Tour there isn't a 500-meter sign, but I was looking for it. How long can 500 meters be? I was so happy to see the top."

While the media concentrated on Gerdemann, another 24-year-old Tour rookie quietly completed an even more remarkable effort. Breaking clear of the peloton halfway up the Colombière, when the gap to Gerdemann was 5:08, Soler quickly disappeared into the no-man's-land ahead of the peloton where riders from the morning break were dropping back. The TV cameras were focused on Gerdemann at the front, on the two chasers behind, and then on the favorites back down the road. No one was with Soler.

The only people watching the lone Colombian were the fans lining the upper slopes of the climb, and they probably thought he was a member of the original break getting his second wind. But the unheralded Barloworld rider was climbing as fast as Armstrong. Over the last 8km of the Colombière, on slopes varying from 7 to 10 percent, Soler averaged 25kph, equivalent to a power output of 450 watts for the roughly 18 minutes he was climbing at that speed. He gained more than a minute on the pack by the top and took almost three minutes out of Gerdemann in the same distance. Soler's effort enabled him to close to within 2:14 of the young German by the finish line, which the Colombian crossed in fourth place and moved to fifth on GC, after gaining 1:24 on the race leaders.

At the time, it wasn't known whether Soler could repeat his effort on future stages. For now, the Colombian was still off the radar.

That wasn't the case with Gerdemann, who was already being heralded by the media as "a breath of fresh air," or "the next Jan Ullrich." Both were headlines in the next day's newspapers.

Gerdemann possessed a Boy Scout image in a sport crippled by doping scandals, particularly the revelations in Germany. Gerdemann represented a modern but clean image, and he was not afraid to talk about cycling's doping past and express a desire to help lead the sport toward a cleaner future.

"For sure cycling has a big problem," Gerdemann said in his winner's press conference. "I think it's really hard for young riders to take all the responsibility now. We want to leave the past behind."

Also in a sign of the times, Gerdemann had been forthcoming about his past relationship with the controversial Italian trainer Luigi Cecchini. "[Gerdemann] joined us in January of 2006," said T-Mobile sponsor liaison Christian Frommert. "We heard [later] that he worked with Dr. Cecchini, and before we could call him, he called us in May and said he wrote Cecchini an e-mail and quit working with him."

The son of wealthy parents, the baby-faced German doesn't fit the image of an unscrupulous, win-at-all-costs rider from the old school of European cycling. Gerdemann, who lives with his student girlfriend in Kreuzlingen, Switzerland, is also an expert downhill skier. He reportedly showed up at his first pro team training camp sporting Louis Vuitton luggage.

T-Mobile team manager Bob Stapleton took a slight risk in bringing him to the Tour, but that bet paid off handsomely as Gerdemann became the 12th German to wear the yellow jersey. "We brought Linus to get some experience for the future and he's taken full advantage of the opportunity," said Stapleton. "We wanted Linus to succeed, but we couldn't imagine the stage victory and the yellow jersey. It shows that riders can do great things in a clean way. It's a great message for the future of cycling."

While the T-Mobile personnel were congratulating themselves, with Gerdemann in yellow and team leader Michael Rogers moving up to 14th on GC, one second behind Evans, there was a darker mood in the Rabobank camp. Rasmussen, who was eighth over the Colombière, 19 seconds ahead of the favorites, said he had wanted to attack earlier in the stage. He was reportedly angry about who was calling the shots between team director Erik Breukink, team leader Denis Menchov, and team captain Michael Boogerd. "Well, maybe I was a little too ambitious," Rasmussen said. "I felt I had too good of legs not to chase for victory. . . . It was the first day where we were climbing a little bit. Everyone was looking at each other."

In the end, Rasmussen took 10 KOM points on the Colombière before drifting back into the group on the descent. But it was clear that the Danish climber, whose contract with Rabobank was due for renewal, didn't want to be restricted to helping out Menchov, as he did in 2006.

When no real battle developed on the Colombière, the relative strengths of the predicted contenders in this unpredictable Tour remained unknown. Astana's injured Andreas Klöden and Alexander Vinokourov had comfortably finished with the main group in Le Grand Bornand, so it was assumed they were still the top favorites, followed by Evans, Contador, Leipheimer, and Alejandro Valverde, while Rasmussen, Rogers, and Christophe Moreau of Ag2r remained ambitious.

It was hoped that stage 8, which featured three long category 1 climbs in the final 88km, would clear the air somewhat. It did, but unexpectedly.

The day's key move (perhaps the key move of the whole Tour) came half-way up the 20km, two-part Cormet de Roseland. At that moment, on an 8 percent section of the climb, winding high above the forested Beaufort valley, where the day's early 18-man move was breaking apart with a 1:45 lead, Rabobank climber Rasmussen accelerated clear of the peloton. The skinny Dane was chased by two Spaniards, Toni Colom (for Astana leaders Klöden and Vinokourov) and David Arroyo (for Caisse d'Épargne's Valverde).

There was no other opposition to the attack because most teams believed that Rasmussen was just starting out on another of his annual long-distance raids to put him in the polka-dot jersey. Rasmussen was joined by Arroyo and Colom within 4km. On a fast run around a lake before the second part of the climb they bridged the two-minute gap to the front to the last three members of the original break: T-Mobile leader Rogers, Austrian climber Bernhard Kohl of Gerolsteiner, and French veteran Stéphane Goubert of Ag2r. With the Rabobank team no longer leading the chase, the reinvigorated break's lead ballooned to 5:10 by the time the sextet topped the bare summit of the 6,452-foot Roselend.

That seemed to be a huge gift for potential contenders like Rogers and Rasmussen, though two more giant climbs loomed before the finish, still 74km away.

Earlier in the stage, in the hectic downhill start to the day from Le Grand Bornand, there was a move that, besides Rogers, included Astana's Klöden and Andrey Kashechkin and Ag2r's Moreau. "That was a bit of panic," admitted Discovery's Leipheimer. "But Rabobank had no one [in the attack] so they controlled it and brought those guys back. So having Michael [Rogers] up there wasn't great for us, but it was a manageable situation."

Discovery sport director Yates gave another opinion on why teams hesitated to chase Rogers and Rasmussen. "Obviously nobody wants to commit their troops at the front before they have to," he said. "So it's a bit of a bluff. Once you commit, you're lumbered."

But just when the prospect of Rogers (who was 40 seconds ahead of Rasmussen on GC) taking over the yellow jersey from T-Mobile teammate Gerdemann began to look possible, it was cruelly ended on the notorious Roselend descent to Bourg St. Maurice. The narrow road, fast downhill straightaways, and erratic turns have often combined to cause crashes. In 1996, current Discovery manager Bruyneel shot over a parapet and landed in the trees, while Swiss contender Alex Zülle slammed into a wall, got going, and then crashed again.

Eleven Tours later, Rogers was the 2007 contender who lost control of his bike and crashed into a wooden guardrail. "It was a really dangerous descent," Rogers said, "but I wasn't pushing it too hard. I just overcooked it on a left-hand turn. There was nothing I could do about it; my back wheel was where my front wheel should have been. I got back up and tried to ride but realized I was hurt."

Right behind the tall Aussie, breakaway companion Arroyo hit the same guardrail and did a Bruyneel, his fall being stopped by the trees. Amazingly, both men continued and caught up to Rasmussen and the other two break-aways by the end of the descent. Arroyo wasn't badly hurt, but Rogers had injured his right wrist and shoulder. The pain prevented him from pulling on the bars. And as soon as the next climb began, the 15km Hauteville, Rogers was dropped. He stopped by the roadside in tears and, after his race numbers were removed, climbed into his team car. It was a sudden, emotional plunge from envisioning yellow to being out of the Tour.

"Needless to say it is a massive disap-pointment," Rogers wrote on his daily blog to an English newspaper. "I could see the yel-low, I could taste it—now it's gone. It's bad luck, but I'll be back. I'm writing to you from Italy where I am having treatment for a dislo-cated shoulder."

> **"Needless to say it is a massive disappointment. I could see the yellow, I could taste it—now it's gone. It's bad luck, but I'll be back."**

On the same twisting descent of the Roselend, three others also crashed. Rabobank's Grischa Niermann needed three stitches in his left elbow; Liquigas's Charlie Wegelius got a headache and superficial cuts and bruises. And then there was Rogers's countryman, Stuart O'Grady. After being dropped on the climb, the daredevil descender picked up several water bottles from his CSC team and was speeding past stragglers on his way to the main group containing his team leaders Sastre and Schleck. Then he crashed heavily at about 80kph.

He was helicoptered to the hospital in Moutiers, 35km away, where a body scan revealed that O'Grady suffered three broken vertebrae, five cracked ribs, and a broken scapula. He also had a punctured lung. But there was no damage to his spinal cord, and he was said to be out of serious danger.

While others were crashing on the Roselend descent, Discovery's Leipheimer was having troubles of a different kind. "My chain came off and got wrapped in the derailleur," he reported later, "and I had to do the last 5K of the downhill without pedaling. . . . When I came to the town at the base, where the car was [finally] behind me, I was a long ways behind. I got my spare bike, but it wasn't right, and they had to fix the spare bike."

There were just 3km of flat roads before the Hauteville climb began, so to get back to the pack Leipheimer made liberal use of the age-old method of holding on to a water bottle held by the team car driver while the car acceler-ates. The commissaires decided he held on too long and levied a 10-second

STAGE 8: LE GRAND BORNAND–TIGNES

penalty, but as Leipheimer said, "[I]f I hadn't gotten back it would have made a bigger difference."

While Leipheimer was chasing back and Rogers was abandoning, Rasmussen increased his lead to 6:15 on the steady 5 percent grade of the Hauteville, which was the first 15km of the famous Little St. Bernard pass before the course turned right onto a narrow side road and headed back down to the Isère valley. Colom and Arroyo sat on the Dane's wheel during the Hauteville climb and descent until he left them effortlessly when the road kicked up again 20km from the finish in Tignes.

Rasmussen lost half of his six-minute lead riding into a headwind up the wide, steadily climbing highway, leading to the finish, but he still won comfortably to take over the yellow and polka-dot jerseys.

Rasmussen's Rabobank team director, Breukink, later said his team would work to defend the race lead, while Rasmussen was talking more ambitiously. "Two years ago I came pretty close to ending up on the [final] podium," said Rasmussen, who was lying third that year until he dropped to seventh on the penultimate day after a disastrous series of falls and bike changes in the final time trial. "Of course it crossed my mind that year that at one point in the future, if the *parcours* were in my favor, I could make the podium. I think this could be the year."

He then added, "We still have 110km of time trialing to do, [and] I've shown in the past that that's not exactly my specialty. I haven't trained any time trialing at all this year. I'm a pure climber, so I think if I have to go all the way to Paris, I'll have to climb faster than I have ever done in my life. I don't think my TT skills have improved that much."

While Rasmussen was enjoying his victorious ride through Tignes to the finish in the Val-Claret ski resort, the first real battle of the Tour was taking place behind him. As soon as the climb up to Tignes began, a blitz of accelerations came from "Le Grand" Moreau, who was still on the great form that won him the Dauphiné Libéré and French championship. His attacks split the pack of contenders into three.

In the first group, which also included Evans, Valverde, Moreau, Schleck, and Kashechkin, a revived Iban Mayo attacked on the last steep section of the long climb to take second place, 2:47 behind Rasmussen. "It's satisfying to be at the front again," said Saunier Duval's Mayo after the stage. "I knew that if I could finally have my health back I would return to my position among the favorites. Last year I came here very strong but I got sick. Some lost faith in me, but I never did."

Valverde rode strongly to finish 3:12 back, taking the chase group's third-place sprint. Contador would likely have been with them had he not flatted with 4km to go, and had to take a wheel from the Mavic neutral support vehicle before his Discovery team car could reach him; he lost 18 seconds to the Evans group. "I tried to get back but I lost my rhythm," said Contador. "I was going well and it's unfortunate to have this bad luck. You have to remember there's a lot of racing ahead of us, but when you lose time like this when you were right up in the front with the best, it makes you mad."

Behind, Leipheimer ceded 3:59 to Rasmussen (and 33 seconds to teammate Contador), while Klöden waited for teammate Vinokourov, who was struggling with his knee injuries, and lost 4:29. Soler showed his inexperience by neglecting to eat enough during the long stage; he couldn't follow the accelerations and dropped 8:48 to stage winner Rasmussen.

Meanwhile, Pereiro—the rider who was still waiting to hear whether he would inherit the 2006 Tour crown should Floyd Landis fail in his bid to clear his name of doping charges—finished 15th, 4:13 back, to remain within shooting distance of the overall favorites. "I believe that many people were expecting to see what I was able to do in this difficult mountain stage," Pereiro said. "I think I showed that I was there and feeling well. The general classification is clearer tonight, but the gaps are not very important yet. I think that a rider like Vinokourov, who had a hard time today, remains among the favorites for the final win."

As for the Discovery tactics, team director Bruyneel cautioned that it was too soon to talk about Contador as a podium candidate, but he said that having two riders [Contador and Leipheimer] within striking range for the Tour's final podium played perfectly for the team's role as outsiders. "Levi is our leader for the GC because he's the most experienced, and he has the resistance to fight for three weeks," Bruyneel said. "Alberto is still young and we have to see how he can do in the third week of the race."

At that moment, with the riders about to enjoy their first rest day, the third week seemed a long way off. But the dynamics of the race were already changing, especially with Astana's two leaders conceding more time. There were even questions whether Klöden truly wanted to shoot for the overall victory. One observation on Klöden's seeming abdication of his yellow jersey hopes by waiting for Vinokourov came from Discovery directeur sportif Yates. "Vino's the captain," said the blunt Brit, "but, Christ, you've got to be a bit clever. . . . It's an easy option just to wait for Vino and say, 'I was told to wait.' Klöden would have been the favorite if he'd gone with [the Moreau group]. He's never won a grand tour. Maybe he doesn't want the pressure."

— ◉ —

One rider who would be happy to have such pressure was French champion Moreau, who was one of the stars of the grueling stage to Tignes. His best Tour finish to date was fourth in 2000. After eight stages of the 2006 Tour he was lying seventh overall, 3:06 down on race leader Rasmussen, but on a par with main contenders Valverde, Evans, Schleck, and Menchov.

At a rest day press conference in the alpine village of Les Brevières, in a narrow valley below Tignes, the Ag2r team leader explained why he was so aggressive on the previous day's final climb. "I be lieved a lot on this climb that I could create some time gaps and see who was and wasn't competitive," Moreau said. "I was probably the only one who believed we could challenge the [Tour's] big act—Astana, Vinokourov, Klöden. It was interesting to try. I had to try something, because I was a little alone in thinking that.

"It's true I used up a lot of energy in attacking but if I hadn't have done that the time gaps would have been much smaller, and most likely leaders like [Vladimir] Karpets, Vino, and Klöden would have gotten back to us, and it would have been another stage without much happening."

Moreau added that he was "very tired" from his aggressive day in the saddle and that the other contenders would now pay him much closer attention, but he said he was proud of what he was doing in the Tour. "I gained confidence from [winning] the Dauphiné and when you have good legs you have to try something. Otherwise what's the point of racing," he said.

Moreau, 36, said he was enjoying his second season with Ag2r after four years with Crédit Agricole and six with the infamous Festina team. He was one of the nine Festina riders in 1998 who confessed to doping, but he saw that as a turning point in his career and now wanted to be an example to younger riders.

When asked about his thoughts on the recent revelations by T-Mobile riders who had doped in the mid- to late 1990s, Moreau said, "I was out of the country [racing] in Spain when that news came out, so I didn't pay much attention. Since then though, I've followed the developments, the news, but what more can you say? It was up to them. What they said makes cycling look bad. We don't have any need for that, and we should continue in a positive direction."

Getting back to the Tour, Moreau was asked whether he had a legitimate chance at making the Paris podium. "I hope," he replied. "I hope. I want to. Now, I know the Tour very well, it's my wish that I don't have a bad day. I'm able to pace myself better now but you can't *always* be at your best, and I'm thinking here of the Pyrénées, which are difficult in the final week.

"For now, everything is going well and I'm recuperating well, but between the difficulties, the strategy, and the recuperation, it's necessary to have a little mélange of all three to succeed, and get a chance at the podium. And I know I will have to attack to get on the podium, as I'm not great at the time trials right now. But we'll see."

Moreau's stage 8 performance and his burning ambition resonated with the French media, particularly *L'Équipe*, which featured a huge portrait of Moreau on its broadsheet front page and ran a full-page article inside, asking whether he could become the first Frenchman to win the Tour since Bernard Hinault in 1985.

A panel of experts intimated that he could. Hinault himself said, "I believe that he can win . . . but he has to go for broke and tell himself that at 36 he has nothing to lose and everything to gain. Physically, he's ready."

Two-time Tour winner Bernard Thévenet said it would be hard for Moreau to win but added, "The retirement of Lance Armstrong has kind of liberated him. He finds himself in a position that he's never been in before, like in childhood with all his dreams rediscovered. I was like that in 1975, when I was able to match Eddy Merckx in the mountains. . . . Moreau is in a similar position. He understood in the Dauphiné that if he takes the initiative he can win races. And why not the Tour?"

The most pessimistic view came from another two-time Tour winner, Laurent Fignon, who said, "Moreau made a beginner's error in attacking six or seven times [on the climb to Tignes] because the gradient wasn't steep enough and there was a headwind. He can't make another mistake like that. You can make one error in the Tour, but not two."

Moreau would have a chance to show what he could do in this Tour on the tough stage coming up, the last in the Alps, which would feature the two highest mountain passes of the race: the Col de l'Iseran and the Col du Galibier, both over 8,600 feet.

— ◎ —

A die-straight 13 percent wall-like street, almost a kilometer long, faced the survivors of stage 9 on their way up to the finish in Briançon, the highest city in Europe. It was a tough ending to three dramatic days of racing in the Alps that left riders in varying states of fatigue and fortune.

Poker-faced Soler, the winner of the stage, was hurting from his massive solo break over the Col du Galibier but forgot his pain as his overwhelmed Barloworld team personnel greeted him with open arms at the finish. The young Colombian was a farm boy when he took up cycling only seven years earlier, but with two brilliant performances in the Alps—the other came on the Col de la Colombière on stage 7—Soler had put himself in the forefront of Tour climbers.

While Soler's star was soaring, that of prerace favorite Vinokourov was sinking. The wounded Kazakh finished 4:29 behind Soler after failing to follow the attacks made by his main rivals on the Galibier. When the Astana team leader pulled to a halt in Briançon, his face was bright red from the pain of fighting an obstinate rearguard action after being dropped, and from fighting back tears of delusion as his victory hopes took a dive. Vino even spoke to his teammates about abandoning the Tour.

The verdict of the Alps was more positive for Evans. After taking third place on this rugged stage—Valverde outsprinted him for second place, 38 seconds behind Soler—the Aussie was mobbed by the media. Before escaping to his distant team bus, Evans was pinned to the barriers by a five-deep semicircle of camera- and microphone-wielding reporters. The Aussie talked about his brash ride over the Galibier that moved him from sixth to fourth on GC, only 2:41 behind race leader Michael Rasmussen, and put the Paris podium in his sights.

A few meters away, two reporters were waiting to talk to Discovery Channel team leader Levi Leipheimer when he stopped to recover from the huge effort he had just made on the steep climb to the finish. He was breathing heavily, bent over his bars, with his head down.

As one of the interviewers handed him a bottle of water, he asked, "Where's the bus?" He'd have to ride back down the hill to find it. "That was a hard finish," said the other reporter. "Yeah, I couldn't get my chain into the little ring there at the bottom of the hill. That cost me because I had to come back to those guys and they're already sprinting. I was suffering . . . but the stage win was gone, right?"

Right.

After his chain problem, Leipheimer found himself tailed off by the chase group of 10 riders at the foot of the wall. But the American recovered quickly. He overtook Moreau and Euskaltel's Mikel Astarloza, then went past new race favorite Klöden, Sastre, and T-Mobile's Kim Kirchen, before jumping across to race leader Rasmussen and runner-up Mayo. At the line, Leipheimer was two seconds behind teammate Contador and four seconds back of Evans and Valverde. No wonder the American needed time to recover from his late effort on the wall at the end of another day of baking temperatures.

Discovery's early policy of patience seemed to be paying off, because the American-based team had the strength to employ textbook tactics on this stage from Val d'Isère to Briançon. Its Ukraine hard man, Yaroslav Popovych, attacked on the opening climb of the Col de l'Iseran—the highest pass in the race at 9,088 feet—before he was joined on the long descent by his Russian teammate Gusev and four others.

The tactic forced Rasmussen's Rabobank team to ride tempo down the Maurienne valley for the next 100 minutes, resulting in the six-man break being only 3:30 ahead when it began the day's *pièce de résistance*: the 30 or so kilometers of continuous climbing up the Télégraphe and Galibier passes, which were separated by just a five-minute downhill.

His stage 8 time loss meant that no one chased Soler when he made a sudden attack on the Col du Télégraphe. On his own, the 6-foot-2 climber crossed a 2:40 gap to the Popovych-led break, went straight past them, and charged up the Col du Galibier to take a two-minute lead on Popovych and the pursuing Contador, who had jumped impressively clear of the group of favorites.

Soler was timed at 1:25:45 for the 34.8km separating the base of the Télégraphe from the top of the Galibier, which includes 6,860 feet of vertical climbing. That's an average speed of 24.41kph and is an all-time record, 1:05 faster than the time set by Marco Pantani on his winning solo break over the Galibier to Les Deux-Alpes in 1998. Had Soler not lost so much time on the previous stage, he would now be in second overall and not down in 17th place, 6:49 back. But making mistakes was part of the learning process for this young Colombian in his first grand tour.

While not much attention was paid to Soler when he set out to bridge to the breakaways halfway up the 12km Télégraphe, all the contenders were looking when Valverde attacked 9km from the Galibier summit. "When he went, it just exploded the whole group into pieces," said Chris Horner, who was doing sterling work for his team leader Evans. "And from then on you got to watch some incredibly good bike racing."

Evans was the first to respond. "Valverde surprised me with his attacking," said the Aussie. "That's good. I need someone to break things up a bit for me. I can't do it on my own. Lance Armstrong had the whole team to do it, but I don't."

Vinokourov was the first of the favorites to drop back, while Leipheimer and Mayo quickly moved up to Evans and Valverde. But, as Leipheimer

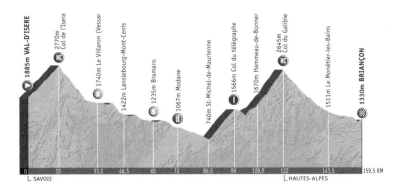

STAGE 9: VAL-D'ISÈRE–BRIANÇON

observed, "Moreau had problems, Menchov had problems, even at one point Rasmussen cracked a little bit. Vice versa, I didn't feel all that great but I seemed to be one of the better guys on the climbs."

The Galibier continued to take its toll, notably when Contador made a fierce attack 6km from the summit. "Alberto's phenomenal. When he hit the gas on the Galibier . . . nobody could stay with him," said Leipheimer. Their team boss Bruyneel explained, "Alberto said he felt good on the Galibier, and knowing that Popo was in the front, he made a smart move."

When Contador made his initial attack, Evans dug deep to catch him. The Aussie said he didn't plan to attack on the Galibier, but when he saw that most of the other race favorites were riding without teammates he tried to take advantage. "I saw everyone was isolated [and] I had the legs to go with Contador when he went," Evans said. "For me, he was one of the strongest guys, particularly on the steeper climbs. He's one to watch, so when he went I thought I'd go with him, but I couldn't stay with him. [With] his position and his team, he can sit a bit more relaxed before the real attacks come, but he's very mature for his age."

After Contador raced clear, Evans continued with his solo effort on the steepest grades of the Galibier, hoping to catch the Spaniard over the top. "Yesterday, everyone was asking me why I didn't attack [on stage 8's climb to Tignes]," Evans said at the finish. "But the Galibier was the first climb we've done [an extended] 7 percent gradient in the Tour. I had a little bit of an attack today; [the steeper climbs] suit me best."

At the summit, with 36km of downhill before the kick to the finish, Contador had caught teammate Popovych, while Evans was within 15 seconds of joining them. Perhaps the two Discovery men should have slowed a little and then worked with the Predictor rider. That would have improved their chances of closing a two-minute gap on Soler and staying clear of the unorganized chase group, which started the descent 1:10 back. Instead, Evans continued solo on the long descent and was eventually caught by the Valverde-Leipheimer-Rasmussen chase group.

So Soler hung on to take his excellent victory—five years after the last stage win by a Colombian, Santiago Botero, at nearby Les Deux-Alpes—and the chasers all regrouped in the final 5km before battling up the Briançon "wall" to the border town's 300-year-old citadel.

Rasmussen, despite some faltering on the Galibier, was more firmly in yellow because his teammate Menchov dropped almost four minutes to the other favorites.

"Things are clear now," said Rabobank team director Breukink. "Menchov is no longer the team captain. Now it's all for Rasmussen. That's too bad for us because it would have been better to have two options. Menchov had an off day. If you have one bad day at the Tour, you cannot win the Tour."

But it would be hard to have a "bad day" on the upcoming menu of flatter stages stretching out across the south of France before the next big rendez-vous, stage 13's long individual time trial. The favorites could rest easy for a few days. Or could they?

STAGE 7: BOURG-EN-BRESSE–LE GRAND BORNAND

1. Linus Gerdemann (G), T-Mobile, 4:53:13
2. Inigo Landaluze (Sp), Euskaltel-Euskadi, at 0:40
3. David de la Fuente (Sp), Saunier Duval-Prodir, at 1:39
4. Juan Mauricio Soler Hernandez (Col), Barloworld, at 2:14
5. Laurent Lefevre (F), Bouygues Telecom, at 2:21
6. Fabian Wegmann (G), Gerolsteiner, at 3:32
7. Juan Manuel Garate (Sp), Quick Step-Innergetic, at 3:38
8. Xavier Florencio (Sp), Bouygues Telecom, same time
9. Christophe Moreau (F), Ag2r Prévoyance, s.t.
10. Alejandro Valverde (Sp), Caisse d'Épargne, s.t.

STAGE 8: LE GRAND BORNAND–TIGNES

1. Michael Rasmussen (Dk), Rabobank, 4:49:40
2. Iban Mayo (Sp), Saunier Duval-Prodir, at 02:47
3. Alejandro Valverde (Sp), Caisse d'Épargne, at 03:12
4. Christophe Moreau (F), Ag2r Prévoyance, at 03:13
5. Fränk Schleck (Lux), CSC, at 03:13
6. Cadel Evans (Aus), Predictor-Lotto, at 03:13
7. Andrey Kashechkin (Kz), Astana, at 03:13
8. Alberto Contador (Sp), Discovery Channel, at 03:31
9. Denis Menchov (Rus), Rabobank, at 03:35
10. Carlos Sastre (Sp), CSC, at 03:35

STAGE 9: VAL-D'ISÈRE–BRIANÇON

1. Mauricio Soler (Col), Barloworld, 4:14:24
2. Alejandro Valverde Belmonte (Sp), Caisse d'Épargne, at 0:38
3. Cadel Evans (Aus), Predictor-Lotto, at 0:38
4. Alberto Contador Velasco (Sp), Discovery, at 0:40
5. Iban Mayo Diez (Sp), Saunier Duval, at 0:42
6. Michael Rasmussen (Dk), Rabobank, at 0:42
7. **Levi Leipheimer (USA), Discovery, at 0:42**
8. Kim Kirchen (Lx), T-Mobile, at 0:46
9. Andreas Klöden (G), Astana, at 0:46
10. Carlos Sastre (Sp), CSC, at 0:46

GENERAL CLASSIFICATION AFTER STAGE 9

1. Michael Rasmussen (Dk), Rabobank, 43:52:48
2. Alejandro Valverde Belmonte (Sp), Caisse d'Épargne, at 2:35
3. Iban Mayo Diez (Sp), Saunier Duval, at 2:39
4. Cadel Evans (Aus), Predictor-Lotto, at 2:41
5. Alberto Contador Velasco (Sp), Discovery, at 3:08
6. Christophe Moreau (F), Ag2r Prévoyance, at 3:18
7. Carlos Sastre (Sp), CSC, at 3:39
8. Andreas Klöden (G), Astana, at 3:50
9. **Levi Leipheimer (USA), Discovery, at 3:53**
10. Kim Kirchen (Lx), T-Mobile, at 5:06

RIDER DIARY

CHRISTIAN VANDE VELDE | JULY 15

The mountains, Chicken, and losing Stuey

The mountains started in earnest today and they didn't disappoint.

Yesterday offered a little taste of things to come with the Col de la Colombière. Today, though, was the real deal, with six categorized climbs. There were attacks from the gun and they didn't let up until we crossed the line.

Racing up and then down the climbs made for a really hard and stressful day. One of our lieutenants is out of the race because of the descent down the Cormet de Roselend.

It was scary as hell and I am not too much of a man to admit it. Stuey and Fabian go really fast downhill; they put Valentino Rossi to shame. The only problem is that some of us can't stay out of their way. Fabian passed the entire peloton and we were already flying to begin with.

So Stuey is out and we are all more than sad to lose him as he is strong,

CHRISTIAN VANDE VELDE | JULY 15 *continued*

smart, and funny, all traits that make for a great teammate and friend. I know I am speaking of him like he died but he is really busted up badly. We will miss him big time.

The rest of the race played out a lot like other massive mountain days with all of us chasing Chicken through the Alps. Usually when he decides to launch we rarely catch him. He now owns two jerseys and might not relinquish either of them.

We are now done with the first third or so of the race. We held the jersey for seven of those stages and maybe we burned some matches, but who cares? Like I said the other day, it hurts whether you're at the front or the back. ⊗

RIDER DIARY

SIMON GERRANS | JULY 14
Bastille Day blues

The word "pressure" doesn't do justice to what you feel racing on a French team in France's biggest sporting event on their national holiday, Bastille Day. There was a rather large emphasis in the pre-race team meeting on having at least one Ag2r rider in the breakaway.

Once again the stage started at a cracking pace. My teammates and I were doing a good job of following the breaks until after around 40km of rac-ing, when a big group went clear with no Ag2r riders. Luckily Martin counter-attacked and was able to get across to the front group, saving our asses from a postrace ribbing.

A couple of teams who missed the move then set tempo on the front of the group until the base of the Col de la Colombière, where the bunch broke up. I didn't have the legs to do anything, so cruised in with the *gruppetto*. ⊗

SIMON GERRANS I JULY 15

Climbing legs

I knew what I was in for today. This was one of the stages we rode in the Ag2r pre-Tour training camp. Not sure if this was a good idea or not.

After the way I felt in the first—and one of the easier—mountain stages yesterday, I must admit I was a little concerned about how I was going to survive today. However, I think the hit-out was exactly what I needed to find my climbing legs.

The pressure was on once again to have guys in the break. We figured if the race blew early on, Moreau would have teammates waiting for him up the road ready to help out.

Things panned out pretty well. We landed Gouby and Arrie in the breakaway. I felt really good and was able to stick with Moreau until the base of the final climb, where he was the one who blew what was left of the front group to pieces.

Christophe really got people talking today. The way he attacked the race favorites, he showed that he is in top condition and a real contender.

Most of my Aussie mates in the bunch didn't have such a good day. Robbie missed the time cut, still struggling with injuries from his crash on stage 1. Mick fell heavily while in the winning break, hurting his shoulder and being forced to abandon the race. To top it off, Stuey fell on the descent of the Cormet de Roselend, which to be honest with you frightened the hell out of me. Stuey flew past me with a jersey stuffed full of bidons on the descent. I next spotted him a few corners later wrapped around a pole on the side of the road, not moving. I could tell straightaway he'd really hurt himself. He finished his Tour there and then with more broken bones than I care to mention. Today's stage left only Cadel and me flying the Aussie flag. No pressure. ⊗

RIDER DIARY

SIMON GERRANS | JULY 17

A day of chasing, a day to forget

Stage 9 was one of those days I'd rather forget! I always seem to struggle the day following a rest day, and today was no exception.

Starting from kilometer zero we climbed the Col de l'Iseran, where the bunch split into several groups. I ended up in the second group for a short while until the peloton regrouped.

Knowing my legs weren't fantastic, I thought I'd do my best to place my teammates at the front of the group for the Col du Télégraphe. So I took a bit of wind for the boys leading into the base of the climb.

It turned out to be just as well I didn't have high hopes for myself. As soon as the gradient increased and I changed down to my small chainring, the chain dropped off completely and I came to a standstill. By the time I got moving again I was well out the back and had a fair chase in front of me just to catch the *gruppetto*.   ⊗

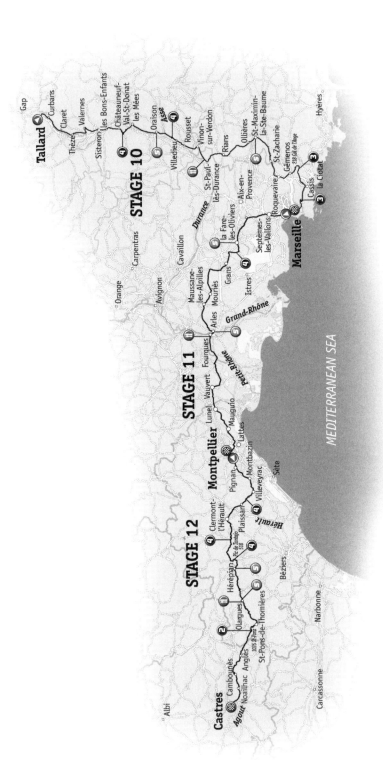

9

Dark Days in the South

*After a tough time in the Alps, the Tour heads for
three easy days of transition that are anything but.*

"This Tour pleases me a lot because it's very indecisive. We don't know who's going to win. It's a fabulous Tour."

This was five-time Tour de France winner Bernard Hinault talking in Tallard, a sleepy town nestled in dusty vineyards on the northern edge of Provence. It marked the start of the 2007 Tour's third phase: three flat stages across southern France leading to the first major time trial.

Hinault remarked that eight or nine riders still had a chance of making the Paris podium, including Ag2r's homegrown Christophe Moreau—known as *Le Grand*—who had been on the front pages of every French newspaper since his combative ride on the stage to Tignes. The crowds in Tallard easily spotted the sixth-place Moreau in his blue-white-red tricolor jersey of French national champion, and greeted him with loud cheers and applause as he threaded his way through sunbaked medieval streets to the start in the shadow of Tallard's massive tenth-century castle.

In contrast to Moreau's warm reception, contenders like second-place Alejandro Valverde, fourth-place Cadel Evans, and ninth-place Levi Leipheimer were barely recognized by the fans. Even race leader Michael Rasmussen, pedaling slowly to sign in with his yellow helmet looped over his stem, merited just a few polite claps.

The most popular figure was Alexander Vinokourov, who rode to the start behind Russian teammate Sergei Ivanov. The Astana leader, still riding with big bandages on both knees, looked very sad. He would say later, "I almost abandoned [yesterday] but I said to myself I'll go for another day and perhaps it will get better. I'll always remember that my riders gave me a lot of courage.

I know that without them I wouldn't have gotten through the Alps." But at 21st overall, 8:05 behind Rasmussen, Vino would need a miracle to get back into overall contention.

T-Mobile, which had been on a roller-coaster ride in the Alps, was already out of contention. On stage 8 into Tignes, Linus Gerdemann lost his yellow jersey to Rasmussen, rookie Mark Cavendish abandoned his first Tour, and team leader Michael Rogers left the race after the crash that stopped him from taking a potential yellow jersey. Then, following the stage, team rider Patrik Sinkewitz went to the hospital with a broken nose and an injured jaw after a freak collision with an elderly spectator. Then, on stage 9, another of T-Mobile's Tour rookies, Marcus Burghardt, struck a loose dog on the descent of the Col de l'Iseran and finished the stage with cuts, scrapes, and bruises.

If the team's American manager, Bob Stapleton, thought things couldn't get any worse, he was wrong. Just before the stage start in Tallard, he was met by a pack of journalists when the T-Mobile team bus pulled into the starting area. The media hounds asked for his comments on a report that Sinkewitz had tested positive for an elevated testosterone-to-epitestosterone ratio from a drug test conducted by the German Cycling Federation a month before the Tour. The news, which had been leaked to German television reporters, was sprung on Stapleton as he stepped out of the bus.

Although he had not received any official notification from the German federation or its antidoping agency, Stapleton was forced to defend his team, its internal testing policies, and the movement to clean up the sport. "Clearly we are disappointed that one of our athletes has breached his code of conduct and is involved with some form of doping," Stapleton said. "Part of this validates what we've been pushing for all along, which is more testing, more out-of-competition testing, and testing all athletes on all teams. And not relying solely on what individual teams do in their own test procedures. So on one hand, we feel like this is consistent with the actions we want to see in the sport, and that is the part that is showing promise that the more tests there are, the more they apply to everyone, the more pressure there is to change the doping culture in sport."

Sinkewitz, who won the 2004 Tour of Germany, was still recovering from his injuries in a Hamburg hospital. He said he had no idea how he could have tested positive for testosterone. But after the Tour, Sinkewitz admitted to using a testosterone gel and was subsequently fired by T-Mobile. He was the first T-Mobile rider to test positive through an independent antidoping agency since the squad introduced its new antidoping policies. Earlier in the year, the team sacked Sergei Gontchar after the team's internal testing program identified blood abnormalities in the Ukrainian time trial specialist.

Asked why Sinkewitz hadn't been caught by the team's internal testing, Stapleton explained that the team focuses on searching for signs of blood doping and the use of EPO. "We do blood-based tests to screen the athletes for any unusual circumstances, and then do follow-up tests if we see anything unusual [as with Gontchar]," he said. "The teams were never intended to do antidoping tests. The independent antidoping agencies should do these tests."

Adding to the gravity of the situation, German TV stations ARD and ZDF announced they were suspending coverage of the Tour de France until the Sinkewitz case was clarified. "We can't screen an event involving some teams and riders under suspicion of doping," explained ZDF chief producer Nikolaus Brender. "We want to show by this gesture that we're ready to support cycling only if it's clean, that's to say without banned doping substances."

Patrice Clerc, the president of the Tour's parent company ASO, failed to comprehend the German decision, especially in light of cycling's proactive stance in the fight against drugs cheats. "It's a paradox," he said. "Why is the Tour de France being punished, when we are sticking with our efforts to clean up the sport? Would they prefer that there are no surprise tests, that we do nothing? If you don't look you don't find anything. We've decided to take another attitude; we're fighting against doping, and yet we're being sanctioned because cheats are being found!"

Stapleton had a similar view, saying that now was not the time to abandon cycling. "Everyone has their own business interests that they are pursuing," he said of ARD and ZDF. "That's their choice. There is obviously a lot of scrutiny in Germany around doping, and I think that is fair and valid. I think every magazine, newspaper, television channel, and person needs to make their own decision on where they stand on these issues. Do you want to stay and fight? Do you really want to try and make a difference? Or do you want to throw up your hands and walk away? That's a decision for everyone here to make on their own. My decision is to stay and fight."

Stapleton added that while the past few days at the Tour had been difficult, the news of Sinkewitz's positive test eclipsed the trials and tribulations the team had faced during the race. "I would have said up until today that all these challenges we've faced in this Tour would have made us stronger," Stapleton said. "I think this is extremely difficult for the athletes to bear. I think they believe their livelihoods are at stake. I think they feel that all the personal commitments they've made to this team have gone for naught. We had only a brief time to talk before the departure. Of course they are devastated. They signed a code of conduct that says if we think you are screwing around, we can fire you. They have subjected themselves to the blood volume tests, which are not pleasant. I think they feel absolutely betrayed."

Team CSC's "elder statesman" Jens Voigt, who once lived in the German Democratic Republic, said the TV channels were acting like dictators in the old DDR. "It's just like the old East Germany," he said. "There are only a few people in control of making that decision, and it's not right. Let people watch the Tour. If they don't want to they can turn off their television or change the channel."

— ◉ —

That a huge kerfuffle was being made of a minor rider testing positive weeks before the Tour, which he had already abandoned, raised questions about what would happen if a major star was caught cheating; the Sinkewitz affair was already drowning out news of the race, which was a shame, because stage 10 from Tallard was another fast one, despite the 90-degree heat on a marathon 229.5km trek across the low hills of Provence to the Mediterranean coast at Marseille. "It was a long, hot day and a lot of guys were suffering in the heat," said Rasmussen, who retained the overall lead. "The heat takes a toll on everybody."

The long stage didn't give Vinokourov and the other injured riders much chance to relax, especially early on when both the speed and the sun were at their hottest. "The start was quick 'cause there's like 150 guys who realized that the break was going to go today," said Brit Charlie Wegelius of Liquigas.

Sure enough, riders eagerly tried breakaways right from the gun, and the peloton averaged almost 50kph until an 11-man break went clear 80km into the stage. "It was really hard on those little small roads, and, yeah, hot," said Wegelius. "But hot is nice. It's better than rain."

The cloud cover on the coast didn't cool the racing. Over two category 3 climbs on either side of the fishing and wine village of Cassis, five men burst clear from the break and stayed together until the long finishing straight in Marseille. CSC was hoping that Voigt could take the win, but the German couldn't get clear of the faster finishers in the group, and it was Quick Step's Cédric Vasseur, 36, who came from the back to take the lead and just hold off countryman Sandy Casar of Française des Jeux to give France its first stage win of the race. Vasseur's success was well received by the home crowd, especially as this was his farewell Tour and his victory came exactly 10 years after his only other Tour stage win. The peloton arrived more than 10 minutes later.

A similar result—a small breakaway finishing well ahead of the pack—was anticipated the next day when, after another 50kph opening, a five-man break reached ancient Arles, halfway through the 182.5km stage, with a 7:30 lead. Powered by German national champion Fabian Wegmann of Gerolsteiner, Brit David Millar of Saunier Duval, and Belgian Philippe Gilbert of Française des Jeux, the break seemed set to increase its lead all the way to Montpellier. Then came one of cycling's classic moves: a sudden acceleration by one team in echelon formation to take advantage of a strong crosswind.

"You knew it was going down all day," said Predictor's Chris Horner. "It slowed down just a little bit [when the Millar break went clear], but when we went through the feed zone the crosswind was so strong you just had to stay at the front."

The Liquigas team had tried something similar on stage 5, but the wind direction didn't cooperate. On stage 11, though, the infamous mistral wind was blowing straight from the Mediterranean across the bean-flat marshes of the Camargue and hitting the riders on the left hip, slightly from behind. The seasoned Vinokourov, feeling better each day, recognized that conditions were perfect for such a move. "The wind was really strong. We saw some bad faces in the bunch so we decided to attack," Vinokourov said after the stage.

"It was a lot of crosswind, and nobody knew where the crosswind was stronger and [where] a little bit less," said Vino's Astana directeur sportif Mario Kummer. "We heard from our soigneurs that the crosswind in the feed zone, and just after the feed zone, was very strong. I told the riders to pay attention, and to stay at the front.

"Vino told us he wanted to try something. We translated to the other riders, and then they were together and they did the initial [echelon]. We didn't know [who] was behind, but we expected we could drop somebody. The peloton was very long in this situation, and we were riding full-on."

> **"There are days like this ...The Tour is far from finished. It could have been even worse. I could have broken something."**

Half of the 170-strong bunch was caught out by the sudden acceleration, including Moreau, who had just three teammates to help him in his desperate pursuit: the Swiss Martin Elmiger, Spanish veteran José Luis Arrieta, and French climber Stéphane Goubert.

"You can say whatever you want about this," said T-Mobile's Bernard Eisel, who was also caught out by the move. "Astana tried it, it worked out. I think Ag2r is not happy at the moment because Moreau crashed [earlier] today. And then Astana attacked when everybody still had a feedbag around his neck. It's not gentlemanlike, but what's gentlemanlike in this Tour?"

Moreau said he broke a cleat in his crash, and he had to change a shoe just before the feed zone. But the Frenchman wasn't resentful. "There are days like this," he said. "The Tour is far from finished. It could have been even worse. I could have broken something. I was well supported by my team, because at one moment I was near a breaking point, psychologically. In the Tour, you have to get over these sorts of days, even if it isn't easy. Perhaps something good may come out of the bad. Perhaps now I will have more chances of an opening, more room to move. It's a black day that I will have to forget."

Discovery Channel team director Johan Bruyneel commended Vinokourov for his fighting spirit. "We were not expecting it at all," Bruyneel said. "There was a strong tempo in the peloton straight after the feed zone. We had two guys who missed their feedbags, [Egoï] Martinez and [Sergio] Paulinho. All of a sudden Astana started to go. We were in a good position. We had five guys up there."

Discovery team leader Leipheimer was up there, of course, thanks in no small measure to the team's seasoned veteran, George Hincapie, who said at the finish in Montpellier, "I pretty much rode the whole day in the wind in front of Levi. It was a really tough day for me."

Bruyneel added that the Astana team tactic was just one more example of how GC riders like Leipheimer must be constantly vigilant. "The Tour de France is three weeks long," he said. "You have to be there in the flats, in the time trials, in the mountains, and in the downhills. You have to be everywhere. You always have to keep fighting. It was a good try from Astana today."

Aside from Moreau, none of the other 18 men in front of Vinokourov on the overall classification lost any time on the stage. Nonetheless, Vinokourov felt good after his team's surge. In fact, with 4km to go, he had the gall to attack the peloton and the legs to hold them off for nearly a kilometer. "It's a big boost to my morale," Vinokourov said. "My legs are much better than yesterday. I almost abandoned yesterday, but the team doctor worked on me overnight. I feel a lot better today."

Moreau eventually conceded 3:20 to the Astana-led pack. Also trapped behind were five of the Tour's best remaining sprinters: Eisel, Thor Hushovd, Erik Zabel, Robert Förster, and Sébastien Chavanel. So, with the 80 lead riders hurtling into Montpellier together, the chances for the stage win looked good for green jersey leader Tom Boonen, while his likely challengers looked to be Barloworld's Robbie Hunter, Crédit Agricole's Julian Dean (normally Hushovd's lead-out man), Predictor-Lotto's Fred Rodriguez (whose teammate Robbie McEwen was out of the race), and Saunier Duval's Francisco Ventoso.

That was the theory, but reality changed after the racers sped in a long line down a narrow ramp off a highway and took a sweeping left turn around a traffic island, 750 meters from the finish line, and then came to a chicane that was not shown on the map in the official road book.

Boonen said he was confident of taking his second stage win of the Tour. "I was on the wheel of four Liquigas guys and in a perfect position to get points that would put me well ahead of Zabel and Hushovd in the classification," he said. "Then this rider comes through at 75kph into a 90-degree turn. That person was Julian Dean."

Rodriguez, who had just about recovered from the injuries he sustained in the stage 2 crash, was also well positioned. "I was right behind Boonen," said

ABOVE More than a million people witness the London prologue, including these fans outside the Queen's London residence, Buckingham Palace.

RIGHT He won't win the prologue in London, but Andreas Klöden puts fear into the other prerace favorites with an impressive second place to time trial specialist Fabian Cancellara.

Between lines of yellow-clad British club cyclists, the ceremonial start of stage 1 is celebrated on historic Tower Bridge over the river Thames.

ABOVE With 200 meters to go in the ferocious stage 1 sprint, Bernhard Eisel (right) is still leading, but Robbie McEwen (in pink), Thor Hushovd (green), and Tom Boonen (blue) are about to pounce.

RIGHT In this image from race TV, race leader Fabian Cancellara (in yellow) has just landed (left) on the pile of bodies that resulted from the giant pileup, 2.5km from the stage 2 finish in Ghent.

RIGHT TOP Discovery's Egoï Martinez pushes weeping teammate Tomas Vaitkus to the stage 2 finish line after the big Lithuanian broke his right thumb in five places in the Ghent pileup.

ABOVE On the cobblestones at Compiègne, yellow jersey Fabian Cancellara squeezes between Robbie Hunter and the barrier moments before launching his final-kilometer attack to win stage 3.

BELOW In Joigny, South African Robbie Hunter's final thrust just fails to catch stage 4 winner Thor Hushovd.

ABOVE The peloton speeds through the Chablis vineyards as stage 5 of the Tour heads south toward Autun.

LEFT Knees bleeding after his stage 5 crash, Alexander Vinokourov grits his teeth in the slipstream of his Astana teammates, vainly trying to catch the pack.

ABOVE Linus Gerdemann is overjoyed as he wins stage 7 in Le Grand Bornand to take the overall race lead in the Alps.

BELOW Multiple fractures of ribs and vertebrae will be the verdict for Stuart O'Grady after his stage 8 crash descending the Cormet de Roselend.

RIGHT Michael Rogers was the virtual yellow jersey leader when he crashed down the Cormet de Roselend and had to abandon the Tour with a dislocated shoulder.

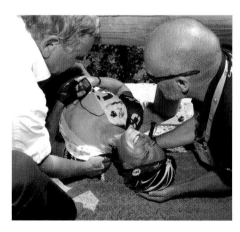

ABOVE An attack by Christophe Moreau on the final stage 8 climb to Tignes draws out Alejandro Valverde, while in the distance Cadel Evans prepares to chase them.

BELOW On crossing the stage 8 finish line in Tignes, Alexander Vinokourov (right) thanks teammate Andreas Klöden for waiting and then pacing him up the last climb.

LEFT Colombian revelation Juan Mauricio Soler has the finish line in his sights as he races up the steep climb in Briançon to win stage 9.

BELOW With a strong crosswind from their left, Astana team riders form a fast-moving echelon that splits the race apart on stage 11 across the flat roads of the Camargue.

TOP Riding a brand-new BMC time trial bike, Alexander Vinokourov speeds through the damp country-side around Albi to win stage 13.

ABOVE Alberto Contador makes one of his signature uphill accelerations on his way to winning the critical Plateau de Beille stage ahead of the beleaguered Michael Rasmussen.

ABOVE In the final gesture of his Tour (and maybe his career), Alexander Vinokourov comes back from his stage 14 defeat to win stage 15 in Loudenvielle.

RIGHT On the toughest slopes of the stage 16 finishing climb to the Col d'Aubisque, Levi Leipheimer puts on the pressure ahead of Rabobank's Michael Rasmussen and Discovery teammate Alberto Contador.

ABOVE Cadel Evans never gave up in his bid to finish on the Paris podium, and he clinches second place with a battling performance in the stage 19 time trial.

LEFT In what he called "the time trial of my life," Levi Leipheimer blasts along the rolling road between Cognac and Angoulême on his way to winning stage 19—and almost winning the Tour.

At the end of an astonishing Tour, yellow-clad Alberto Contador is about to consecrate his victory below the Arc de Triomphe.

After all the battles, heart-aches, and scandals, Alberto Contador can celebrate his shock victory ahead of Cadel Evans (left) and teammate Levi Leipheimer.

the Californian. "There was a chicane and nobody had any idea [it was there] and we were coming in so fast. People came in out of control and I just went into the barriers; we had nowhere to go."

The crash took out Dean, Ventoso, Boonen, and Rodriguez, which left Hunter with an easy shot at the win. The South African started his effort going into the final turn with 250 meters to go, and he finished well ahead of the runner-up, first-week race leader Fabian Cancellara. It was the first stage win by a rider from the African continent in Tour history.

As Hunter was celebrating, Rodriguez was lying flat on his back, writhing in pain. And later, when he had struggled to his feet and crossed the line seven minutes after Hunter, the veteran sprinter again criticized the race organization, just as he did at Ghent 10 days earlier. "They do it every time. They don't care," said an angry Rodriguez. "It's the Tour de France and they have no respect for the riders. I'm sick of it."

Boonen escaped without injury, but Dean had multiple cuts and bruises, particularly around his right knee. Ventoso was taken to a hospital for x-rays on his left hand. As for Rodriguez, with his right leg dangling and a greasy black chainwheel imprint on the calf muscle, he was pushed by a Predictor team soigneur for the 500 meters to his team bus. Holding back tears, Rodriguez spoke quietly, his voice breaking with emotion. "I can't move it right now," he said about his leg.

When a reporter said the crash was tough luck, an angry Rodriguez said, "It's not tough luck. The Tour de France has to start paying, has to start paying for this. They have no respect for their riders."

In 2006, Rodriguez crashed out of the Tour after hitting an unmarked pothole in Belgium on stage 3. Then came the huge pileup in Ghent in this Tour that almost forced Rodriguez to abandon again. It also resulted in him berating Tour officials for serving up another dangerous finish. "My crash in last year's Tour was worse," he said. "But it's going back to the same thing; it's proven that the Tour de France isn't worried about the safety of the riders. I've written complaints and I've contacted the riders' representatives. They've never responded."

While the angry, frustrated Rodriguez was being pushed slowly to his team bus in Montpellier, a group of back markers drifted in to the finish, more than 10 minutes behind. Among the 14 stragglers was one of stage winner Hunter's Barloworld teammates, Welsh rookie Geraint Thomas, who had a different tale to tell. He first spoke about the Astana coup right after the feed zone.

"I was just having something to eat, and all of a sudden it was like, bang! I was like, 'Fuck, man. Thanks for that.' I was at the back and just couldn't move up before it split. Then it split again, and I was in the back again," Thomas said.

"It was a really long, hot day. The heat is really getting to me now after the last two days. It's just unbelievable. I've never been in heat like this before. I'm really tired now, wasted. Everyone says these days are flat and whatever, but they're harder than the mountain stages to be honest. You can't sit up because there's still 100K to go and you'll be outside the time limit [if you don't ride]. It's so hard."

One rider did finish outside the time limit: Dave Zabriskie crossed the finish line 31:26 back. The CSC rider had been struggling with knee pain since the Tour began, attributing it to a team-mandated decision to switch shoes during the Giro d'Italia in May. "The pain is in my left knee, the one that was damaged in a car accident [in May 2003]," Zabriskie said. "The screws in there are just too sensitive to change."

Zabriskie had hoped to recover during the flat stages between the Alps and the Pyrénées but found the pace too difficult. "After the Galibier day I really struggled to try to get better," he said. "I was hoping on these few flat days I could nurse it back to health, but the Tour is not the kind of race where you can fix yourself. Today was a really hard day, and my knee couldn't handle it. I came off when Astana finally did their rotation in the wind."

CSC team director Kim Andersen said, "For us it's too bad that Dave is not at his best. He has to try and make himself useful, and there hasn't been too much of that so far. We hoped he would get better. He's also disappointed that he hasn't been able to help the team like he'd hoped."

The old city center of Montpellier is one of Europe's jewels with its nearly 500-year-old Arc de Triomphe. Many of the streets are paved with polished stone, leading to the magnificent Place de la Comédie, named for an eighteenth-century theater. The centerpiece of this pedestrianized square, which is fronted by sprawling open-air bars and restaurants, is the Fountain of the Three Graces.

Before the start of stage 11 of the 2007 Tour de France, the place was neither graceful nor comedic. The European media at first surrounded the Rabobank team bus parked under the plane trees of the elegant Esplanade that adjoins the square and then pinned race leader Rasmussen to the bus door with boom microphones and TV cameras, before three burly policemen cleared the way for him to reach the sign-in platform.

Why all the fuss? Well, it wasn't because the shaven-headed Dane was wearing the yellow jersey for the fourth consecutive stage but because he was at the center of a suspected doping scandal. Overnight, news had come through from the Danish Cycling Union (DCU) that before the Tour it had informed Rasmussen that he would not be selected for the 2007 world championships nor the 2008 Olympic Games, because of at least two warnings he had received (one from the DCU, the other from the UCI) for not informing the authorities of his correct whereabouts for out-of-competition drug tests.

DCU director Jesper Worre, who raced professionally from 1982 to 1992, told the DR1 TV station, "We consider this case with great seriousness, and the executive of the DCU decided that Michael will no longer be part of the national team and he was informed of this on June 26. It is confidential information, but people have the right to know that the DCU fights for a clean sport. The DCU is not saying that Michael tested positive, but there are a number of question marks over his behavior and attitude."

Rasmussen said he had received just one warning, but Worre insisted there had been several. "I have tried to give my explanations to the DCU," Rasmussen told the Danish media, "but they haven't accepted them."

Specifically, Rasmussen was first called to order on March 24, 2006, for being late to inform the UCI about his whereabouts for the upcoming three months. That was the time when the UCI updated its Web site and several riders are said to have updated their upcoming travel plans by letter. Rasmussen said the letter arrived late, and hence came a warning. More than a year later, on April 6, 2007, a few days before he started the Tour of the Basque Country, Danish federation testers arrived at Rasmussen's house on Lake Garda in Italy for an out-of-competition test. He was not there, having left for the race a day earlier than planned, but he appears not to have received a warning for this infringement. Finally, on June 28, just over a week before the 2007 Tour, he missed another scheduled test (was he training in Mexico, as he later claimed, or in Italy?), and he did receive a warning from the UCI—a decision reported to the DCU.

In the UCI regulations, Article XIV.V.86 states that a rider who receives three such warnings within 18 months is liable to be suspended from competition for between three months and two years.

Despite the media pressure, Rasmussen started stage 12 from Montpellier to Castres as if nothing had happened. "I'm calm and very relaxed," he said before signing on. "All this seems out of proportion. I can confirm that I've not had a positive result at any antidoping control. I was tested out of competition in June, and the result was negative."

The stone-faced Rasmussen did indeed appear calm as he pedaled off through the packed streets of Montpellier on a day of bright sunshine and blustery winds. The race headed west through the Languedoc vineyards before swinging into the hills bordering the Massif Central. After the usual attacks, two riders emerged in front: Frenchman Pierrick Fédrigo of Bouygues Telecom and the young Spaniard Amets Txurruka of Euskaltel.

They rode well to get a maximum lead of 11:30, and they still had five minutes on topping the day's major climb, the category 2 Montée de la Jeante. The peloton rolled up the 10.4km, 6.1 percent hill, led by eight riders from Liquigas, hoping for another stage win by Pozzato. But all the main sprinters were still in the pack 47km later when the two breakaways were passed just before the 1km-to-go archway at Castres. It was a straight run to the finish this time, and Quick Step's Boonen easily dispatched all comers in a mass sprint to take his second stage win of the race, ahead of Zabel and Hunter.

The weather changed. There were clouds and a misty drizzle in the forest of beech and pines after the Jeante climb, where the temperature was a meager 52 degrees Fahrenheit. It was still only 68 degrees at the finish.

The race climate changed too. Bernard Hinault was no longer calling the Tour "fabulous," even though the outcome was more uncertain than ever. With the ongoing Sinkewitz and Rasmussen doping stories, the media was on the hunt for any juicy tidbits of controversy. After the stage, reporters again pursued Rasmussen to his daily news conference to ask difficult questions. Despite his repeated denials of wrongdoing, it was clear that they were not going to leave it at that. Indeed, there had been rumors during the day of more damning news about to emerge. It arrived in an exclusive story posted on the velonews.com Web site:

A former amateur mountain-bike racer alleged Thursday that Tour de France yellow-jersey holder Michael Rasmussen (Rabobank) attempted to trick him into carrying illegal doping products to Europe in 2002.

Whitney Richards, 38, a one-time Colorado-based cross-country racer, told VeloNews that in March of 2002, Rasmussen asked him to transport a box containing cycling shoes. But the shoebox, according to Richards, actually contained bags of an American-made human blood substitute. None of the information Richards provided VeloNews involves allegations of current doping.

Asked by VeloNews about the charges at a postrace press conference following the Tour's 12th stage on Friday, Rasmussen said he was familiar with Richards's name but declined to comment further on the allegations.

"I cannot confirm any of that. I do know the name," Rasmussen said.

The allegations come on the heels of a decision by the Danish cycling federation to exclude the Rabobank rider from that country's world-championship and Olympic teams, citing a dispute over Rasmussen's failure to notify the agency's antidoping officials about his whereabouts in the months leading to the Tour.

Richards said he decided to go public with his allegations after he heard the Tour leader comment on doping in the sport, promising that cycling fans could "trust me."

Richards said he and Rasmussen developed a friendship when the Dane came to the United States to prepare for the 2001 world mountain-bike championships in Vail. Rasmussen won the world cross-country title in 1999, then started his transition to road racing in 2001 when he signed a stagiaire contract with CSC.

That friendship, said Richards, continued for several months until the American moved to Italy to live with his girlfriend in March of 2002.

Rasmussen was also living in Italy at the time, and according to Richards, Rasmussen asked that Richards bring over a pair of cycling shoes he had left in the United States. Richards agreed and two days prior to his departure, a mutual friend delivered a box purportedly containing the for-gotten cycling shoes.

In an effort to fit all his belongings in his luggage, Richards opened the box to discard it and just bring the shoes—he said he then discovered the bags. Richards said he immediately called a friend—a Ph.D. physiolo-gist—to help him decide what to do.

"I was blown away," Richards told VeloNews. "This wasn't a pair of Sidis . . . it was frickin' dog medicine or something."

That friend, Taro Smith, Ph.D., confirmed Richards's recollection of the incident.

"I came to his house to figure out what was in the package," Smith told VeloNews on Friday. "The box was packed full of silver Mylar packages la-beled with 'Biopure.' Once you opened them there were clear plastic IV sets with what looked like blood inside. The box was packed full of these. That's all I know. I don't have first-hand knowledge of where they came from or who delivered them to Whitney, but I do know what was in the box."

Richards and Smith decided to cut open the bags and pour the con-tents down the sink.

"There was no way that I would carry that on to an airplane or carry that through customs for anyone," said Richards.

According to labels, the bags were filled with a hemoglobin-based oxygen carrier (HBOC) known as Hemopure, manufactured by the U.S.-based Biopure Corporation. The product is made from hemoglobin mole-cules that have been removed from the red cells of cow's blood. Originally designed as an emergency blood substitute that requires no refrigeration, Hemopure has only been approved for human use in South Africa. U.S. clinical trials were recently suspended over safety concerns, but a similar product is currently used for veterinary purposes.

Endurance athletes were said to be using the product as a substitute for blood-doping or EPO use, though no one has ever been convicted of using Hemopure or other HBOCs. Its use is banned under the World Anti-Doping Code and the World Anti-Doping Agency developed a low-cost screening test in 2004.

A few weeks later when Richards arrived in Italy, he says he confronted Rasmussen about the package and its contents. He claims Rasmussen admitted it was poor judgment, but then asked Richards what he had done with the hemoglobin substitute. Richards said Rasmussen became very upset when Richards explained he had disposed of it, asking him if he had "any idea how much that shit cost?"

"[Then Rasmussen] stormed upstairs . . . and I decided at that point to just go to the train station and go home," Richards recalled. "Really, he's lucky I didn't follow him upstairs and punch him in the face right then and there.

"The nerve of the guy," Richards added. "Not only is he a drug cheat, but he didn't give a damn about anybody else. He was willing to put me out there to carry that crap through customs . . . into Italy at a time when they were investigating Dr. [Michele] Ferrari and people were lobbing accusations at Lance Armstrong. Think about what it would have been like for Italian customs to catch an American with a bunch of bike gear and cow's blood at the border."

Richards was offended, so much so that he contacted VeloNews later that same year. However, he asked that the conversation be off the record, declining to be named and asking that Rasmussen also not be mentioned in any way that he might be recognized. Because of those restrictions, VeloNews did not publish his story.

Several years later, after being put in contact with Sunday Times *of London reporter David Walsh, Richards again offered details of the story, but continued to insist that neither he nor Rasmussen be identified.*

"I really just wanted someone to know," said Richards. "But I didn't exactly know how they might use the information. I didn't feel comfortable going totally public with this because I knew his girlfriend—now his wife—and I didn't see a reason to bring her into it. My friends who were pro mountain-bike racers have always told me I should, because it's guys like that who are ruining their careers by cheating. Still, it's not a decision you make lightly."

Walsh opted to use the story as an anecdote in his recently released book, From Lance to Landis, *but respected Richards's insistence that both parties remain anonymous.*

Indeed, that's where the story would have stopped, except that Rasmussen moved into the yellow jersey at the Tour de France on Sunday, after an impressive solo ride to Tignes. Richards said that it wasn't the stage victory or even the yellow jersey that prompted him to go public with his story. Instead, it was Rasmussen's recent "trust me" comments during the Tour's rest day on Monday that prompted Richards to speak out.

"[Rasmussen has] won Tour stages before," Richards said. "It's not that. It was the press conference on Monday that got to me. Someone asked him about Bjarne Riis's involvement with drugs and he went on about how he's clean and then added, 'You can trust me.' That's what set me off."

Richards said he finds it offensive that a rider he knows "for sure is mixed up with doping" is leading the Tour de France when the race is fighting for its survival.

This story, written by velonews.com editor Charles Pelkey, was soon translated and posted on Web sites and printed in newspapers all over the world. The allegations and information contained in the report added fuel to the fire that had already singed Michael Rasmussen's reputation. Everyone was wondering how it would affect him in the coming days, starting with a crucial 54km individual time trial at Albi.

STAGE 10: TALLARD–MARSEILLE

1. Cédric Vasseur (F), Quick Step-Innergetic, 5:20:24
2. Sandy Casar (R), Française des Jeux, s.t.
3. Michael Albasini (Swi), Liquigas, s.t.
4. Patrice Halgand (F), Crédit Agricole, s.t.
5. Jens Voigt (G), CSC, s.t.
6. Staf Scheirlinckx (B), Cofidis, at 0:36
7. Paolo Bossoni (I), Lampre-Fondital, at 0:36
8. Marcus Burghardt (G), T-Mobile, at 1:01
9. Aleksandr Kuchynski (Blr), Liquigas, at 2:34
10. Juan Antonio Flecha (Sp), Rabobank, at 2:34

STAGE 11: MARSEILLE–MONTPELLIER

1. Robert Hunter (Rsa), Barloworld, 3:47:50
2. Fabian Cancellara (Swi), CSC, s.t.
3. Murilo Fischer (Brz), Liquigas, s.t.
4. Filippo Pozzato (I), Liquigas, s.t.
5. Alessandro Ballan (I), Lampre-Fondital, s.t.
6. Paolo Bossoni (I), Lampre-Fondital, s.t.

7. Claudio Corioni (I), Lampre-Fondital, s.t.

8. Philippe Gilbert (B), Française des Jeux, s.t.

9. William Bonnet (F), Crédit Agricole, s.t.

10. Kim Kirchen (Lux), T-Mobile, s.t.

STAGE 12: MONTPELLIER–CASTRES

1. Tom Boonen (B), Quick Step-Innergetic, 4:25:32

2. Erik Zabel (G), Milram, s.t.

3. Robert Hunter (RsA), Barloworld, s.t.

4. Daniele Bennati (I), Lampre-Fondital, s.t.

5. Thor Hushovd (N), Crédit Agricole, s.t.

6. Bernhard Eisel (A), T-Mobile, s.t.

7. Sébastien Chavanel (F), Française des Jeux, s.t.

8. Nicolas Jalabert (F), Agritubel, s.t.

9. Robert Förster (G), Gerolsteiner, s.t.

10. Andrey Kashechkin (Kz), Astana, s.t.

GENERAL CLASSIFICATION AFTER STAGE 12

1. Michael Rasmussen (Dk), Rabobank, 57:37:10

2. Alejandro Valverde (Sp), Caisse d'Épargne, 2:35

3. Iban Mayo (Sp), Saunier Duval-Prodir, 2:39

4. Cadel Evans (Aus), Predictor-Lotto, 2:41

5. Alberto Contador (Sp), Discovery Channel, 3:08

6. Carlos Sastre (Sp), CSC, 3:39

7. Andréas Klöden (G), Astana, 3:50

8. **Levi Leipheimer (USA), Discovery Channel, 3:53**

9. Kim Kirchen (Lux), T-Mobile, 5:06

10. Mikel Astarloza (Sp), Euskaltel-Euskadi, 5:20

RIDER DIARY

CHRISTIAN VANDE VELDE | JULY 18

That burnin', burnin', burnin' ring of fire

Today's 230km went by as fast as it possibly could, given the conditions.

Out on the road it was more than 100 degrees all day and the pavement was rough. Some of us were still a bit tired after the mountain day yesterday that took us over the famed Galibier. It was a great mountain stage that started at the bottom of the Col de l'Iseran in the ski town of Val-d'Isère. The Iseran goes straight up to 2,770 meters (9,088 feet) and there ain't so much air up there.

I went with a few attacks and every extra effort was rewarded with a straight-up bout of dizziness. Then we raced down to the bottom of the Télégraphe, which then leads straight into the Galibier which goes higher than the latter before descending down to the town of Briançon. That's 45km of climbing, combined with insane downhills. It sure made for a great stage. The favorites all established themselves and maybe showed a few cards, but nothing really changed.

Today, Cedric Vasseur saved the day for the French, winning the stage. He's about to turn 37 and 10 years have elapsed since his first stage win. On top of that, he has the honor of being the first French stage winner of the year. It was long and brutally hot but that didn't stop the teams who lacked a stage win from attacking for the first hour and a half.

Finally, a group got away and we could peacefully ride to the finish. It was boring and uncomfortable and I now have a horrible tan.

While the 11 guys up the road were riding off to a stage win, we settled in for a long ride on baking roads. Zabriskie lost his mind under the hot sun, much to the amusement of those of us around him. And, of course, we all got sunburned.

I did manage to catch up with a few friends and tossed water bottles at cars. Fabian had an impressive John Paxon-style three pointer today. He pointed out a van on the side of the road with the door open. Once he had our attention, he hucked one across the road, right into the backseat. I was impressed as hell that the Swiss bear could shoot so well. I did my best Bulls' announcer impression, but it was completely lost on ol' Toblerone. Making a shot like this is not as easy as it sounds. We are rolling at about 25 to 30, so you really have to time your throw or else you could put it somewhere you shouldn't, like where I did when I tried to copy his shot. I mean, I . . . well, no comment. Suffice it to say, I'll stick to golf.

So, all is well, we are chugging along in the guts of the race right now. Some in the peloton are thinking of what could have been and some of the guys

CONTINUED →

still have big dreams. One big loser of the week—and I use that term in the broad sense when it comes to him—is Patrik stinky pits (sorry, I don't know how to spell his last name).

He smashed his face after the race the other day and then found out he turned a positive test this morning. And you thought *you* were having a bad week?!?

Not that I feel for him in the slightest. Frankly, if he needs any help re-breaking his nose, I know a lot of people who would love to give him a hand.   ⊗

RIDER DIARY

SIMON GERRANS I JULY 18

Attack, counterattack

I'd marked today as one of the few stages I would try and have a go. Now that Rabobank has taken control of the race and is defending the yellow jersey, it was obvious they would let a non-threatening breakaway go to contest the stage win.

So I was on the front line and ready to rumble in the neutral zone, and when the race officially started I was ideally placed to follow the first attack. Sure enough, 20 meters into the stage Philippe Gilbert got things going. I was straight onto it and in no time I broke clear of the group with five others. We quickly established a good gap of 20 seconds, 30 seconds, 40 seconds, and then I got word over the race radio that Bouygues were getting organized on the front of the peloton to chase us back.

Our lead, however, kept increasing out to 1 minute 30 seconds. "They're los-ing momentum," I heard over the radio. "That's it," I thought, "we've made the break." Our lead was out to 1 minute 40 seconds and we needed to back off a little; otherwise we were going to blow ourselves up. Then I heard, "Gerolsteiner have joined Bouygues on the front." F@#K IT! The inevitable started to happen: our gap started to come down, and the morale and momentum of the breakaway quickly followed. Soon enough we were caught by the peloton. I was really disappointed. I was too spent to follow any more attacks for the stage, and one of my few chances for this year's Tour had passed me by.

The attacks continued until a group of 11 riders formed in the front, without any Ag2r riders. I can tell you Vincent Lavenu, our team manager, was far from happy. We copped a massive serving of abuse over the race radio. ⊗

RIDER DIARY

SIMON GERRANS | JULY 19

Surprise, surprise

In the Ag2r camp, we thought we had our dose of bad luck yesterday. How wrong were we!

Today's stage started out super quick. There was a lot of crosswind and we had riders at both ends of the group. Arrieta was off the front and in the first break of the day, while Calzati was yo-yoing off the back struggling with knee problems. But it was around 35km into the stage when the group came back together that our real problems started . . .

There was a touch of wheels at the front of the group and Christophe went down. At the exact same moment, someone turned left at the back of the group to avoid Christophe's crash and took my front wheel straight out from under me, sending me sliding up the bitumen. Fortunately neither of us was badly hurt and we both got going again pretty quickly. The whole team sat up to tow us back to the group. I think I was kind of lucky the team dropped back for Christophe as I'm sure I wouldn't have got the same treatment if I'd crashed by myself.

We caught the peloton at the base of the day's only categorized climb at the 38km mark. Unfortunately Calzati, who was already suffering, started the climb at the back of the bunch and got

CONTINUED →

dropped immediately. Alone out the back with 140km still to race, he soon realized he was going to be a long way outside the time limit, and so he pulled out.

A break finally went clear and things settled down just before the feed station, so we all started to relax a little. The team was spread out to go through the feed zone and Christophe had just joined the group after stopping to change a shoe that he'd broken in the crash. Then as we exited the feed zone, I heard a crackle over the radio. Nothing unusual—someone probably missed his musette, I thought. But then the pace picked up really quickly. I soon realized a team had started riding on the front to take advantage of the crosswind. I was way out of position. The bunch quickly broke up and

I was in the second of I think four groups. No big deal I thought; we had Christophe in the front with four or five teammates. I was hurting from my crash and looking for an easy ride to the finish.

Twenty or 30 kilometers later, when the front of the race was over two minutes ahead of my group, I saw a small clump of riders in the distance that had been dropped from the front. As they got closer I realized that it was mostly made up of my teammates, including Christophe! I raced to the head of the group and started riding on the front to limit the time loss as much as possible. I worked with the guys until I had nothing left and got dropped with 15km to go. They finished at 3:20 from the leaders. ⊗

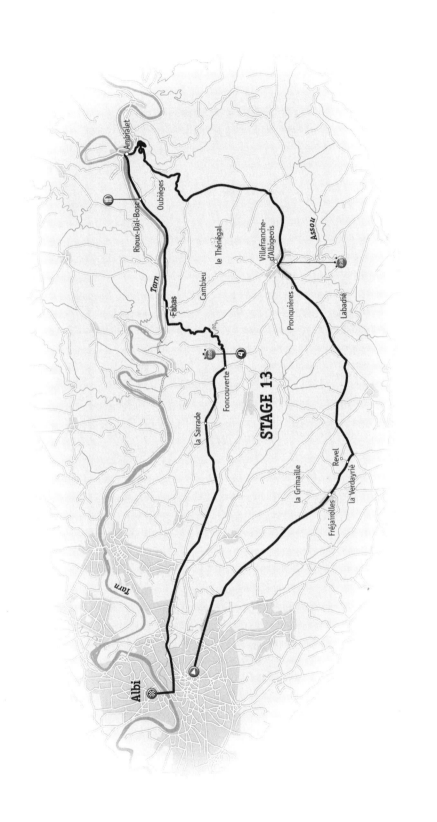

10

Fireworks Follow the Tour

*The cloud of uncertainty hanging over the Tour
clears somewhat with the stage 13 time trial.*

The Tour de France is not just the world's biggest annual sporting event; it is also a social phenomenon that brings people together to celebrate summer and the French countryside. One of the event's former race directors, Xavier Louy, in his new book, *Sauvons le Tour* [Let's Save the Tour], had just started a campaign to have the Tour recognized by UNESCO's World Heritage committee.

The Tour's popularity was clear in Castres, population 47,000, which was clogged with people who had come to watch stage 12 that Friday afternoon. Most would stay for the evening, enjoying the open-air cafés and bistros around the ancient Place Jean Jaurès, a three-block town square lined with plane trees and timbered, terraced houses dating from the eighteenth century. Later, starting at 11:00 p.m., came a gigantic fireworks display next to the ornate gardens fronting the world-famous Goya Museum. Thousands watched as the cascading colors of the fireworks were reflected in the still waters of the Agout River.

Seven Tour teams were lodged in the town, trying to sleep through the explosions. One of the favorites for the next day's time trial, Cadel Evans, was staying with his Predictor team at the Campanile, on the Route de Toulouse. Two other favorites likely to move up the standings, Discovery Channel's Alberto Contador and Levi Leipheimer, were getting a better night's sleep 30km away in Sorèze, a village in the foothills of the Black Mountains, at the exclusive Logis des Pères—a former monastery where the luxury bedrooms were once cells occupied by Dominican fathers.

The other race favorites were staying in Albi, where the time trial would start and finish. Saunier Duval's Iban Mayo and CSC's Carlos Sastre had salubrious digs close to the noisy city center. Caisse d'Épargne's Alejandro Valverde was staying in a small room at the budget Kyriad Hotel, while Rabobank's race leader, Michael Rasmussen, and Astana's Andreas Klöden and Alexander Vinokourov were all at Albi's middle-price Campanile.

Being relaxed and fully prepared for the crucial 54km time trial was essential; a poor result would shoot down a rider's hopes for the final podium. While the controversial Rasmussen had a 2:35 lead on current runner-up Valverde, only 74 seconds covered the next six contenders: Mayo, Evans, Contador, Sastre, Klöden, and Leipheimer. Vinokourov, a much longer shot, had to make up four to five minutes to get back in the picture before the Pyrénées.

Good news for all the contenders, cool temperatures were forecast, a far cry from conditions at the 2003 Tour time trial, which finished 10km north of Albi, at Cap'Découverte. That day, temperatures hit a humid 100 degrees Fahrenheit around a 47km loop north of the Tarn valley. Lance Armstrong experienced one of the worst days in his seven-year reign as Tour champion, although despite severe dehydration he still managed to place second on the stage to Jan Ullrich, a yawning 96 seconds slower than the German.

On one 8km section toward the end of his time trial, Armstrong was conceding four seconds every kilometer to Ullrich. After finishing the stage with shaky legs and his mouth ringed with salt, the American said, "I had an incredible crisis. I felt like I was . . . going backward. I ran out of water. It was the thirstiest I've ever been in a time trial." Armstrong needed three days to recover and then made an amazing comeback at Luz-Ardiden to clinch the yellow jersey.

The same day Armstrong struggled near Albi, Vinokourov rode his best-ever Tour time trial: He took third place on the stage and moved up to third overall—the position he would maintain until Paris. Four years later, the Kazakh needed an even better ride to get himself back into contention.

Things were looking up for Vinokourov. His Astana team had retaken control of the race, as its sensational acceleration in the stage 11 crosswinds proved. The injuries from Vino's first-week crash had almost healed, and he would ride the time trial with lighter dressings. So surprising was Vino's return to form that when Astana team manager Marc Biver was asked whether Vinokourov (still 8:05 behind Rasmussen) or Andreas Klöden (3:50 off the pace) would be the team leader for the upcoming Pyrenean stages, the Swiss official carefully replied, "After the time trial the positions will be clear."

Vino and the rest of the Astana team would race on brand-new time trial machines from Swiss manufacturer BMC. Their backup machine was BMC's original model, which the company had since upgraded, improving the $12,000 frameset's carbon fiber modulus and eliminating the top layer of carbon formerly used to finish the bike. The new frame was made entirely from unidirectional carbon, which shaved roughly 750 grams off of the old bike. The 2007 Tour model also had a new seatpost and a one-bolt top clamp that offered a greater amount of adjustment than the older one.

More importantly, BMC had made a special set of time trial specific components for Astana, including three of its custom time trial cranks. These were first used by Floyd Landis's Phonak team at the 2006 Tour. "We made 10 pieces last year for Phonak," said BMC's product manager Andrew James, "and we made another three for Astana [riders Vinokourov, Klöden, and Andrey Kashechkin]."

James conceded that BMC started with a crank by Campagnolo and then added a massive amount of carbon to it, which gave it both considerable stiffness and better aerodynamic qualities. That increased stiffness counted as a structural component, and therefore the crank conformed to UCI rules concerning gratuitous aerodynamic features.

"We have done a very limited run of them," said James. "The crank is fully enclosed; there's a carbon piece in between the [chain]rings and a carbon-backing piece. You can't take it apart without breaking it. We use the most common chainring gearing [for a time trial], which is 54/44."

Riding the new bike wasn't expected to be a problem for Klöden despite his coccyx injury. "The saddle position is even easier because you sit more on the upper part of the seat. I don't have any worries about that," said team manager Marc Biver, who added that he was optimistic for the time trial because Klöden's moodiness was improving. "I was a long time with him yesterday in the room. We talked about the weather, the family, and occasionally about his condition. He's getting better and better, and he's sleeping very well. He was very relaxed. I haven't seen him so relaxed in a long time."

The Swiss manager said there was no conflict between Klöden and Vinokourov over team leadership. "Absolutely not," he said. "The team is going to do the strategy day by day. There are no instructions so far. Klöden and Vino are protected, and the one who has the better chance in the GC will be the leader. That's a decision we take day by day."

Biver added that he didn't expect miracles in the time trial. "I don't think we can take the yellow jersey in Albi." As for his heroic leader, Vinokourov, Biver said, "Vino is like a wounded tiger; he's even more dangerous now."

— ◉ —

Riders woke up on Saturday morning to cloudy skies, cool temperatures, and a light breeze from the west. The main favorites (for the stage and the GC) rode the course in the morning to see the challenges they'd face. The course had many technical sections, and total concentration would be needed to avoid trouble. A heavy rain set in around midday, making the mainly country roads extra slick.

The time trial's looping 54km course was far from simple. The official route inspection revealed 27 dangerous passages, nine roundabouts, nine traffic islands, four very narrow sections, two railroad crossings, and a number of speed bumps.

It began on the Rue Hippolyte Savary, a stone's throw from the house where French painter Henri de Toulouse-Lautrec was born, and within sight of Albi's magnificent red brick cathedral. The riders would first head east on long, straight roads through grassy fields, where the slight tailwind would help them on a gradually ascending road to the first time check at the village of Villefranche d'Albigeois (18km). After a further 5km of steady uphill work they would reach a limestone plateau, which offered long views across the narrow, deep valley of the Tarn to the north. The riders then faced the most difficult technical section: a 5km descent, very steep in places, which included many curves and two switchback turns, ending in the village of Ambialet (29km).

There the narrow road slalomed downhill to a short tunnel cut through a rocky peninsula that's topped by a ruined medieval castle and church, with the fast-flowing Tarn River to the right. After a sharp left and right through the village, the flattest 5km section of the course led the riders along the valley between green pastures before they turned left to start the day's main climb, the Côte de la Bauzié, to the next time split (38.5km). The 3.4km climb had an average grade of 4.7 percent, but there were a couple of 8 percent pitches on the narrow, newly paved road that twisted its way up a wooded side valley. The following 12km were mainly downhill on a smooth highway back into Albi. Once in town, the riders had to negotiate several roundabouts and a couple of narrow streets before crossing a wide bridge over the Tarn to finish on a 1.4km straightway along the Avenue Albert Thomas.

The course seemed to favor a specialist like world time trial champion Fabian Cancellara of CSC, frequent rival David Millar of Saunier Duval, or perhaps the newly confident Bradley Wiggins of Cofidis. Wiggins had yet to put together a great long time trial, but he clearly had the potential for lifting his sights beyond short prologues, as he showed by his marathon solo breakaway on stage 6.

Of the GC contenders, the advantage appeared to be with Vinokourov (starting three minutes after Discovery strongman Yaroslav Popovych), Klöden (starting three minutes behind Leipheimer), Evans (three minutes behind Contador), and, assuming he'd be transformed by the yellow jersey, Rasmussen (three minutes behind Valverde). But if experts such as five-time Tour winner Bernard Hinault proved correct in predicting that Rasmussen

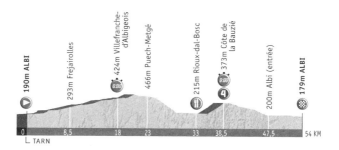

STAGE 13: ALBI—ALBI TIME TRIAL

would lose five minutes to the top riders, then either Klöden or Evans could be in yellow by the end of the day.

But the Tour is not raced on paper. This particular stage was being raced on a road full of risks and in changing weather conditions that would greatly affect the results, as demonstrated by the performances of two early starters in the time trial, Belgian Leif Hoste and Bradley Wiggins. Hoste was the ninth starter and was told to race flat out to produce detailed time splits to help his Predictor team leader, Evans; Wiggins started 10 places and 20 minutes later.

Both of them raced on dry roads to the first checkpoint after 18km, which Hoste reached in 24:25; Wiggins was 1:06 faster. Just when the Brit seemed set to turn in a sensational time, the first drops of rain began to fall. Hoste, 20 minutes ahead of him, had cleared the difficult descent to Ambialet before the roads greased up, and the strong Belgian completed the middle section of the course in 20:52; it took Wiggins 21:33. So instead of continuing to gain 3.6 seconds per kilometer as he had at the start, the Brit lost 2.3 seconds per kilometer while negotiating the dicey descent on wet roads.

When both of them raced in steady rain into a slight headwind over the final sections of the course, Wiggins was again faster than Hoste. At the line, Hoste recorded 1:09:30, the fastest until Wiggins came home in 1:08:48, at a still excellent average speed of 47kph. Had the Brit raced in the same conditions as the Belgian, his final time would likely have been a minute faster.

The rain increased through the early afternoon, with Cancellara and Millar hitting the worst of it. Wearing his world champion's rainbow-striped jersey, Cancellara crashed twice, first on one of the descent's switchbacks and then as he took the sharp left turn emerging from the short tunnel in Ambialet. He ended his ride with a gashed left knee that left him hobbling the next morning. The big Swiss time-trialist recorded a miserable 1:15:19, while Millar, who didn't fall but had to race through low clouds and fog on the Ambialet downhill, did a 1:10:01—good enough for 20th place. Not the result he was expecting.

— ◉ —

By the time Vinokourov set out from Albi at 3:24 p.m., the clouds were beginning to break up and the rain had eased off; the fastest time still belonged to Wiggins, who had started more than four hours earlier.

Riding his sleek new bike and wearing a long-sleeve skin suit, with a gauze bandage on his right knee (nothing on the left), Vinokourov looked like the race favorite he set out to be in London two weeks earlier. With his gloved hands touching at the wrists as he held the ends of his aerobars, and with his forearms parallel to the road, he zoomed though the first time check in 23:09—10 seconds faster than Wiggins's previously unmatched split.

The rain and wind had practically stopped by now, but Vinokourov, like the rest of the favorites, would still have to be extra careful on the wet descent. Predictor's Chris Horner, who started three places ahead of Vino, said, "The descent is just crazy slippery. The really hard right where everyone's slipping, I went through at a crawl speed, and still the bike slipped out from underneath me. I kept it up, I didn't slide too dramatic, but I definitely slipped." Horner, a team rider saving his legs for the next day's huge mountain stage in the Pyrénées, finished in a highly respectable 1:10:55, eventually the 30th best.

> "The descent is just crazy slippery. The really hard right where everyone's slipping, I went through at a crawl speed, and still the bike slipped out from underneath me."

Four minutes later, another team worker who rode exceptionally well, Popovych of Discovery, finished in a time of 1:08:50, only two seconds outside of Wiggins—still the day's fastest. Then, only 44 seconds behind Popovych (they started three minutes apart), Vinokourov blasted across the line in 1:06:34. The wounded tiger had obliterated the field.

Vinokourov's time splits showed that he rode the fastest section of the course—the 10.5km from the top of the Bauzié climb to the outskirts of Albi—in just 10:31, a 60kph average! Admittedly, that section drops 567 feet at a mean gradient of 1.4 percent, but few cyclists have ever ridden at that speed for a sustained period, especially after racing 40km on a difficult course in challenging conditions.

When Vinokourov finished, all of the other GC contenders had started their time trials, but only two had reached the first time check. Vino's teammate Klöden was 34 seconds slower, while Leipheimer's deficit was already 1:31—a stunning loss of five seconds a kilometer on that mainly flat 18km opener!

The American would say later, "At the beginning, I thought I was okay, but I was a little stunned to see that first time split. Vino went fast, but I thought

I heard on the radio that he was a lot faster than everybody else. So I just tried to keep pushing."

As Leipheimer and Klöden continued their efforts, Vinokourov was being mobbed at the finish. Stuck in the middle of a sweaty media scrum on a muggy afternoon, Vino was blowing as hard as a stallion after the Kentucky Derby. He slowly removed his aero helmet, took a towel from his bodyguard to dry his face, and then said in his heavily accented French, mixed with his own patois and occasional grunts, "I can say [my time trial] was almost perfect. The legs felt good, and the finish went very well. And, *bon*, I'm happy with this performance."

The interviewer for French TV, Jean-René Godard, summed up everyone's feelings when he said to Vino, "Only a few days ago you collapsed in tears, you had suffered so much and showed so much courage, and made the whole world feel your emotion. Today, it was a wonderful Alexander Vinokourov we saw—a fighter who can still win the Tour."

Looking somewhat embarrassed by Godard's eloquence, Vino sighed and replied: "*Oui* . . . I almost abandoned that day. Me, I said to myself I'll go for another day and perhaps it will get better. Now, I have re-found my legs and I'm ready to attack in the Pyrénées."

Godard next asked, "Things will now change between you and Klöden?"

"We'll wait for the finish and see how Andreas does," Vinokourov answered, avoiding the question. "In any case, I'm happy with my performance."

Godard, trying to elicit the reply he wanted, asked one more question: "So, the Boss is back?" Vino replied, "I'm happy because lots of people have already eliminated me [from the Tour], but I don't think the race is finished yet."

The next of the favorites to cross the line was Leipheimer, who recorded a 1:09:13. The intermediate time breakdowns later revealed that the American lost time to all of his rivals in the opening 18km except for Rasmussen (who was 11 seconds slower), but he was faster than all of them (except for Vinokourov, who was only four seconds quicker) over the final 15.5km.

"I felt good at the end," Leipheimer confirmed, with a wry smile. "Bit by bit, move up the classification, that's the goal. I don't like losing two and a half minutes—but considering I used to lose five minutes to Lance [Armstrong], it's not that bad."

Reflecting his cautious approach to the Tour and to this stage, Leipheimer added, "I took it really easy [on the descent]. But it still slipped a little bit. I mean, it's better to lose 20 seconds than to crash. And obviously the end was really good. I definitely felt good from the bottom of the downhill to the finish."

The next finisher, Klöden, who was exactly a minute faster than Leipheimer at the end, also took it carefully. But on the course's trickiest descent, he still crashed on the tight right-hander, taking a slow-motion fall onto his right hip. Klöden's 1:08:13 was just five seconds better than that of his teammate Kashechkin; they would place third and fourth behind Vinokourov, the eventual stage winner, to complete a dominant afternoon for the Astana trio.

"I have a mixed feeling today," Klöden said later. "On the one hand, I finished third and my place in the overall ranking is now fourth. But on the other hand, I fell on my right side and that means new pains for me."

— ⊙ —

Of the final starters, Contador, Evans, and Rasmussen were all putting in rides they'd be proud of. Contador was half a minute faster than teammate Leipheimer over the first half of the course, while Evans had a 1:18 margin over the American before reaching the category 4 climb. Significantly, Contador and Evans were the only two riders to race up the 4km hill in less than six minutes, almost 10 seconds faster than Rasmussen.

Contador completed his 54km effort in 1:08:52 for seventh on the stage, just two seconds short of teammate Popovych and 21 seconds ahead of Leipheimer. Evans finished faster than Klöden but slower than Leipheimer, to claim second on the stage, 1:14 behind Vinokourov.

But what really took everyone by surprise was Rasmussen's shocking effort over the final 15.5km, which the skinny Dane completed with a body-rolling, head-shaking effort 11 seconds faster than Contador, two seconds faster than Klöden, and only two seconds slower than Evans. Rasmussen even caught his three-minute man, Valverde, just inside 3km to go, and dropped him by 13 seconds before the line.

The race leader's finish was enough to give him 11th place on the stage and keep him in yellow by one minute over the new runner-up, Evans. Contador climbed to third at 2:31, Klöden to fourth at 2:34, and Leipheimer to fifth at 3:37.

"That was the time trial of my life," Rasmussen said at his official press conference, where he refused to answer any questions not connected to the race (i.e., anything to do with missing out-of-competition antidoping controls). "For the first time in my life, I raced a time trial at 100 percent. I decided to put the last few days behind me, and just look ahead. Starting last with the yellow jersey was an extremely strong motivation. I'm surprised to have kept so much time on Evans."

Evans was mobbed as he finished, but he was whisked away by Tour security to doping control before the media could get answers to their questions. The Aussie later said that he was very cautious on the slick roads. "I took every turn twice as slow as I would have liked. I knew that lots of riders had fallen before me," he said.

Saying he was pleased to move up into second place, Evans added, "The best is yet to come. [But] Astana now has three in the top ten, and Discovery Channel two in the top five . . . ."

Evans left his sentence hanging but implied that holding on to his second place, or even shooting for the yellow jersey, was going to be tough in the upcoming stages.

— ◎ —

With Contador sitting two places higher than Leipheimer after two weeks of racing, it was fair to ask again, Who is the Discovery team leader, and who is the lieutenant?

Contador repeated that he recognized his place. "I'm surprised by how well I performed today," said the young Spaniard. "I can't believe that I finished on top of many rivals. I want to enjoy this moment. But Levi is the sure bet for this team. He will be stronger than me in the final time trial. I still would like to try to win a stage."

Looking forward to the mountains, Leipheimer said he embraced a lieutenant like Contador who was also a threat overall. "We will keep doing our own race," Leipheimer said. "We have the full support of the team. We don't have the lead, so it's not like one has to sacrifice for the other. [Contador] looks good, and if I were the other guys I would be worried because I don't think anyone in the race can climb with him. I think Rasmussen has got to be getting tired. I don't know if anyone can go uphill with [Contador]."

Meanwhile, two other Spanish climbers, Valverde and Mayo, had dropped behind Vinokourov, who moved up to ninth place on GC. Mayo shrugged off his poor time trial performance with trademark indifference to media inquiries. The Basque climber finished 46th on the stage, 6:04 slower than Vinokourov, and sank like a rock from second to twelfth overall, 5:48 back. No worries, said Mayo at the finish line, "I already said I would lose a lot of time. Now I am approaching my favored terrain, and we'll see if I can't win a stage. The time that I lost today, maybe I can gain back in the Pyrénées. But if it's to finish sixth or seventh in Paris, I'd prefer to win a stage."

Valverde also saw his podium chances dashed after a disappointing performance. The ballyhooed Spanish rider was hoping to stay within three minutes of the specialists, but he never expected to lose twice that amount. "I knew it was a bad day," Valverde said. "This morning I felt good, but when the time trial started, I felt that my legs were not that good. And when my director told me the intermediate times, I understood that I was going to lose plenty of time today. But the Tour and cycling are like that: one day you win, and the next you lose."

The Caisse d'Épargne leader tried to put a philosophical spin on his third Tour start, though injuries had stopped him from finishing the first two. "I am here to learn and before being able to win the Tour, I believe that one has to learn to know it. As I have already said, this year, the most important for me is to arrive in Paris. Now, three stages await us in the Pyrénées, and we will see how each of us recovers, starting with me."

With Valverde and Mayo out of the top 10, the balance of power had returned to Astana (three in the top four on the stage), while Discovery was still improving (with three in the top nine of the time trial). Overall, the only other team with a rider within five minutes of Rasmussen was CSC, with its leader Sastre, who placed a disappointing 16th on the stage and was now sitting seventh overall, 4:45 back.

Sastre said he knew his dream of finishing on the podium was fading, but he would continue to fight. And even though he was two places, and 25 seconds, ahead of Vinokourov overall, he felt that the Kazakh was still a big threat.

"It's obvious that Vinokourov is back in the race," Sastre said. "He's dangerous in any race. And we all know he wants to win the Tour. We saw two days ago he was feeling stronger. Now he's going to attack. We'll have to be alert in the Pyrénées and try to stay with him. It won't be easy."

Discovery's most experienced rider, George Hincapie, expressed a similar view. When asked to pick five riders he thought had the greatest chance to make the podium in Paris, the American said, "Cadel, Vino, Contador, Klöden . . . and hopefully Levi."

Astana's team manager Marc Biver agreed. "Cadel Evans is the biggest threat," he said. "Cadel is dangerous because he is very regular on the Tour. He has proven that in the past. He is strong in the mountains, and good in the time trial. He's a guy who is very solid on the bike. I believe very much in Cadel Evans."

Even though the overall picture seemed clearer, the Tour was headed back into the high mountains the next day, and the balance of power could change once more. Looking ahead to the three Pyrenean stages, the favored Evans noted, in an understatement, "They're all hard. None of them is a walk in the park, that's for sure."

STAGE 13: ALBI–ALBI TIME TRIAL

1. Alexander Vinokourov (Kz), Astana, 1:06:34
2. Cadel Evans (Aus), Predictor-Lotto, at 1:14
3. Andréas Klöden (G), Astana, at 1:39
4. Andrey Kashechkin (Kz), Astana, at 1:44

5. Bradley Wiggins (GB), Cofidis, at 2:14

6. Yaroslav Popovych (Ukr), Discovery Channel, at 2:16

7. Alberto Contador (Sp), Discovery Channel, at 2:18

8. Sylvain Chavanel (F), Cofidis, at 2:38

9. Levi Leipheimer (USA), Discovery Channel, at 2:39

10. Mikel Astarloza (Sp), Euskaltel-Euskadi, at 2:42

GENERAL CLASSIFICATION AFTER STAGE 13

1. Michael Rasmussen (Dk), Rabobank, 58:46:39

2. Cadel Evans (Aus), Predictor-Lotto, at 1:00

3. Alberto Contador (Sp), Discovery Channel, at 2:31

4. Andréas Klöden (G), Astana, at 2:34

5. Levi Leipheimer (USA), Discovery Channel, at 3:37

6. Andrey Kashechkin (Kz), Astana, at 4:23

7. Carlos Sastre (Sp), CSC, at 4:45

8. Mikel Astarloza (Sp), Euskaltel-Euskadi, at 5:07

9. Alexander Vinokourov (Kz), Astana, at 5:10

10. Kim Kirchen (Lux), T-Mobile, at 5:29

RIDER DIARY

CHRISTIAN VANDE VELDE | JULY 21

The Motorcycle Diaries

The Tour is one big moving circus.

The smallest portion of the whole thing is the peloton: 180 or so guys on bikes. Even when you add all of the staff and gear from the teams themselves, that still makes up only 10 percent of the Tour caravan.

Add in journalists, police, publicity caravan, the dudes who put up the barriers, and you easily bump that to more than 5,000 people who cover the Tour from start to finish. Some are more visible than others and some are taken for granted. Like the guys who put up the signs for the race. When do they do that? Or the guy who paints the finish line and does the timing.

These are things I take for granted. What? It's not *normal* to have a finish line in every town? You mean it's not *normal* for French towns to have 25, 20, 15, 10, 5, 4, 3, 2 and 1 k-to-go signs? They don't just appear?

Shit, it's 11:00 in the morning on Saturday before the TT and it just started to rain. Sometimes it's the best to go off first in the time trial. Get your ride in early and then just lie in bed and watch the race on TV. Really, if you beat the rain you can watch everyone else tiptoe through corners that you absolutely flew through. But I don't go till 2:30. It will be nice and dry by then, right? Don't think so.

CONTINUED →

Okay, back to my thought. The reason I brought this all up in the first place are the gendarmes—the French police—that patrol the race. There are all sorts of different genres of police in France and these guys are the *top* moto guys.

They point out dangerous traffic islands and corners and pass back and forth through the peloton almost invisibly. They are like the Blue Angels on BMW motorcycles, all uniformly driving massive bikes through holes that don't exist without interrupting the race. They even drive in formation to and from the race every day, making them look more impressive and classy even when they aren't working.

I have known the chief of this squad for the last 11 years; he likes to practice his English and has always hung out with the Americans since the days of Jonathan Boyer. So he tells us some of the behind-the-scenes stuff about their jobs and what it's like year-round, at the Tour and otherwise. All these guys do are bike races, parades, and some other duties.

They are badass and I will never take those boys for granted.   ⊗

RIDER DIARY

SIMON GERRANS I JULY 21

Trial time

My motivation for a 54km time trial is not great at the best of times, let alone doing one or two days after a crash and in pouring rain.

I set my sights on just riding a steady tempo to make the time limit, and also on staying upright in the wet and very slippery conditions.

Today was going to be a real test for Christophe. He didn't do a great time trial in the Dauphiné and he couldn't afford to lose any more time here to the favorites before the Pyrénées. He was obviously still suffering from his crash, as he lost a lot of time and effectively dropped out of contention for his goal of a podium finish.

Vino showed everyone that he has recovered from his crash on stage 5. He won convincingly and made it quite clear he is still a contender for the overall win. ⊗

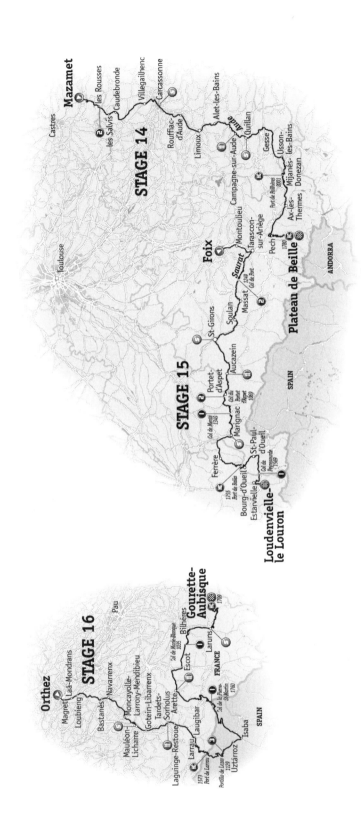

High Climbs and Misdemeanors

Three giant stages across the Pyrénées are ready to designate the Tour winner, but some things get in the way.

Riders were apprehensive about the stages in the Pyrénées. The earlier mountain climbs in the Alps had been challenging enough, but both the team leaders and their troops agreed: "Just wait for the Pyrénées. They're much tougher than the Alps this year. That's where the race will be decided."

Those stages would be even more difficult for the top men because of the effort they had made in the Albi time trial. After finishing that stage, going to the antidoping control, conducting media interviews, and then dealing with heavy traffic leaving town, some of them didn't get back to their hotels until 7:30 p.m. Then came the long daily massage session and perhaps time with the team chiropractor or doctor to treat wounds before a leisurely dinner and calls to loved ones. To help them relax, roommates might watch a movie on a laptop before getting to bed around midnight.

Daily life on the Tour becomes a ritual, but that doesn't always mean you wake up feeling refreshed. The 165 survivors from the 189 starters in London had already raced 14 stages, and they didn't always find it easy to face another very long day. The day after the time trial, the riders would be on the go for another 12 hours. With a scheduled 11:40 a.m. start for stage 14 from Mazamet to Plateau de Beille, breakfast would be 7:40 to 8:40, suitcases in the foyer soon after, on the bus by 9:40, and arrive in the start area by 9:40. Then would come the team meeting, sign-in, media interviews, and, at last, the start of the 197km mountain stage. That would probably mean six hours in the saddle for most riders, only to return along the same road they had just climbed to reach the team bus and another long ride to another hotel.

You've got to love racing your bike to do that day after day. And the race leaders must always be at or near their best performance level on every single stage. Of course, some of them can't stand the pressure and have what the French call *un jour sans* [a day without]. Whose turn would it be today? Would the huge effort Alexander Vinokourov made to win the time trial rebound? Would runner-up Cadel Evans recover enough to answer the expected attacks at day's end? Or would race leader Michael Rasmussen be the one to crack, especially after the lashing he had been getting from the media, from other riders and teams, and even from the race organizers, over the antidoping controls he missed before the Tour.

The Tour can be a grind, but everything becomes manageable when you have a good organization, good teammates, and lots of self-discipline.

One racer who exuded this last quality in his 14 years as a professional was French star Laurent Jalabert. He never won the Tour (fourth place was his best finish), but he took the green jersey twice, the polka-dot jersey twice, and he won four stages. Elsewhere he won the Vuelta a España (and 18 stages), took three stages of the Giro d'Italia, won six other top stage races, six major classics, and the world time trial championship. He retired in 2002 and now provides commentary at the Tour for French TV from the backseat of a motorcycle and works as a consultant for Look Cycles. For fun, he ran the 2005 New York Marathon in 2:55:39 and completed the 2007 Ironman® Switzerland in 9:12:00.

Jalabert was born, grew up, and became a bike racer in Mazamet, a town of 13,000 where stage 14 would start. It's also the hometown of his younger brother Nicolas Jalabert, a member of the Agritubel team, who had crashed in the Albi time trial and was nursing wounds to his right knee and elbow. The younger Jalabert was warmly welcomed by the crowds at the start line but would get dropped in the very first kilometers of the stage that opened with an immediate 9km category 2 climb over a ridge of the Black Mountains. It was an ignominious homecoming for the local hero.

A climb from a dead start on stiff legs is a tough opening to any day. Chris Horner knew that when he stepped down from the Predictor team bus in Mazamet and said, "I don't have much time to talk. We're going for a warm-up." And off he went with his teammates, including Evans. That was exactly the sort of thing Laurent Jalabert would have done in his exemplary career. Also, Evans knew that feeling good on a difficult opening climb would give him a mental boost before tackling the two *hors-catégorie* giants awaiting three hours down the road.

— ◎ —

The Discovery Channel pair of Contador and Leipheimer was also looking to play a more aggressive role. "Today's a summit finish [on the Plateau de Beille] and the best climbers in the race have got to try to make it happen there," said their directeur sportif Sean Yates. "We want to win a stage and at the same time put us into a better position overall."

Spanish climbers Mayo and Valverde were hoping to get back in the GC mix after their poor time trials. Valverde put a Caisse d'Épargne teammate, Ivan Gutierrez, into the day's main six-man breakaway that pushed to a 10-minute lead on the valley roads through Carcassonne and Limoux. That move also included Astana's Toni Colom, who might be a useful ally for his team leader Vinokourov should he carry out his threat "to attack in the Pyrénées."

As for Mayo, he sent his Saunier Duval men to the front along the deep limestone gorge that slices into the mountains to set a ferocious tempo. Their efforts cut the early break's lead to 6:30 before they turned right out of the valley to tackle the first of the day's two *hors-catégorie* climbs, the very demanding 17km Port de Pailhères. Mayo's marquee teammate David Millar then took over on the narrow climb with its tight, steep switchbacks, putting in an impressive solo effort at the head of the pack. His fast tempo cut the break's gap in half before he dropped back and ceded pace making to the Rabobank trio of Thomas Dekker, Denis Menchov, and Michael Boogerd, who were duty bound to work selflessly for Rasmussen as long as he kept the yellow jersey.

Among the scores of riders who couldn't follow the fast pace on the Pailhères was Ag2r's demoralized Christophe Moreau, who had gone from a podium favorite to pack fill in three short days. And then a grim-looking Vinokourov, his jersey zip pulled to the waist to help cool him on this hot, sunny afternoon, drifted out the back, while teammates Daniel Navarro and Sergei Ivanov dropped back to help guide him though the stage's remaining 57km.

No attacking today for yesterday's winner. "I had nothing left in the legs. I had no more power," a disillusioned Vinokourov said later. "Since the start of the stage, I [was] flat. This was one day too many. Now I know that it's over. Miracles can't last for two weeks."

Vinokourov and Moreau weren't the only team leaders having a hard time on the pitiless Pailhères. Toward the top, after team workers like Discovery's Egoï Martinez, Yaroslav Popovych, and George Hincapie fell back, the ambitious Mayo couldn't follow the Rabobank pacesetters. The demise of the Saunier Duval captain wouldn't be too popular with teammates like Millar; all that effort for naught.

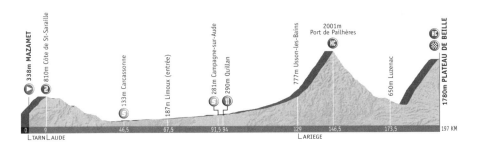

STAGE 14: MAZAMET-PLATEAU DE BEILLE

One rider who was feeling good was Barloworld's Juan Mauricio Soler, who sprinted over the 6,565-foot summit 15 seconds ahead of the small group of leaders to take a temporary lead from Rasmussen in the King of the Mountains competition.

With Astana unexpectedly in trouble after Vino's collapse, the onus on challenging Rasmussen for the overall lead fell to Discovery—and the American team stepped up impressively. Hincapie and Popovych chased back to the Rasmussen-Evans-Contador-Leipheimer group on the breathtaking descent to the deep valley of the Ariège, where Hincapie motored along as he did in the Lance Armstrong era to keep the pace high until the village of Les Cabannes. Hincapie then dropped back and passed the relay to teammate Popovych, who led up the Plateau de Beille's opening sequence of backbreaking turns at a ferocious pace. The Ukraine rider led for half of the 16km, 8 percent climb before eventually peeling off, leaving just six riders to contest the stage: Contador, Leipheimer, Evans, Rasmussen, Soler, and CSC's Carlos Sastre.

"The first 5km at the bottom were very fast," Leipheimer said. "There were still teammates at the bottom pulling for their captains, so everyone was really suffering."

That was the effective end of Mayo's and Valverde's GC chances, but not Klöden's. The lean German fought through hip pain from his heavy fall in the time trial, and he wasn't able to follow the strongest climbers, but he battled his way to the windswept summit to keep his GC hopes alive. Klöden would finish sixth on the stage and slide back to fifth overall, 4:38 off the pace.

Discovery had the advantage in front, the only team with two riders. Contador was looking strong, but this was the first time he had raced up this long, long finishing climb. Leipheimer, nine years older than his Spanish teammate, had many (mixed) memories of the Plateau de Beille. He first climbed it in a time trial at the Route du Sud stage race in June 2002; he won the time trial and the race. A month later, at the Tour de France, he rode solidly to finish stage 12 in 13th place, but 2:27 behind the solo stage winner, Armstrong.

In 2004, the Beille climb saw the finish of another stage, at the end of a vicious six-climb day through the Pyrénées. "It was probably the hardest stage I've ever done," said Leipheimer, who struggled home in 19th place, this time conceding 6:35 to stage winner Armstrong. "Little by little I ran out of gas. I had nothing left. I was completely empty."

Perhaps those mixed memories were filling Leipheimer's mind as the six leaders fanned out across the road before the defining confrontation in this 94th Tour. Only three previous Tour stages had finished here. Each time, the stage winner—Marco Pantani in 1998 and Lance Armstrong in 2002 and 2004—went on to win the Tour. Was history going to repeat itself?

Knowing he was with Contador—who was wearing the white jersey of best young rider—Leipheimer was the first to make a probing attack. The other five responded. Contador counterattacked to keep the pressure on for Discovery. Next, Soler accelerated in the style of a crane taking off, his long neck stretching outward. Then Rasmussen attacked in what was becoming an intensified version of the free-for-all seen on the alpine climbs to Tignes and the Galibier a week earlier. As before, Evans tried to follow Contador's vicious attack, but only race leader Rasmussen could stay with the exciting Spanish prodigy. Evans went into the red zone again but fell back, unable to stay with Sastre, Soler, and Leipheimer when they came by him. The Aussie would ride the rest of the climb with a hurting Klöden.

Contador and Rasmussen passed the last of the day's early breakaways, Colom, inside 3km to go. Shortly afterward, as they headed into a strong gusting wind blowing off the exposed plateau above, the two men were seen talking and nodding their heads in agreement. The Dane appeared to make a deal with Contador, perhaps to concede the stage win to the Spaniard for his cooperation in sharing the work into the wind. Rasmussen clearly led out his rival in the final kilometer, but with less than 500 meters remaining, the race leader upped the pace, and a shocked Contador struggled to come around him to take the win.

Contador's impressive victory left observers wondering whether the Plateau de Beille stage winner was going to follow Armstrong and Pantani to the top of the podium in Paris. The quality of his ride was emphasized by the time he and Rasmussen took to make the final climb, albeit after a huge effort from Popovych at the beginning. Contador was timed at 44:08 for the 15.9km (a speed of 21.6kph), which was the second fastest in Tour history, compared with 43:30 by Pantani and Armstrong's two winning times of 45:43 and 45:30.

— ◎ —

I n the minutes following the stage finish, Contador initially told Spanish radio that he and Rasmussen had made an agreement that would benefit them both. "We spoke about the stage in the last kilometers. I was surprised at how hard Rasmussen went at the end. I was able to come around to win the sprint," said Contador. He then added sarcastically, "So he is really a man of his word."

Rasmussen brushed off the notion that the discussion between him and Contador before their duel to the line was to arrange who would win the stage. "No, it was definitely not," Rasmussen said. "This is the Tour de France, and there are no gifts here. Contador deserved his win."

Asked about it a second time, Rasmussen said he and Contador shared a common interest to widen the gap on their GC rivals, but that was all. "Obviously Contador was the one making the race at the end," Rasmussen said. "I tried to take advantage of that. When we got close to the finish we were racing 100 percent to the line. This is Plateau de Beille, where riders like Pantani and Armstrong have won before. Both of us wanted to be added to the list of winners. In the end he was in a better position and got me in the last 20 meters."

Following his Spanish radio interview Contador changed his tune, saying he and Rasmussen had simply wanted to increase the lead on their rivals. "We still fought for it," Contador said. "Rasmussen attacked first, then I managed to counter him in the final 200 meters."

In a postrace statement, Contador returned to his original story, telling his publicist that he was saddened by Rasmussen's finish line surprise. "It disappointed me," Contador said. "He attacked me in the last two kilometers and has demonstrated to me that he is not a man to keep his word."

The man from Madrid then said, "To win a stage of the Tour in front of all the world, on a weekend, in front of my fans and my family, which have been pushing me, it's everything for me. It is as if already the Tour has finished, independently of how it ends. It is the same for me if tomorrow I have a bad day."

Though Leipheimer couldn't match the pace of Contador and Rasmussen, he rode a sound race. Throughout the round of repeated attacks, Leipheimer stayed within himself. Once separated from Contador, the Discovery leader rode with Sastre and Soler but wouldn't help them in the chase. And after Soler jumped clear to take third place on the stage, Leipheimer stayed with Sastre until the CSC rider withered. Leipheimer finished fourth, 40 seconds down.

"When the accelerations went, I couldn't follow," Leipheimer said. "I have trouble with those fast accelerations that Contador and Rasmussen can do. I tried to stay steady and within my own pace. I didn't want to go too deep. But I am pretty happy with my performance today. I took some time out of Klöden and Evans."

After Evans blew, he linked up with Klöden, but they both conceded more than two minutes (including time bonuses) to Contador and Rasmussen, and almost a minute to Leipheimer. The Aussie was in tears after the stage, saying his legs were fatigued from the previous day's time trial. "Rasmussen and Contador were the best today, and I couldn't go with them," he said. "But Klöden and I aren't through. We can make something up in the last time trial."

Asked if he made a mistake in trying to stay with the fastest two climbers, Evans replied, "A lot of people are suggesting that, but I don't think so. No, no. If I'd let them go earlier they would have maybe taken more time, which would have been more disadvantageous, and it's now good having Discovery in the position to take a bit more responsibility in the race."

Almost a half hour after the leaders finished, a dejected Vinokourov coasted across the line and fell from ninth overall to thirtieth, 34:12 back. His ignominy was heightened by an incident near the finish. Riding in a seven-man group, the injured and defeated Vino was being led by teammate Ivanov when crazed spectators jamming the narrow passage ran alongside him. A fan's flag became entangled in Ivanov's wheel, and both he and Vinokourov went skittering to the ground. A Tour doctor stopped to treat Vinokourov while the driver of the medical car chased down the spectator, who was hiding among the crowd behind a car. The fan pleaded that the incident was a mistake.

With Vino's virtual elimination and Klöden's setback, Discovery Channel took the lead in the overall team classification from Astana. Team boss Johan Bruyneel could also boast of having his top men in second and fourth overall. Commenting on the day's developments, Bruyneel said, "We prepared a strategy in the morning and it worked to perfection. The team was like the old days, not in the sense of the domination but how we achieved our goals as we stated them. We wanted the stage to conserve the white jersey and push Levi and Alberto closer to the podium, so it was a successful day. I believe in both Alberto and Levi."

"Certainly the Discovery Channel team has two cards to play," race leader Rasmussen commented. "Leipheimer is close on GC but Contador is the biggest rival."

Leipheimer didn't disagree but said confidently, "This third week is really hard; some people are going to start to crack. I'm not going to be one of them."

— ◎ —

After two tough days of racing, no one knew what to expect on stage 15, which would take the Tour east from Foix across five mountains (two category 2s, two category 1s, and an *hors-cat*) to Loudenvielle. The biggest unknown factor was the *hors-catégorie* Port de Balès, a climb new to the tour that awaited the field 36km from the finish of the 196km stage. It was 19km long, the first 7.5km at an easy grade of 3.2 percent, followed by 11.7km of narrow switchbacks climbing at 8.1 percent, with some 13 percent pitches thrown in. Adding to the mystery, the summit would be covered in thick mist when the race went though later on the day.

A week earlier, when 7,000 amateur cyclists rode this same course, many of them found the grades on the Balès so steep they had to dismount and push their bikes. The first finisher in that so-called *étape du Tour* was a former pro racer, Nicolas Fritsch, who completed it in 6:21:19.

"It's quite hard, it's quite hard. . . . It'll be another good one," said Evans, who scouted the Balès before the Tour. "I think there are a lot of tired legs in the peloton today."

Tired or not, everyone wanted to get up the road in the early breakaway, especially those who lost time the day before. One of those riders, a revived Vinokourov, was in a group of seven riders that moved clear on the opening category 2 climb, the Col de Porte, but they were caught over the summit. Vino was also in the move that did stick: a breakaway of 25 riders that included his two Astana teammates, Ivanov and Navarro, who rode with him at the back of the field on stage 14. Now off the front, these team workers helped push the break's lead to nine minutes on the downhill and flats between the day's first and second climbs.

Discovery Channel cleverly inserted Hincapie into the attack, guessing that he would come in useful in the later part of the stage. The best-placed riders in the big front group were Euskaltel's Haimar Zubeldia (13th at 12:15) and T-Mobile's Kim Kirchen (14th at 13:16), who would both move up into the top 10 overall—and stay there till the end of the Tour.

On this particular day, Kirchen and Zubeldia would finish in second and third place respectively, 51 seconds behind the stage winner—Vinokourov. Kirchen, a gentle Luxembourger, said that Vino "broke my legs" when he attacked on the final climb, the Col du Peyresourde, with 15km to go. Vino's time for the stage was 5:34:28, some 47 minutes faster than the top amateur the previous week.

When Kirchen was asked by the Luxembourg reporters if he considered his second place to be worth a victory, in consideration of Vinokourov's miraculous comeback, he would reply, rather mysteriously, "Work out your own results. I do mine."

Five minutes behind the front-runners, Hincapie did valuable work for his team when he waited at the top of the Peyresourde for Contador, after the Spanish climber had attacked hard out of the chase group, and only Rasmussen had had the strength to go with him. Descending is not Contador's strongest suit, but it *is* Hincapie's, and so Contador was more than grateful to have his

STAGE 15: FOIX LOUDENVIELLE–LE LOURON

teammate pace him (and Rasmussen) down the flying downhill to the Louron valley before a last 1km climb just before the downhill finish, where he out-kicked Rasmussen to take 10th place behind the nine riders who survived the early break.

After Evans took the sprint for 13th place at the head of a 10-man group including Leipheimer, Klöden, Valverde, Sastre, and Andrey Kashechkin, both Leipheimer and Evans had some frustration to share with the press.

Leipheimer illustrated his dilemma of coleading the Discovery team by recounting the situation over the Peyresourde when Contador relentlessly attacked Rasmussen. "I would have liked to have been able to go with Rasmussen and Alberto on the Peyresourde," he said. "Once they were away, it seemed like [Evans and Klöden] conceded the first two spots in the GC. It wasn't my responsibility to chase down my own teammate. I tried to go across, but they were sitting on my wheel. I didn't push it very long because I am not going to pull them up there. They are both good time trialists, and that would hurt Alberto."

Discovery team director Bruyneel said he had discussed every tactical situation with his riders, saying there was no internal power strug-gle between the two captains. In fact, Bruyneel

> **"Levi started the Tour as the leader of the team. I feel bad because he's having his best Tour ever ..."**

lauded Leipheimer's professionalism and sense of commitment to the team.

"Levi started the Tour as the leader of the team. I feel bad because he's having his best Tour ever," Bruyneel said. "Our goals are very high. With Alberto, if we come into a situation, we have to make sacrifices. [Levi] will do that. He's able to deal with it. He's very professional."

At the same time, Evans expressed his frustration in not getting help from top-10 riders Valverde, Klöden, and Kashechkin in chasing Contador and Rasmussen. The Aussie said they "rode like amateurs." Evans then added,

"Unfortunately I had to race conservatively. It's not what I wanted to do, but I was completely on my own. I was looking to Astana and the other guys to follow. What am I supposed to do when I am on my own? Riders like [Kashechkin and Hincapie] that can pull back breaks cost a lot of money, and not every team can afford them."

Evans's sole support in the mountains had come from his teammate Horner, but ultimately the American was not the sort of rider who could attack or chase down pure climbers like Contador and Rasmussen. "For that reason I didn't try to go with [Contador and Rasmussen]," Evans continued. "As they did yesterday, they cooperated together against me. When I have half of the peloton against me with their teammates, what am I supposed to do? I'm on my own. Astana has teammates, Caisse d'Épargne, CSC, they've all got teammates and they're not riding. They don't seem to want to win the Tour de France."

Later Evans revealed, "A lot of dirty words were said by me after that stage. I was disappointed in the Astana and Caisse d'Épargne teams. I was all alone chasing Contador and Rasmussen, and both teams had riders there. For me, that was where I lost the Tour de France."

At the end of the day, another question being asked was why none of the race leaders took advantage of the difficult Port de Balès to launch attacks and attempt to isolate Rasmussen, who had teammates Dekker, Menchov, and Boogerd still pacing him on the final climb, allowing the race leader to remain completely fresh until he had to chase Contador only 13km from the finish. Admittedly, it would have been hard to get rid of the Rabobank trio of workers, but had Leipheimer and Contador ganged up on Rasmussen they would at least have made the Dane work much harder; and if they had isolated him before the Peyresourde, the two Discovery men could have attacked in turn, and perhaps shifted the Tour in their favor.

Instead, Rasmussen was looking stronger than ever in the yellow jersey, despite all the pressure still coming his way.

Dogged by allegations and innuendo, Rasmussen was trying to stay focused on a race that no one seemed to want him to win. "Everyone takes shots at number 1. That's just a normal reaction from everybody," Rasmussen reasoned. "Lance Armstrong was under pressure for seven years in a row, but he still managed to win."

What was sure was that the upcoming rest day in Pau would be anything but carefree for the Rabobank rider. Rasmussen reluctantly agreed to hold a press conference when he would have preferred not to face an increasingly antagonistic media. After efforts to broadcast a videotaped message were shouted down by Dutch journalists, Rasmussen would confront the media at the press center the following day.

Not only the journalists were unhappy. After Rasmussen received warnings from the UCI over his whereabouts during critical pre-Tour training periods, UCI president Pat McQuaid seemed to be distancing himself from the controversial rider with comments that the brewing media storm was "bad for cycling." With the sport still reeling from other doping controversies and continuing doubts over 2006 winner Floyd Landis, even the Tour de France organizers didn't want to see the stained Rasmussen potentially spoiling their final podium.

Before stage 15, ASO president Patrice Clerc told reporters that Rasmussen didn't "deserve to wear the yellow jersey."

Even Rasmussen's Rabobank team appeared halfhearted in supporting his yellow jersey run. The riders were doing their job to help Rasmussen on the road, but there was no joy around the team bus, no sense of celebration. The team brass had held off extending Rasmussen's contract, which was due to expire at the end of the 2007 season. One team official told a Dutch journalist that Rabobank had worked more than a decade to be in a position to win the Tour, but "the dream of winning the Tour is turning into a nightmare."

Other riders were also upset. In that day's *L'Équipe*, Saunier Duval's David Millar criticized Rasmussen, claiming that his failure to notify cycling authorities of his whereabouts for out-of-competition testing had spoiled things for the whole peloton.

Millar told the French newspaper, "It is unacceptable that Rasmussen did not manage to give notice of his whereabouts. He started the race knowing what would happen but did nothing to rectify the situation, and now we are all screwed, and the Tour is in the shit. He took no notice of warnings from the UCI though he deserved to be punished. He has either been unprofessional or has used the system."

With Rasmussen's press conference scheduled for the next day, rest day was certain to be another busy one for the media. But no one knew *how* busy.

Before the media gathered at the pressroom in Pau from their hotels in the city of 82,000 people and the surrounding region in the Pyrenean foothills, most of the reporters read the morning papers to see what their colleagues were writing. One front-page headline read, *Le Tour en péril?* [Is the Tour in peril?].

That question was going through many heads by the time the news conference convened. Like foxhounds on a hunt, the hundreds of reporters streamed into the rest-day pressroom, which was set up in the Palais Beaumont, an elegant empire-style palace with a terrace looking out toward the high peaks of the Pyrénées. Most were skeptical about the outcome: Would there be any answers?

Rasmussen attempted to quell the growing controversy by bringing along a Rabobank team lawyer to sit next to his team manager, Theo de Rooy, but they provided few answers to the media's chorus of questions.

The attorney's long-winded opening, detailing Rasmussen's pre-Tour whereabouts, and the occasions of his written and recorded UCI warnings, provided a smokescreen instead of an explanation, leaving the press corps struggling to follow and the pressroom translator at a loss as to where to begin.

At one point during the conference de Rooy told the press that Rasmussen had been fined for his administrative mistake. Asked by a reporter what the amount of the fine had been, Rasmussen's response was to immediately look to de Rooy, as if in need of an answer. De Rooy fielded the question, telling the press the team had fined Rasmussen 10,000 euros. For his part, de Rooy seemed to be part of the attempt to deflect any investigation, insisting that he stood by his rider and stressing that confidentiality over Rasmussen's warnings should have been respected.

At another point a reporter from *L'Équipe* asked the Tour leader how it felt to know that no one believed his story. His answer was something to the effect of: "I hope what I've explained today has clarified everything about my missed tests." It had clarified nothing.

As the news conference broke up, the Beaumont Palace's banquet hall, which doubled as the pressroom, was abuzz with the chatter of hundreds of journalists sharing their views on Rasmussen's "administrative errors." Many were filing stories or editing tape before sending the news to newspapers, magazines, Web sites, and TV and radio stations around the world. At the entrance, the *International Herald Tribune*'s Samuel Abt, who was taking a short break, said the news conference was much too technical and that the words spoken by Rasmussen's team didn't convince him that the race leader was blameless in his failure to report his whereabouts correctly to the anti-doping authorities.

Many reporters dismissed the conference and headed out to the nearby Discovery Channel team hotel, the elegant four-star Villa Navarre, where Leipheimer was waiting to answer questions about the race. He said that though he was closer than ever to realizing his lifetime goal of reaching the Tour de France podium, he was prepared to sacrifice those dreams to help his teammate Contador shoot for the *maillot jaune*.

"If there's a chance to win the Tour with Alberto, we have to make some sacrifices," Leipheimer said. The 33-year-old American found himself in a contradictory position as the Tour headed toward the expected climactic stage 16, with its mountaintop finish on the Col d'Aubisque. Leipheimer was poised fourth overall, 5:25 back of Rasmussen, but his 24-year-old teammate was still sitting in second, just 2:23 behind the race leader.

With Contador's superior climbing legs, Discovery knew that its best bet to win the Tour lay with him. That meant that Leipheimer would have to subordinate his personal ambitions to the team's larger interests. "I don't see Alberto's position helping me at all," Leipheimer said. "In fact, it could play out quite the opposite."

Clipping Leipheimer's wings were the GC positions of Evans (third at 4:00) and Klöden (fifth at 5:34). Both had been dropped consistently by Contador on the climbs, but both were superior time-trialists to the Spanish mountain goat. And Contador needed to gap Evans just as much as he had to try to lose Rasmussen. That meant that Leipheimer's interests were squeezed in the middle.

But the American said he hadn't abandoned hopes for the podium. If he could attack Klöden and Evans, and not hurt Contador's chances, he'd still go for it. "It's going to be a really, really hard stage tomorrow," he concluded. "It's possible that we both could gain time."

Back at the palace, sunshine was streaming into the pressroom, even though a black thunder cloud had started to drop over the snow-streaked peaks of the Pyrénées. Yet another press conference was under way, with Saunier Duval-Prodir team manager Mauro Gianetti presenting a diplomat from the West African nation of Mali with a check that would pay for another 300,000 trees in the team's "a million trees for Mali" environmental program.

Moments later, in a question-and-answer session with Saunier Duval riders Mayo and Millar, a journalist asked Millar to comment on a report just posted on the Web site of *L'Équipe*. The story said that Vinokourov had tested positive for homologous blood doping following his stage 13 time trial victory—and that the prerace favorite had already left Pau.

Millar was shattered, his voice breaking with emotion as he said that Vino was one of his heroes, and that if indeed he had been caught cheating, then everyone at the Tour should pack their bags and go home.

The Vinokourov story shot like wildfire through the pressroom. Dozens of reporters homed in on Millar to get more of his thoughts, while others hastily packed their camera and computer bags and headed out to the three-star Hotel La Palmeraie on the edge of town hoping to get photos and catch some quotes from the Astana team. They discovered that the riders had left and the French police had arrived to remove boxes of evidence concerning Vinokourov's alleged doping case.

The facts of the case were that after stage 13, Vinokourov's blood sample was tested at the French antidoping laboratory near Paris that had recently acquired the apparatus and expertise needed to identify homologous blood transfusions. This is the illegal method of taking blood from a compatible donor and transfusing it to boost the red blood cell count of an athlete, who can then perform at a much higher level.

Previously, the World Anti-Doping Agency's lab in Lausanne, Switzerland, was the only one in Europe accredited to do this test—which had not been used in cycling since two positive tests in September 2004 involving then Phonak team riders Tyler Hamilton and Santi Perez. Both were given two-year suspensions from the sport despite Hamilton's lengthy appeals process in which his legal team alleged the test was untried and inaccurate. The test was first put together for the 2004 Olympic Games in Athens.

While reporters swarmed around the Astana team's hotel, staff back at the pressroom prepared for yet another press conference, this one by the Tour's big boss, Amaury Sport Organisation president Patrice Clerc, and his sidekick, race director Christian Prudhomme.

Late-evening sunshine bathed the terrace outside the palace's tall picture windows, while the dark cloud over the mountains intensified, lending a dramatic backdrop to the pronouncement by Clerc and Prudhomme that Vino's positive test and the suspicions concerning Rasmussen had sent the Tour into "a black period."

Clerc began the press conference by explaining that he had spoken with Astana team manager Biver by phone earlier, and requested that he and the Astana team leave the race. Biver accepted the request without hesitation, Clerc said. The ASO president was then asked if the news of Vinokourov's positive, combined with the cloud of suspicion hanging over Rasmussen, had prompted ASO to consider canceling the Tour. Clerc replied that the thought had "never crossed my mind."

"We have started a war on doping, and unfortunately in war there are losses, but it is out of the question to quit," Clerc said. "There was never a question the Tour would stop. Then the cheaters would win."

Cycling needed "an ethical revolution," Clerc said, adding that he now regretted inviting Astana to the race. At the end of 2006, because of its ongoing battle of words with the UCI, ASO did not accept the Astana team as a member of the UCI ProTour, but it did invite the Kazakh-sponsored, Swiss-registered formation to the Tour as a wild-card squad. So this was one development that ASO couldn't blame on the UCI.

"We have to be careful of the reputations within a team [like Astana]," Clerc said, likely referring to the suspensions of the team's Eddy Mazzoleni and Matthias Kessler in the weeks prior to the Tour. "Astana had some of the best riders in the world. We told Astana about the risks. We thought they had a place [in the Tour]. Yes, I regret inviting them. I regret being cheated."

Prudhomme said he had told the riders before the start in London that this Tour was "a fantastic opportunity to start over again." He added, "The riders are playing Russian roulette. They have to get this through their heads. They need to understand that their determination is total. It doesn't make me happy, but in a certain way it shows that the system is working."

"[Vinokourov] crossed the yellow line," Clerc stated. "He cheated. I believe the public no longer needs racers who cheat. And it makes me more committed than ever in the fight against doping."

Clerc also had harsh words for Rasmussen, saying the Dane should not have been allowed to race in the Tour and was not a good example. "In a period of crisis [for cycling], such as we are living in at the moment, a champion must be a good example," said Clerc. "His attitude, his lack of respect shown to the administrative rules, which is unacceptable, should have been made known to us, and we would have refused his participation, because he is not a good role model for the others in the peloton."

Clerc added that major changes were needed to save marquee events like the Tour. And he concluded optimistically that the Tour remained "a beautiful event" and that it would survive this latest dark period just as it had done in the past.

Reporters agreed that cycling was at a crossroads. It was believed that perhaps half of the Tour peloton—including reformed riders like Millar—was vehemently against the cheaters and their doping methods. The other half was probably on the edge, not sure whether doping was still a viable option for helping them perform at a higher level.

Despite the long day of mixed emotions, the press corps seemed optimistic. With reporters still banging out stories on their laptops, a Danish sportswriter brought two bottles of wine into the pressroom with a half dozen glasses. He filled a glass and raised it, toasting, "to Vino!" That could have been a toast to thank Vinokourov for making it more likely that cycling would be a cleaner sport in the future, or it might have been thanking the Kazakh for giving him a big story to report on what should have been a quiet rest day.

That night, after filing their stories, a dozen American and British reporters dined at a sidewalk bistro in the old part of town to honor Paris-based journalist Samuel Abt, who was reporting his 31st and what he said was his final Tour de France. His story as a race follower is as much a part of the Tour de France as the exploits made by the racers. The festive meal was a good time to enjoy the flavors of France and exchange memories of a Tour that was in its 104th year . . . and counting.

To answer the question in that morning's paper: No, the Tour was not in peril. It was the cheaters who were in peril. And the more of them that were caught, the better.

— ◉ —

All of cycling's epic qualities were on display during the final day in the mountains: hundreds of thousands of spectators along the 218.5km course that crisscrossed the Pyrénées; a spectacular 150km breakaway by climbers Soler, Sastre, and Mayo from the foot of the day's first climb, the incredibly steep and long Port de Larrau, to the day's final ascent, the Col d'Aubisque; a total of 16,555 feet of climbing that all but one of the 151 starters survived; and a battle royal between the four men who already topped the general classification, Rabobank's Rasmussen, Discovery Channel's Contador and Leipheimer, and Predictor-Lotto's Evans.

The riders would cross the finish line weary from their nearly seven-hour ordeal under a broiling sun, battling grades as steep as 15 percent, negotiating perilous descents that twisted down forested hillsides, and reserving their hardest efforts for the 17km haul up the spectacular Aubisque, whose grueling upper reaches are carved from a near-vertical mountainside.

Soler attacked from the main pack after his eight teammates had set a torrid tempo to the foot of the *hors-catégorie* Port de Larrau, which averages 9.4 percent for its opening 10km—the steepest sustained climb in the whole Tour. After he was joined by Sastre (sixth overall at 6:46) and Mayo, this trio gained 4:20 by the time they caught the day's early four-man break on a flat section of road in Spain, halfway through the stage.

"When the Sastre break went," said Discovery team director Bruyneel, "we let it go to force Rabobank to work."

And work they did. The Rabobank team workers had to pull the pack for hour after hour as riders were being shed from the back on each of the day's four climbs, until the group was only 30-strong and the gap was down to two minutes approaching the Aubisque. One by one, Soler, Mayo, and Sastre were caught by the chasers until just Contador, Evans, Leipheimer, and Rasmussen were left at the front with the steepest slopes still to come.

"On the last climb, Alberto [Contador] attacked with his heart, but he didn't have the strength," said Bruyneel. "That's normal. He's young and you can't ask the impossible."

Contador's first sortie came with about 7km to go, but Rasmussen coolly reeled him in, later saying he had learned something from the previous climbing stage over the Peyresourde. "I saw [then] that I wasn't able to follow Contador's accelerations, so we changed our tactic today, and I rode more at my own rhythm," said the Dane.

The race leader had no trouble catching Contador in his subsequent accelerations as the climb pushed higher, and the Spaniard started to run out of steam. Leipheimer also tried several attacks, but each time Rasmussen closed the gap.

STAGE 16: ORTHEZ GOURETTE–COL D'AUBISQUE

"With three or four kilometers to go," said Bruyneel, "when I called up from the car for [Contador] to attack, and he couldn't, that's when I realized it was over."

"I could see he was tiring," said Rasmussen. "When I attacked in the final kilometer, he blew up."

Behind the Dane's winning effort, Leipheimer was the stronger of the two Discovery men, and he crossed the summit 26 seconds back, while Contador coasted across the line in third, at 35 seconds, and tipped his hat to Rasmussen.

"I started today's stage to try to win the Tour, but now I end it seeing that my chances are lost," said Contador, now 3:10 back on GC. "I wasn't at my best today. I can't do anything now but congratulate him. Now I will fight to keep my second place."

With no room for team buses at the summit finish, soigneurs waited with towels, bottles of water, and clean jerseys for the riders to wear on their way back down the mountain. It was a raw reminder of how cycling used to be.

"It was very, very hard," said Saunier Duval's Christophe Rinero, a 33-year-old Frenchman who was 48th across the line, 21:36 down. He had been in the day's first break for three hours until caught by the Soler-Sastre-Mayo move and then worked hard for his team leader, Mayo, for another hour or so before making his way to the finish as best he could.

"I'm really cooked," Rinero continued, "but I worked hard for the team, and it's a pity Mayo didn't win the stage [he faded to 16th]. I did my maximum. Now I'm dead, dead, dead."

Team CSC's Jens Voigt came in 59th at 29:20, a victim of a spectacular crash on the vertiginous descent of the day's third peak, the lofty Col de la Pierre–St. Martin on the Spanish-French border. The 36-year-old German's jersey was ripped at the left shoulder while his left leg was streaked with coagulated blood.

No less than 73 riders were in the *gruppetto* that arrived almost 42 minutes behind the leaders. Finishing near the back of this giant bunch was Britain's Bradley Wiggins of Cofidis. He had placed fifth in the stage 13 time trial a few days before, and looked to have a chance to podium at the last time trial in three days' time. His bare chest glistened with sweat before he toweled it dry and put on a warm top.

Wiggins, whose face was tight with anger, refused to talk about his day. He had just learned that his Italian teammate, Cristian Moreni, had tested positive for testosterone after stage 11 in Montpellier, and that team management was probably going to pull the whole team from the Tour. [It did.]

Wiggins, an outspoken critic of doping, had raced the Tour with distinction. He had just finished the most grueling day of the race. Now it was over because of a doper on his own team. All that effort for nothing. No wonder he was angry.

Moreni ended his day in the back of a police car waiting for him at the Cofidis team bus after he coasted down from the Aubisque summit.

Moreni ended his day in the back of a police car waiting for him at the Cofidis team bus after he coasted down from the Aubisque summit. He was charged with breaking France's tough laws against using and trafficking in doping products. The 35-year-old former Italian champion admitted to administering himself a synthetic version of the male sex hormone and did not ask for his B sample to be tested.

The news came as a heavy blow to the Cofidis team manager, Eric Boyer, who for years had spoken out against the evils of doping in cycling. "Cristian apologized for having hurt us, and he also apologized to his family, his teammates, and the organizers of the Tour de France," Boyer told *L'Équipe TV*. "He is assuming responsibility, and is absolving the team, including our medical personnel, from responsibility. I blame myself and take responsibility for not having been present in the difficult moments when he gave into temptation."

French teams have long been seen as the ProTour's cleanest squads, largely the result of federally mandated monitoring of all French-licensed riders following the 1998 Festina Affair. Cofidis, however, was embroiled in its own doping problems in 2004, with a scandal that involved a series of confessions, accusations, and even the arrest and suspension of Millar for admitted EPO use.

But the French team said it had taken steps to correct that history, and Cofidis was one of seven teams that announced the previous day the formation of the *Mouvement pour un Cyclisme Crédible*, demanding strict application of the UCI code of conduct, signatures of the UCI antidoping pledge by all team managers, directors, and doctors, and total transparency concerning riders' therapeutic use exemptions.

These teams had staged a small protest at the beginning of this long day to denounce Rasmussen's continued presence in the race, holding up the start in Orthez for several minutes. The contrast of Cofidis riders protesting the use of doping products at the stage start with the image of Moreni leaving the race in police custody many hours later was just another unimaginable moment in a Tour de France that seemed to grow more surreal by the hour.

The French team's protest resonated with the crowds lining the climb to the Aubisque summit, with many of them whistling or booing Rasmussen as he passed by. The condemnation of Rasmussen wasn't universal, and when he appeared on the Aubisque podium to receive his 10th consecutive yellow jersey, most spectators on the mountaintop applauded politely. He held aloft the little lion of jersey sponsor LCL like a symbol of his dominance, in which he toyed with and tamed his opposition.

Some felt that Rasmussen's slowing on the steepest climbs to turn and stare at his last rivals before sprinting away to victory was reminiscent of countryman Bjarne Riis, the 1996 Tour champion, who confessed just before this race that his victory came with the aid of blood-boosting EPO.

Rasmussen didn't admit to anything like that, but he mentioned hearing the booing. "It did happen during the stage," he said. "I believe there's a lot of frustration among the people and in the peloton about what's going on. After what happened to Vino, since he is not here, people are taking their frustrations out on me." Rasmussen was wrong in thinking those boos were meant for the disgraced Vinokourov, because he was loudly booed when he went to the morning's sign-in ceremony in Orthez. The podium announcer momentarily stopped his endless banter as the skinny Dane signed his name to the start list.

The intense negative feeling toward Rasmussen reminded many of the divisiveness provoked by Armstrong's dominant victory run. "Now I understand what Lance Armstrong went through for seven years. My respect for him is growing day by day," Rasmussen said. "The only good thing about the Vinokourov situation is that it proves the system is working. To that, I can only add that I've had 14 negative tests on this Tour."

If the boos weren't enough, a wasp stung Rasmussen on his lower lip during the descent off the Port de Larrau, and he rode the rest of the stage with his mouth swollen "like I had a golf ball in it." At least the swollen lip hadn't come from a fan's sucker punch.

STAGE 14: MAZAMET–PLATEAU DE BEILLE

1. Alberto Contador (Sp), Discovery Channel, 5:25:48
2. Michael Rasmussen (Dk), Rabobank, s.t.
3. Juan Mauricio Soler Hernandez (Col), Barloworld, at 0:37
4. **Levi Leipheimer (USA), Discovery Channel, at 0:40**
5. Carlos Sastre (Sp), CSC, at 0:53
6. Andréas Klöden (G), Astana, at 1:52
7. Cadel Evans (Aus), Predictor-Lotto, at 1:52

8. Antonio Colom (Sp), Astana, at 2:23

9. Andrey Kashechkin (Kz), Astana, at 2:23

10. Yaroslav Popovych (Ukr), Discovery Channel, at 3:06

STAGE 15: FOIX LOUDENVIELLE–LE LOURON

1. Alexander Vinokourov (Kz), Astana, 5:34:28

2. Kim Kirchen (Lux), T-Mobile, at 0:51

3. Haimar Zubeldia (Sp), Euskaltel-Euskadi, at 0:51

4. Juan Jose Cobo Acebo (Sp), Saunier Duval-Prodir, at 0:58

5. Juan Manuel Garate (Sp), Quick Step-Innergetic, at 2:14

6. David Arroyo (Sp), Caisse d'Épargne, at 3:23

7. Bernhard Kohl (A), Gerolsteiner, at 4:25

8. Christian Vande Velde (USA), CSC, at 4:25

9. Ludovic Turpin (F), Ag2r Prévoyance, at 5:16

10. Alberto Contador (Sp), Discovery Channel, at 5:31

STAGE 16: ORTHEZ GOURETTE–COL D'AUBISQUE

1. Michael Rasmussen (Dk), Rabobank, 6:23:21

2. Levi Leipheimer (USA), Discovery Channel, at 00:26

3. Alberto Contador (Sp), Discovery Channel, at 00:35

4. Cadel Evans (Aus), Predictor-Lotto, at 00:43

5. Juan Mauricio Soler Hernandez (Col), Barloworld, at 01:25

6. Haimar Zubeldia (Esp), Euskaltel-Euskadi, at 01:52

7. Juan Jose Cobo Acebo (Sp), Saunier Duval-Prodir, at 01:54

8. Carlos Sastre (Sp), CSC, at 02:12

9. Oscar Pereiro Sio (Sp), Caisse d'Épargne, at 02:27

10. Alejandro Valverde (Sp), Caisse d'Épargne, s.t.

GENERAL CLASSIFICATION AFTER STAGE 16

1. Michael Rasmussen (Dk), Rabobank, 76:15:15

2. Alberto Contador (Sp), Discovery Channel, at 03:10

3. Cadel Evans (Aus), Predictor-Lotto, at 05:03

4. Levi Leipheimer (USA), Discovery Channel, at 05:59

5. Carlos Sastre (Sp), CSC, at 09:12

6. Haimar Zubeldia (Esp), Euskaltel-Euskadi, at 09:39

7. Alejandro Valverde (Sp), Caisse d'Épargne, at 13:28

8. Kim Kirchen (Lux), T-Mobile, at 14:46

9. Yaroslav Popovych (Ukr), Discovery Channel, at 16:00

10. Juan Mauricio Soler Hernandez (Col), Barloworld, at 16:41

CHRISTIAN VANDE VELDE | JULY 24

Sulking

Jesus. I was having a great rest day that came on the heels of a successful race for myself and for our team. We went for a nice ride through the countryside and then had a team press conference that ended without one negative question. Then we had a good lunch. Heck, I didn't even mind the out-of-competition blood and urine tests that our team conducted.

Around 2:00 or so I took a nap and after about 30 minutes, I heard all this ruckus in the hall and my phone started to burp, gargle, and ring.

What the hell is going on? I finally answered a call from the States of all places, and my friend was on the other line reading me the news. Amazing, this day and age; someone from Boulder, Colorado, who works in the ski industry is giving me news from Pau, France, about cycling and about a race that I am in!

So Vino and Astana are gone. Obviously I don't know any more than you at this point. I am sad and disappointed, because I thought of Vino as an intelligent, charismatic champion. Then this happens.

I can say one thing positive: the system is working. Now two runners-up who deserved to win have won, with Cadel Evans in the first TT and Kim Kirchen yesterday. They're both great riders, with Kim coming from a team with a strong antidoping program, T-Mobile. Of course, they never got to stand on the podium the way they deserved to, but justice is being served.

What will tomorrow bring? Will it still be hard? Yes. Will there be doubt? Yes. Will I still race as hard as I have every other day? Yes. Can I do anything about these guys playing Russian roulette? No! And that is the most frustrating thing; *we* are at the mercy of the weak.

But the controls are working and there are many. I have been controlled on 13 different occasions this year from our team alone. They look for everything from blood transfusions, EPO, testosterone, HGH, reticulocytes . . . you name it. Then on top of that I have been controlled at races randomly a few times and by USADA at least three times at my home. That brings me up to about 20 times this year, so I have given my fair share of bodily fluids for the sport.

We don't lack tests and they are obviously working, weeding out cheaters and protecting the future of the clean athletes.

Tomorrow is coming fast and I need to get my head straight. It will be a beautiful stage nonetheless and the fans will

CONTINUED →

CHRISTIAN VANDE VELDE | JULY 24 *continued*

still come out in droves to cheer on the riders as we try to scale the mountains in Spain and France . . . all of that despite today's shock.

Cycling will always be a beautiful sport no matter how many people disgrace it. And the Tour de France will *always* be the headliner. ⊗

RIDER DIARY

SIMON GERRANS | JULY 22

Basquet of nuts

I do my best to look on the bright side of most situations, and the bright side of racing through the Pyrénées is the crazy Basque fans. They go absolutely nuts when the race passes by. It doesn't matter if you're up in front racing for the win

or half an hour down in the *gruppetto*, they go ballistic! A cold can of Coke to drink or a bottle of water to tip over your head is only a group of orange-clad spectators away. ⊗

RIDER DIARY

SIMON GERRANS | JULY 23

Down on the farm

Nothing hurts more than an uphill start when everybody wants to be in the break, and today was no exception. The bunch completely shattered on the first climb. Luckily for Ag2r, Ludo was on a good day and made the break.

Once I'd recovered from the effort of passing the first climb of the day with the main bunch, I actually didn't feel too bad. That is, until I collected a hay bale that was right in the middle of the road, protecting a small traffic island. I was looking down at my computer to see how many kilometers until the base of the fol-lowing climb. The bunch parted in front of me, and I looked up at the last second to see I had nowhere to go but straight over the top of the bloody thing. Down I went. Again I was lucky not to hurt myself. I quickly caught the group just in time for the next mountain, where the group exploded and I found myself back with my sprinter friends in the *gruppetto*.

Unfortunately Cyril, who'd been struggling for a few days (since the start, actually) didn't get back on after the carnage of the day's first climb and pulled the pin midstage.   ⊗

RIDER DIARY

SIMON GERRANS | JULY 24

A no-rest day

Rest days are supposed to be relaxing. An easy ride, massage, a visit to the osteopath, and a nap during the day is the usual agenda. Not this rest day, as we were sharing a hotel with Astana . . .

Fortunately I managed to get most of my relaxing done in the morning, as by midafternoon chaos broke out in the hotel.

Vino had returned a positive control for blood doping on the stage of his time trial win. In no time whatsoever, hundreds of journalists arrived at the hotel trying to find anyone from Astana. A hundred or so police arrived soon after and our hotel was on lockdown. No one was coming or going. But the journos and the police were way too late if they were hoping to find any of the Kazakh riders. Martin spotted them climbing out the hotel window hours earlier with their suitcases; he said he thought it was a little bizarre.

I couldn't believe the lengths these journalists would go to get footage or photos or whatever. I spotted one photographer halfway up a tree trying to look in the window of my room on the first floor while I was getting a massage.

Midway through dinner, someone outside discovered the back door to the restaurant where we were eating wasn't locked, so in one mad rush we had maybe 30 journalists storm through the door, cameras blazing. The police quickly escorted them out.

The Astana cook, Willy, was funny, saying, "Last time we checked, no one was murdered here; this is unbelievable!"

I began to ask myself what I was doing here. The Tour de France is hard enough without having to deal with this kind of bedlam.   ⊗

RIDER DIARY

SIMON GERRANS | JULY 25

A protest, a bust

Following the mess we had to deal with yesterday, I really didn't feel like getting off the team bus at the stage start. I knew the only thing everyone would be talking about would be doping. To add to the situation, Vincent had asked the team to be at the start line 15 minutes early, along with all the other French and German teams, to sit down on the road and protest the fact that Rasmussen was still allowed to compete even though he had missed some doping controls prior to the Tour.

All the French and German teams were indeed there early. We didn't sit down and block the road, but we delayed the start several minutes and let the other teams take off first. I hope it had the desired effect. Vincent was happy because it sure created tension in the peloton.

Once the race got under way, I just worried about getting through the stage. Today was arguably the toughest mountain stage of the Tour. The climbs were spread out all the way through, so making the time limit was going to be tricky. The *gruppetto* was organized to form at the base of the first climb of the day. That way we'd get through with safety in numbers. We made it within the time limit; no worries.

There was yet another circus waiting for us at the finish line. Cristian Moreni, from Cofidis, had tested positive for testosterone a few days earlier so the police were there to collect him on his arrival.

Rasmussen won the stage convincingly, putting more time into second place. Unless he gets pulled, I am convinced he will win the Tour. ⊗

Paris

Issy-les-Moulineaux
Meudon
Châtenay-Malabry
Saclay
Saint-Rémy-les-Chevreuse
Les Ulis
Bullion
Marcoussis
STAGE 20
Le Marais

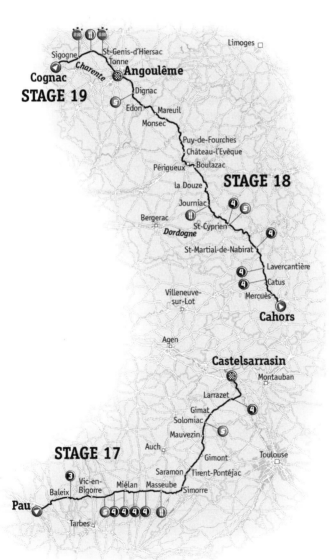

Limoges

Sigogne
St-Genis-d'Hiersac
Tonne
Angoulême
Cognac
STAGE 19
Charente
Dignac
Edon
Mareuil
Monsec
Puy-de-Fourches
Château-l'Evêque
Boulazac
Périgueux
la Douze
STAGE 18
Journiac
Bergerac
St-Cyprien
Dordogne
St-Martial-de-Nabirat
Lavercantière
Catus
Mercuès
Villeneuve-sur-Lot
Cahors
Agen
Castelsarrasin
Montauban
Larrazet
Gimat
Solomiac
Mauvezin
Gimont
Auch
Toulouse
STAGE 17
Saramon
Tirent-Pontéjac
Vic-en-Bigorre
Miélan
Masseube
Baleix
Simorre
Pau
Tarbes

12

Down to the Wire

One race leader departs and a new champion emerges.

I t was 11:20 p.m. on Wednesday, July 25. A full moon had arced its way over the snow peaks of the Pyrénées after a blazing sun had set beyond the misty ridges to the west. Stage 16 of the Tour de France finished here six hours ago, and the workers on the bleak summit of the Col d'Aubisque had just finished dismantling and stacking the crowd barriers with their forklift trucks. Five kilometers back down the mountain pass, half a dozen journalists from the United States were just finishing an impromptu meal of sandwiches, salad, French fries, and multiple sachets of ketchup, washed down with Cokes and beers, at La Grignotine, a sparse café that was the only place still open for business in the ski village of Gourette. Right then, one of the scribes checked his BlackBerry. There was a new e-mail message from the Agence France Presse. He read it out loud to the others: "The leader of the Tour de France, Michael Rasmussen, has been thrown out of the race by his Rabobank team. After a week of suspicion over four missed random doping controls, his Dutch outfit finally cracked after learning that Rasmussen had been in Italy in June, and not in Mexico as he had claimed. In the wake of Rasmussen's exit, Discovery Channel's 24-year-old Spanish climber Alberto Contador, one of the few riders able to keep pace with him in the final kilometers of the mountains stages, will take over the race lead."

The journalists reacted slowly, some thinking at first that it was a joke, while others sat in stunned silence. But it was true. At that same moment, 60km away in Pau, Rasmussen had already packed his bags and was about to leave the Hôtel Mercure. A picture of the grim-faced Rasmussen exiting the luxury hotel wearing a black team sweatshirt with an orange stripe down the sleeves was snapped by French photographer Bernard Papon. It would appear on the front page of the next morning's *L'Équipe* under the banner headline: *Exclu!* [Excluded!]

The Rabobank team sacked the Dane for lying to them about his whereabouts for out-of-competition drug tests. "He broke team rules," explained Rabobank spokesman Jacob Bergsma, who said that team officials believed Rasmussen had lied to them regarding his whereabouts in June, when UCI and Danish Cycling Union officials had been unable to locate the rider for their tests. Bergsma said the team officials learned that when Rasmussen had said he was in Mexico, where his wife's family lives, he had actually been in Italy.

Among the damning evidence was an eyewitness account by Italian TV reporter Davide Cassani, a former pro racer in Italy. Cassani said, "This morning, a Danish colleague came to interview me. He had heard that I said som thing about Rasmussen on Italian television, and wanted confirmation of what I'd said."

Cassani had told his viewers during coverage of the previous week's stage to Tignes that in mid-June ("either June 13 or 14, I'm not sure") he saw Rasmussen training in the rain in the Dolomites. He said it to demonstrate that the Dane was a cyclist dedicated to his profession who deserved the successes he had won at the Tour. But once the news came out from the Danish federation several days later that Rasmussen had supposedly been in Mexico in mid-June, Cassani's comments gained new importance.

The morning after Rasmussen left Pau, a statement was issued by management at team sponsor Rabobank, a major Dutch financial institution. It began: "Rabobank is shocked and disappointed of the fact that Michael Rasmussen gave false information in regards to his whereabouts. Apparently he did not stay at the address that he reported to the UCI and he did not send the report in a timely manner. UCI has issued a rightful warning to Rasmussen for this delayed provision of information. As giving false information in regards to his whereabouts is a flagrant violation of the UCI rules and therefore is unacceptable, Rabobank supports the decision of the Rabo cycling team to pull Rasmussen out of the competition and to immediately dismiss him from the team."

Later in the day, in an interview with the Danish newspaper *B.T.*, Rasmussen questioned the decision by his team manager Theo de Rooy to send him home, and disputed Cassani's claims about his whereabouts. "It's the work of a desperate man who is at the end of his nerves," Rasmussen said about de Rooy. "My boss is mad. I wasn't in Italy, no way. That's the story of one man [Cassani] who thinks he saw me. But there's not the slightest proof."

He added that there was an entire village in Mexico that could verify his presence in June. On the verge of tears, Rasmussen then told the paper that the scandal had left him "broken and destroyed," with nowhere left to turn.

Rasmussen's disgrace, along with the dismissals of Moreni and Vinokourov, left many riders angry. Emotions ran so high before the start of stage 17 in Pau that Rabobank's Dutch veteran Michael Boogerd tried to punch a fan who was booing him at the sign-in podium.

The opinion of CSC's American rider Christian Vande Velde was typical. He said, "I'm full with aggression, and I want to get home. I don't care that these people are trying to wreck it for me. I can give two shits about what these guys have done to us. I've trained my whole year for this race, and I'm not about to give it up."

Vande Velde voiced his frustration that the entire Tour peloton was being painted with the same brush as the riders getting caught in antidoping controls. He pointed to Team CSC's extensive internal testing program as a way for cycling to regain credibility with the fans and media.

"I'm angry. We're trying to do everything we can to make a great race, and there are still people who shit on the sport. Of course I'm angry," Vande Velde said. "At the same time, I am going to try to be positive and make a great spectacle and a great race for myself. There's no reason we should be punished. I'm not trying to be a pessimist. I want to go forth."

> "I'm angry. We're trying to do everything we can to make a great race, and there are still people who shit on the sport. Of course I'm angry."

Discovery team captain George Hincapie said riders were playing Russian roulette with their careers and the sport. "It's tough," he said. "You just wish people would do the right thing. I don't have all the answers to all the doping issues. All I can say is that I am clean, I work hard, and I try to win races. I just hope that everyone can do it the clean way, and stop being stupid."

Rasmussen's dramatic dismissal didn't surprise Cadel Evans, who told the AFP that he had harbored doubts over the Dane's sporadic performances ever since the two competed on the mountain bike World Cup circuit in the 1990s. "I first started racing against him in March of 1996 at the Sea Otter Classic in California," Evans said, "and on that occasion I couldn't go near him. For three years I raced against him in mountain biking, and I always finished ahead of him. And then he won the mountain bike world championship title in 1999, in the elite category. And he rode away from everyone."

Evans said he had had doubts about the Dane's erratic progress then, and also since he took up road racing, especially at the 2006 Tour de France. "It's strange, his progression," Evans said. "It's just observations I have. What can you say? It's not even progression. He has one or two good days a year, and last year he nearly put [70] guys out of the time limit [with his stage win at La Toussuire]. And I heard he had been suffering in the *gruppetto* himself in the Giro d'Italia [the month before]. It's strange."

But Evans stopped short of saying he was glad the Tour got rid of Rasmussen. "I really don't know the truth behind it all," he said. "Just because someone has a good performance you should never accuse them of cheating, because it could be the result of hard work and good training. But I see what I see. I've been beaten by cheats before, and I'll be beaten by them again, I'm sure of that, but I'm not worried about it."

In the meantime, Rasmussen's exit meant that Evans was now sure to finish on the Paris podium, and he even had a chance of winning the Tour outright. The victory would be decided at the stage 19 time trial on the penultimate day of the race.

— ⊙ —

After long-distance breakaways earned stage wins for Lampre-Fondital's Italian sprinter Daniele Bennati at Castelsarrasin and Française des Jeux's French veteran Sandy Casar at Angoulême, Contador would go into the final time trial with a 1:50 cushion on Evans, while the new leader had a 2:49 gap on teammate Leipheimer.

Evans actually cut his deficit by three seconds on the stage 18 finish at Angoulême—the same place the time trial would end 24 hours later. Eight minutes after Casar had sprinted to the stage win from three breakaway companions, the peloton split in the uphill charge to the line, with Evans one of 11 riders (led in by points competition leaders Tom Boonen, Robbie Hunter, and Erik Zabel) that took three seconds out of the rest. Behind the split, Contador actually led in the next group of 57 riders, with Leipheimer four places behind him, so all three contenders for the yellow jersey tested their legs on what would be the next day's time trial finish too.

They would all make a more detailed inspection of the rolling 55.5km route between Cognac and Angoulême in the morning. Their upcoming three-way battle had even the skeptics admitting that this time trial could produce one of the most exciting finale's in the Tour's 104-year history, especially as the course offered enough changes in terrain that Evans had a legitimate shot at snagging the final yellow jersey.

"Evans is the favorite [to win the stage]," said Discovery Channel team director Johan Bruyneel. "Evans is more of a specialist than Alberto, but the *maillot jaune* will give him motivation. I think the [1:50] margin will be sufficient. Evans has to take back two seconds a kilometer. If Cadel has a great day and Alberto has an off-day, maybe he can lose it."

Few people gave Leipheimer a glimmer of winning the whole enchilada, because he needed to gain more than three seconds per kilometer to overcome his teammate Contador. That was a lot to ask. Looking at this possibility, Bruyneel said, "The final time trial of a big tour is different. The first time trial is more for the specialists. The final one, people are more tired and it's not surprising to see the *maillot jaune* have a good final time trial. If both Alberto and Cadel have bad days, Levi could still win the Tour. I hope that Alberto doesn't have a bad day."

With the pressure building on him as Paris approached, Contador knew that he needed to remain calm and focus on preparing for the next day's appointment with history. "I know that tomorrow is a day that can change your life forever," he said. "I also know that it will be the most difficult day of my life. The public was nice with me today. I felt a warm reception along the roads, and it was an honor to ride in the yellow jersey today. I have to take advantage of this opportunity. Tomorrow I will fight to win the race."

Bruyneel was confident that his Spanish protégé would be up to the task. "Now [that] we're in position to win the Tour," he said, "we have to stay calm and do our job tomorrow. The key to a long time trial is to be constant, and to maintain a good rhythm. The first references will be key. Then you can see if you have to go harder or can ease up. I see the *maillot jaune* as ours to lose."

Evans's directeur sportif at Predictor-Lotto, Hendrik Redant, agreed with that view. "I am a realist," he said. "Contador is strong. It will be like at [the] Albi [time trial]. Cadel will gain back some time, but maybe it won't be enough. He's prepared well, he'll give it his maximum. Contador will have the time checks of Cadel, but Cadel will have the references to Levi—who we cannot forget.

"Leipheimer is probably the best time trialist of the three. He can still win the Tour. Contador will have an experienced guy like Bruyneel behind him in the car. That will be important. The pressure is not on us. We can only win. It is Contador who could lose everything. I saw him this morning and he looked nervous. That can be a factor. Cadel is relaxed and confident."

Evans too knew that beating Contador by almost two minutes would be difficult. At Albi, his advantage over the Spaniard was only 1:04 over a similar distance. "I don't know if it's possible [to take the yellow jersey]," Evans said. "It won't be easy. Contador showed he's a strong time trialist. I will certainly try to win the Tour. Everyone has asked me [if I can do it], and I don't have the answer."

Leipheimer noted, "I'm tired but I think everyone else is, too. I'll give it everything I have . . . we'll see. Tomorrow is [Alberto]'s job, and my job. It's all up to us, ourselves. I hope one of us wins."

— ◉ —

The three rivals would start their time trials at three-minute intervals at the end of the afternoon. It was a day of strong winds and squally rain showers blowing in from the Atlantic, though most of the riders would race on dry roads. The course curved northeast and then southeast, so the generally favorable wind became a crosswind in the second half.

Leipheimer, who'd be the first of the three contenders out of the gate, would use the aerodynamic tuck he first used five months earlier to win the critical time trial at the Tour of California, even though his hand position was slightly lower since the UCI modified the regulation concerning bar angles just before the Tour prologue.

Of the four time trials he had ridden in 2007 before the Tour, Leipheimer had won three and finished second the other time. That's why he was disappointed with his first two efforts at the Tour, particularly his stage 13 ride at Albi—though his strong finish there, much faster than Evans and Contador, left him feeling more confident about the modified position.

Leipheimer always had solid time trial ability, but his confidence really grew after his visit in November 2006 to the low-speed wind tunnel facility in San Diego. "I wanted to get in there early and train in that position over the winter," he said. "It's quite a bit different."

The new position was not quite as radical as that of 2006 Tour winner Floyd Landis. "But that's because of the rules," Leipheimer explained. "I can only have my bars as high as the saddle. But for me it works out perfect. It's actually very comfortable. I can't say why, but it's fast. That's what a wind tunnel's for."

Leipheimer added that discovering his new position was somewhat lucky. "We were in the tunnel playing around and I almost left; I almost stepped off the bike to finish [the session]," he said. "and someone suggested trying something [different], and it was like, Wow, that's low, that's a low drag. And right from that moment my motivation has been very good."

His low-down body position enables the lightweight Leipheimer to stay rock solid on the road, in contrast to some of his rides in 2006, when he was blown all over in heavy winds. After his second winning ride in 2007, Leipheimer said, "I tried to stay just one with my bike, to stay as straight as possible and keep the pressure on."

And that's exactly what he needed to do when he set out down the ramp in Cognac, the small town famous for its brandy. "In the back of my head I thought maybe if they both had a bad day I could win [the Tour]," said the 33-year-old American, who had been getting stronger through the three weeks. That improvement was confirmed by Evans, who said, "Leipheimer overall since the Aubisque has been really good—more than I expected of him actually."

The turnaround in his form began toward the end of the 54km time trial at Albi the previous Saturday. After inexplicably losing time to Evans and Contador on the easiest, early part of that stage, Leipheimer finally hit his stride 20km from the finish. Now, a week later, he said, "I just felt awesome."

More importantly, helped by the favorable winds, he got his 54×11 gear rolling early and kept the big ring turning on the frequent false flats along the challenging point-to-point course. Just how fast he was riding was confirmed at the first official time check, 17.5km from the start. The fastest of the previous 138 riders was time trial specialist Vladimir Karpets of Caisse d'Épargne, the tall, long-haired Russian who sped through in a time of 20:15.

Leipheimer was a stunning 39 seconds faster, having averaged 53.571kph despite an opening 10km that included two uphills and two tricky descents, one at 12 percent, on bumpy back roads, and some tricky, tight turns through the narrow streets of the pastel-painted villages of Bertiers and Nercillac.

On this opening stretch, Evans and Contador were able to make use of their snappier fast-twitch muscles on the climbs and out of the corners to limit their losses—14 seconds for the Aussie, 36 seconds for the Spaniard. "I had a pretty good start," Evans told *VeloNews*. "Leipheimer surprised me over the first section, and I had an idea he would be really good over the middle section. I've been racing against him a long time."

Out on smoother, straighter roads, slanting between fields of sunflowers and vineyards that produce grapes for the region's wines and liqueurs, the 5-foot-7, 132-pound American was flying. "It felt like I had all this energy," he said right after finishing. "I wasn't conservative because I got time checks right away, and they were good, and they just kept getting better. And that builds, you know. You're able to push yourself that much harder when you hear that."

Leipheimer's low position enabled him to keep a straight line despite a strong side wind vector to the gusting westerly winds. And there was never any letup in his momentum up the long rollers. "It definitely wasn't flat," said Leipheimer. "There was a lot of long, uphill drags." This was where he was gaining just over three seconds a kilometer on Contador, the rate he needed to overcome his GC deficit . . . while Evans too was challenging for the yellow jersey.

"When [my directeur sportif] Hendrik [Redant] told me over the radio I was 38 seconds from yellow with 15 kilometers to go," Evans recounted, "I thought, 'I'm still in with a chance here, so just keep giving it everything.'"

Hearing the same information, Contador recalled, "At that moment I was worried because my legs were hurting me very bad."

The time checks showed that if—and it was a big if—all three men continued to ride the final 15km at the same pace they had ridden the previous

5km, the final GC result would have been reversed: 1. Leipheimer; 2. Evans, at 0:11; 3. Contador, at 0:22. That's how close this race was becoming.

At that point in his ride, Leipheimer was catching and passing Carlos Sastre for three minutes, so the impossible was starting to look more possible. But the course didn't continue with its wide-open rollers on which the skinnier Contador was losing so much time to the other two. The road, now heading gradually downhill, was more sheltered as it reached the buildings on the outskirts of Angoulême.

Before reaching the hilltop city, the riders crossed the Charente River on an old stone bridge, then headed up the hardest climb of the day, rising 200 feet in a half mile past the Roman city's impressive ramparts, where huge crowds waved flags, banged thunder sticks, and screamed encouragement at the riders. "That little hill was hard," said Leipheimer. "I had to give it everything I had to keep it in the big chainring, and not shift. I thought it was shorter than it was, and I kind of punched it at the bottom, and then came around a turn and saw that I was only halfway up, and I had to sit down for a second."

It was just the terrain and crowd energy that Contador needed. "I started to feel better, and I knew I had to give everything to the end to keep the yellow jersey," said the young Spaniard.

As the race leader was dancing up the ramparts hill, Leipheimer was finishing his effort on the far side of town. He stopped the clock at 1:02:44, two minutes faster than the previous best (by Karpets), for an average speed of 53.081kph, the second fastest for a Tour time trial longer than 50km, behind only Lance Armstrong's 53.986kph over the 58.5km Freiburg-Mulhouse course in 2000.

Leipheimer had done everything asked of him, and more. It looked likely that he was going to take second place from Evans because the Aussie reached the final time check with a GC advantage over the American of only eight seconds. But on the last 5.4km through town Evans matched Leipheimer's split, to dash up the 600 meter climb to the line and hold on to second place by those eight seconds. "I was hurting a little bit the last 5K," Leipheimer later admitted.

Contador resisted too. At the last time split he led Evans by 32 seconds, and though he conceded another nine seconds before the finish, Discovery's black-haired climber turned to see his time and raised his arms in relief and celebration.

He was greeted by Spanish fans chanting his name, just the way they greeted Miguel Induráin during his five-year reign as Tour champion through the 1990s. Also there to sing Contador's praises was team boss Bruyneel and part-team owner Armstrong. The seven-time Tour winner arrived earlier in the day to ride shotgun in the number 1 Discovery car and witness the American team's eighth Tour triumph in nine years.

Armstrong was quickly escorted into the Discovery team camper for a few moments before he stepped out to speak to many of the same journalists who covered his Tour exploits. As expected, Armstrong was more eager to speak of his team's impressive Tour than of the plague of doping scandals that rocked this year's Tour.

"I'm here as a fan of the team, a supporter of the team, and a supporter of Johan," Armstrong said when asked about controversial former race leader Rasmussen. "I'm not here to talk about that."

The former Discovery team leader also had high praise for Contador, who was now poised to win the Tour. "He's a great talent, a great rider," Armstrong said. "He's an explosive climber, able to make a difference quickly on the steep parts. The message you get from Johan is that he's also very poised, very mature for a 24-year-old. If everything goes well tomorrow and he wins to become one of the youngest winners ever, it's a statement."

Leipheimer was thrilled to finally win a Tour stage and stand on the Paris podium, but he seemed sad that his best shot at winning the Tour fell 31 seconds short. "Honestly, I'm happy for Contador," he said, before adding, "I'm very happy for Alberto. He's the next superstar."

Leipheimer would say later, "That for me was the best day of my career. I had the best legs I've ever had. [The confidence] starts to build on itself during the race. You feel good, and I think your mentality changes. It's hard to describe. You just open up."

When Evans reached his team camper van, he hugged his Italian wife Chiara, spoke with the Belgian team owner Marc Coucke, and then replied to some questions from the press. Asked whether he was disappointed at not winning the Tour, the 30-year-old Aussie from the Melbourne area said, "No. All along my objective was to do better than last year. Last year, fifth, this year, second, and I think I rode a really good Tour. But when you're so close to winning, and I'm a very competitive athlete, you always want to win."

The following evening on the Champs-Élysées—after Bennati easily won his second stage in four days in a mass-sprint finish—Evans was happy to be on the Paris podium alongside winner Contador and third-place Leipheimer. Asked if the result might have been different with Rasmussen in the race, Evans said, "That's complicated . . . there's so many different directions the race could have taken. It's not possible to quantify."

What could be quantified is that after surviving everything the dopers could do to falsify the results, the 2007 Tour de France came down to a drama-filled time trial that ended with three superlative athletes providing the race's closest-ever podium.

STAGE 17: PAU–CASTELSARRASIN

1. Daniele Bennati (I), Lampre-Fondital, 4:14:04
2. Markus Fothen (G), Gerolsteiner, s.t.
3. Martin Elmiger (Swi), Ag2r Prévoyance, s.t.
4. Jens Voigt (G), CSC, s.t.
5. David Millar (GB), Saunier Duval-Prodir, at 02:41
6. Matteo Tosatto (I), Quick Step-Innergetic, at 02:43
7. Manuel Quinziato (I), Liquigas, at 03:20
8. Daniele Righi (I), Lampre-Fondital, s.t.
9. Tom Boonen (B), Quick Step-Innergetic, at 09:37
10. Sébastien Chavanel (F), Française des Jeux, s.t.

STAGE 18: CAHORS–ANGOULÊME

1. Sandy Casar (F), Française des Jeux, 5:13:31
2. Axel Merckx (B), T-Mobile, at 00:01
3. Laurent Lefevre (F), Bouygues Telecom, s.t.
4. Michael Boogerd (Nl), Rabobank, s.t.
5. Tom Boonen (B), Quick Step-Innergetic, at 08:34
6. Robert Hunter (Rsa), Barloworld, s.t.
7. Erik Zabel (G), Milram, s.t.
8. Sébastien Chavanel (F), Française des Jeux, s.t.
9. Bernhard Eisel (A), T-Mobile, s.t.
10. Thor Hushovd (N), Crédit Agricole, s.t.

STAGE 19: COGNAC–ANGOULÊME TIME TRIAL

1. **Levi Leipheimer (USA), Discovery Channel, 1:02:44**
2. Cadel Evans (Aus), Predictor-Lotto, at 00:51
3. Vladimir Karpets (Rus), Caisse d'Épargne, at 01:56
4. Yaroslav Popovych (Ukr), Discovery Channel, at 02:01
5. Alberto Contador (Sp), Discovery Channel, at 02:18
6. Ivan Gutierrez José (Sp), Caisse d'Épargne, at 02:27
7. **George Hincapie (USA), Discovery Channel, at 02:33**
8. Oscar Pereiro Sio (Sp), Caisse d'Épargne, at 02:36
9. Leif Hoste (B), Predictor-Lotto, at 02:48
10. Mikel Astarloza (Sp), Euskaltel-Euskadi, at 02:50

STAGE 20: MARCOUSSIS–PARIS CHAMPS-ÉLYSÉES

1. Daniele Bennati (I), Lampre-Fondital, 3:51:03
2. Thor Hushovd (N), Crédit Agricole, s.t.
3. Erik Zabel (G), Milram, s.t.
4. Robert Hunter (Rsa), Barloworld, s.t.
5. Tom Boonen (B), Quick Step-Innergetic, s.t.
6. Sébastien Chavanel (F), Française des Jeux, s.t.
7. Fabian Cancellara (Swi), CSC, s.t.
8. David Millar (Gb), Saunier Duval-Prodir, s.t.

9. Robert Förster (G), Gerolsteiner, s.t.

10. Manuel Quinziato (I), Liquigas, s.t.

GENERAL CLASSIFICATION AFTER STAGE 20

1. Alberto Contador (Sp), Discovery Channel, 91:00:26

2. Cadel Evans (Aus), Predictor-Lotto, at 00:23

3. Levi Leipheimer (USA), Discovery Channel, at 00:31

4. Carlos Sastre (Sp), CSC, at 07:08

5. Haimar Zubeldia (Esp), Euskaltel-Euskadi, at 08:17

6. Alejandro Valverde (Sp), Caisse d'Épargne, at 11:37

7. Kim Kirchen (Lux), T-Mobile, at 12:18

8. Yaroslav Popovych (Ukr), Discovery Channel, at 12:25

9. Mikel Astarloza (Sp), Euskaltel-Euskadi, at 14:14

10. Oscar Pereiro Sio (Sp), Caisse d'Épargne, at 14:25

RIDER DIARY

CHRISTIAN VANDE VELDE | JULY 26

Lenny

Yesterday was a long day.

It started out with a half-assed protest by the French. They only protested within their respective teams and didn't inform us as to what they were doing or what it was they were protesting.

I agree about taking a stand but taking a stand without unity is a waste of time and, from my point of view, embarrassing. They were quick to throw stones and then at the end of the day they had a positive case of their own in Cristian Moreni. Just great!

After the race, our hotel was swarming with police because we were staying in the same place as Cofidis. Then, as if anything couldn't get worse, the Rabobank guys pulled their own yellow jersey out of the race.

Chicken lied to his team and the antidoping authorities and he got caught. I swear I thought that one was a joke or a bad rumor. But no, just a bad movie known as *The 2007 Tour*. If his team doesn't believe him anymore, then we shouldn't either. I was so depressed and shocked, I didn't know whether I should laugh or cry. I did a little of both, but then got it together.

After all of this, there was more energy flowing through our hotel than at an AC/DC concert. I found myself walking from room to room, getting everyone's take on the situation.

I made it to bed around 1:00 a.m. with all sorts of random thoughts flying through my head. I finally focused on my

CONTINUED →

daughter, whom I've not seen in three weeks. That put a smile on my face and I eventually drifted off to sleep.

But after dinner tonight, I had all of this put into perspective by one of my friends from Chicago. He asked me how I was doing and I responded with, "I've been better."

"Yeah, I've been better, too," he said.

He then went on to tell me that our mutual friend and my biggest fan, Lenny, had passed away last night after an ice hockey game. He had a heart attack in the locker room and never came back.

This stopped me in my tracks and made me take a step back away from sport and look at life. Cycling is my life right now and we are wrapped up in a hor-rible situation that is hopefully at the bottom of the curve. But hearing this put cycling on the back burner really quick and made me realize that while the problems within the Tour are huge and horrible, the big picture is much, much bigger.

Today was a great stage as expected and Chicken was forgotten quickly. We don't have any time for people getting in trouble and we will not waste a Tour de France stage on their account. The sport deserves better and so do the fans, who came out in droves to watch today. The race didn't disappoint, as we had some of the hardest kilometers of the Tour.

I was excited for the race today and had plenty of angst to take out on my bike, but tomorrow I'll ride for Lenny.   ⊗

RIDER DIARY

CHRISTIAN VANDE VELDE | JULY 29

With Paris in our sights

The Tour is more or less over and I am already thinking of canoe trips in Wisconsin, buying bait and a case of Old Style at the local store.

Today was the final time trial and it was actually interesting to watch. Levi Leipheimer rode an amazing race, averaging 53kph over 55.5 kilometers. With his ride and that of Cadel, the top three on GC are now all within half a minute of each other.

Obviously it has been a strange Tour and one that I would hope never happens again. I am glad it's over, but I do have one personal regret. In June, during the Dauphiné, I half-jokingly told Alberto Contador that I bet 1,000 euros on him at 50-to-1 that he would win the Tour. Yeah, how stupid am I that I didn't! That would've been a good payout. The fact is that I have had confidence in that boy since I first saw him in 2004. He absolutely destroyed Michael Boogerd in Valencia that year at the tender age of 20, and I have been a fan of his ever since.

This morning I ate my last breakfast of the Tour with our chef, Søren. I had to ask him how much ketchup and honey we had consumed during the month and some quick math equated to 17.5 liters of honey and eight liters of ketchup. That's more than four gallons of honey and two gallons of ketchup. Keep in mind that Dave Z and Stuey went home early; they would've added another gallon to that total. Those boys do like their condiments.

I sat with Alberto this morning on the bus to the train station. He looked a bit dazed but was taking everything in stride, almost like it was nothing new.

We all congregated in the Caisse d'Épargne bus last night after a few beers at dinner. We were drinking Pacharán, a Basque aperitif, but a little faster than it is supposed to be drunk. We all had a good time and it was nice to see some guys in a different atmosphere. We bonded a bit with the Spanish guys and this morning we all had similar stories of waking up in the middle of the night with cotton mouth.

It's amazing what a few drinks will do to break down some barriers with people you detested for a month. Chente Garcia is back in my good graces but I am sure next weekend in San Sebastian we will butt heads.   ⊗

RIDER DIARY

CHRISTIAN VANDE VELDE | JULY 31

The dust settles

Oh my lord, the morning after the Tour is the best breakfast in the world.

It's better than Christmas, as Stuey says. I spoke with the man a few times over the last two days as he coached me to make it through the last night. He is the teacher, after all.

Last night I hurt myself as I always do with friends and foes and now I am crawling back to Gerona on my knees. CSC had the usual post-Tour party, which was fun, but then Discovery went above and beyond by renting the roof of the Hôtel de Crillon (go to www.crillon.com to see the place). Awesome. I won't go into details but I had a good time. Thanks, Alberto.

I did miss my girls last night and I can't wait to see them in a few hours. After the finish yesterday I was so tired that all I wanted to do was crawl into a cave and sleep. Of course, that didn't happen.

Actually, I managed to get a lot accomplished yesterday, officially an-nouncing my transfer to the U.S.-based Slipstream Sports team. I was really apprehensive about talking to my team about it and the media, but now I feel 100 pounds lighter and I am really excited for the next two years. I realized that half of my fear was telling everyone yesterday. After getting that weight off my shoulders, I can see my future in cycling a bit more clearly. Slipstream will be a great team and a nice change of pace as I take on new responsibilities and titles. We have a huge talent pool of young American riders and I am more than happy to offer them some insight along the way, using my trial-and-error handbook on life in Europe as a guide.

The second half of the season still must be raced and we have many more days of pasta to go. But every day of pasta means that I am one day closer to that beer and burger at the Flambeau Lodge in Wisconsin.

Thanks for reading this year.

RIDER DIARY

SIMON GERRANS | JULY 26

More changes on a tough day of racing

I knew today was one of my last chances to make my mark on this year's Tour, but I really didn't want to be there. Overnight, Rabobank pulled Rasmussen out of the Tour for apparently lying on his UCI whereabouts forms. The whole Cofidis team had gone home following Moreni's positive control. No one seemed to care about the race anymore; it was all doping, and I'd had enough of it. There were spectators by the start line who had come along just to yell abuse at the riders. I knew I'd done nothing wrong but I felt like a criminal just for being there.

Once I rolled off the start line and was riding my bike, I managed to clear my head a little to think about the race again and the job at hand.

The stage started super quick. I forced my way up the front. The roads were familiar, as they were the same ones used to start stage 17 in 2005 where I made the break and finished third. This gave me extra motivation.

A group split off the front only a few kilometers into the stage on a small climb. Martin was there already. But there were around 20 riders, so I jumped across the gap, and to my surprise my legs felt pretty good. The break then split across the top of the climb. Martin was in the front with seven others. I looked around and saw that Popovych and Horner had followed the move. They were both well placed on GC, and I knew with these guys there the break would never work, so I stopped working and let Martin's group ride away, disappointed to miss my chance again. We were soon swept up by the peloton while Martin's group stayed away to contest the stage win. Martin did a good job finishing third.

At the end of the day with no more Rasmussen in the race, Contador pulled on his first yellow jersey and Cadel moved up to second overall, well within striking distance.   ⊗

RIDER DIARY

SIMON GERRANS | JULY 28

An impressive TT

Going through the motions in the time trial on a fast but tough circuit. Impressive Discovery and really impressive Leipheimer.

The thing I was mostly looking forward to about today's time trial was, once it was over, I was going to be 55.5km closer to Paris.

I was back at the hotel early and watched the last few guys on telly. What an exciting finish! The Disco boys were really impressive. Contador managed to hang on to his lead and I was cheering for Cadel. But if the time trial had been another 3 or 4 kilometers long, I think Leipheimer might have won the Tour. Boy oh boy, he was flying! ⊗

SIMON GERRANS | JULY 29

First the party, then the race, then the party

The start of the final stage into Paris had a really cool, relaxed atmosphere. The jersey wearers and the Discovery guys drank their champagne as we rolled through the neutral zone. There was more talk of the party that follows the final stage than about the race itself.

The pace of the bunch slowly but surely sped up as we neared the center of Paris. By the time we hit the Champs-Élysées for the first of the finishing laps, we were at full speed. I was keen to get in a break on the finishing circuits. I hadn't been able to make one stick all Tour and this was my last chance.

As we neared the Arc de Triomphe with 40km left to race, I followed an acceleration at the front of the bunch. It split behind and 10 of us got a gap. I'd made the break. There were eight of us working really hard and with a couple of blokes sitting on, we gained a maximum of 45 seconds with 20km to go. At this point I thought we had a real chance of staying away and I began to think about how I was going to try and win the stage. Then the peloton sped up a little and the break became disorganized, causing our advantage to quickly disappear. We were caught by the bunch coming into the final lap. The stage finished in a mass sprint.

So ended my visions of glory for this year's Tour!

As for the final result, I think Contador was a worthy winner. He consistently took advantage of his impressive climbing abilities, while limiting his losses in the time trials. To top it off he also seems like a pretty good guy, and his teammates seemed really pleased to be working for him. It was also a fantastic result for Cadel to finish in second place. He is the first Australian to have an overall podium finish in the Tour. I'm sure this result will motivate him even more to go one better next year.

Following the stage and the lap of honor around the Champs-Élysées, we all rushed back to the hotel for a shower and a change of clothes. Then the entire Ag2r Prévoyance crew and their partners got together at L'Étoile restaurant for dinner. At some point the dining tables disappeared, the turntables came out, and our little restaurant turned into a nightclub. It was great to see everybody unwind and have a good time following the month of hard work we'd all put in.

For me it was also a night involving a lot of good-byes. I'd just signed a contract for next year with French team Crédit Agricole, so the Tour would be the last time I raced alongside many of my teammates. I am really excited about going to Crédit Agricole and looking

CONTINUED →

forward to the change. However, it is difficult to leave Ag2r; the past three seasons with the team have been fantastic and a massive learning experience.

Hope to see you all at the Tour next year!   ⊗

Epilogue

The (Controversial) New Champion

Alberto Contador overcomes—and addresses—problems of his own.

Life changed quickly for Alberto Contador. He came into the 94th Tour de France as a talented young climber with a freelance role for the Discovery Channel squad. He confirmed his great promise with some blazing attacks in the Alps, became the top challenger to race leader Michael Rasmussen in the Pyrénées, and took a spectacular stage win at Plateau de Beille. Then, just as Rasmussen seemed to have the overall victory locked up, the Dane exited the race and Contador was thrust into the yellow jersey—and the spotlight.

After fending off his final challengers in the Cognac-Angoulême time trial, "Cinderella" Contador swept into Paris to claim his throne. But a skeptical public in the capital didn't greet his sudden success with the exuberance they showed in the Lance Armstrong years. Contador's march into the city wasn't quite the "funeral procession" that the German publication *Bild* had predicted a few days earlier "[because] the worldwide audience does not approve, and is angry and disappointed with the cycling liars." But the fallout from the Rasmussen and Alexander Vinokourov expulsions, combined with unseasonably cool, rainy weather, kept many spectators away.

The mood before the final stage was bleak. The rain had turned grassy patches to mud in the start town of Marcoussis, a bland suburban no-man's-land. Crowds were thin. Because of the rain, riders stayed in their buses until the final moments. Many were irritable, only too ready to get out of France, away from the media, away from all the doping scandals and innuendo. The rain only added to the depressing atmosphere. There was a rumor going around that there might be another rider protest against the dopers, but nothing came of it.

Instead of joyously celebrating the about-to-be-crowned champion when champagne was uncorked and glasses clinked between Contador and his team, there was an air of going through the motions as the race slowly headed out of Marcoussis. It didn't help the racers' mood that one of the intermediate sprints was at Châtenay-Malabry, hometown of the French lab where blood and urine samples from the antidoping controls are tested. And when the riders arrived for the final laps around the Champs-Élysées, the crowds lining the storied streets of Paris were much thinner than usual, even though the rain held off.

Light rain resumed falling after the finish, as the staff of the Discovery Channel team sipped champagne and celebrated outside their team truck, while their eight riders trooped off to receive the fans' ovations as the winning team. And for the first time since Team Telekom's Bjarne Riis and Jan Ullrich placed first and second in 1996, two riders from one team, Discovery's Contador and Levi Leipheimer, stood together on the final podium, alongside runner-up Cadel Evans.

There was great enthusiasm from a contingent of Contador supporters, chanting the name of their hero, while the Spanish flag was hanging at the Hotel de Crillon where the Texas flag flew during the Armstrong reign. But Discovery's postrace party at the Crillon's rooftop restaurant didn't have the same excesses as the much bigger celebrations when Armstrong won.

Why was the reception so muted for a young champion the Spanish were greeting as "a breath of fresh air," and whose performances in the mountains had thrilled the world? In short, at a Tour where virtually every rider's status was being questioned by the media, not even the apparently clean Contador was being let off the doping hook.

Before Contador won the Tour, people talked about his promising future or his heartbreaking past. The present was rarely a topic. But his unabashed ambition and unquestioned talent added up to a star package. Others spoke about his back-from-the-brink recovery after doctors discovered a blood clot in his brain in 2004. Whenever the topic was mentioned, Contador would proudly remove his Discovery Channel hat to show off the scar that slices across the top of his skull. A titanium plate acts as a reminder that his promising racing career was almost cut short at age 21.

No one expected Contador to become the fifth Spanish rider to wear the yellow jersey on the Champs-Élysées. No one, it seems, except Contador.

Discovery Channel boss Johan Bruyneel had more realistic goals for Contador's second career Tour start: to improve on his 31st placing from his 2005 Tour debut, take aim for the young rider's white jersey, and maybe win a stage. When the Belgian director sent him a text message with a list of potential white jersey rivals that included Linus Gerdemann and Thomas Dekker, Contador replied with a telling message of his own: "I expect my rivals to be Vinokourov, [Alejandro] Valverde, and Evans." Even if no one else was counting on him, Contador had something else in mind.

Contador's road from cycling prodigy, to the emergency room, to the Operación Puerto list, to Tour champion seemed fitting in a wild Tour that delivered large dollops of everything bad and beautiful about professional cycling. But the 2007 Tour seemed to unfold on two planes, with Contador floating serenely in between.

The first battle was the scintillating, no-holds-barred brawl on the roads, with an anxious peloton scrambling to fill the power vacuum still vacant after seven years of Armstrong's rule. The other struggle was a bitter, sometimes surreal tug-of-war for hearts and minds. While journalists painted a gloom-and-doom picture as if the Tour were dead and the peloton a band of junkies, and while Tour officials and the UCI engaged in an embarrassing game of finger-pointing, Contador shrugged off his own dubious links to Operación Puerto and rode as if born to win the Tour. His 23-second margin of victory—the second smallest in Tour history after the eight seconds that separated 1989 winner Greg LeMond from Laurent Fignon—only underscored the quality of the racing.

The string of doping scandals, however, threatened to drown out any sense of rejuvenation that came with the enthusiastic welcome for the Tour's *grand départ* in London. An already frenzied media lost all sense of propriety as a chain of lies and misinformation about the whereabouts of *maillot jaune* Michael Rasmussen during critical, pre-Tour testing periods spun out of control. When Rasmussen was confronted at a rest-day press conference, the enigmatic Dane succeeded in digging his own grave when he couldn't conclusively demonstrate exactly where he was. Barely 24 hours later, the Rabobank team climber became a dubious footnote in Tour history, becoming the first yellow jersey hounded out of the race despite not failing a doping test.

Just as Rasmussen's world faded to black, Contador's went white-hot as the dazed rider slipped into the leader's jersey at the end of stage 17, his face nearly sullen on the podium. "This is not how I would have liked to have taken the jersey. I would have preferred to have made an attack with 5km to go on the Aubisque," Contador said. "But that's how things have unfolded. I am going to take advantage of the circumstances."

With only three days left to Paris, the world didn't have much time to get to know this young rider that Bruyneel was now calling "the next Lance Armstrong." Contador revealed a few glimpses of his softer side, especially when he talked about his passion for raising canaries, hunting in the mountains west of his hometown of Pinto, south of Madrid, or caring for his younger brother, Raul, confined to a wheelchair with cerebral palsy.

The middle of three brothers and one sister, Contador didn't take cycling seriously until he was 15. Winning Spain's national junior time trial championship helped draw the attention of Manolo Saíz, the now disgraced team manager, who would offer Contador a pro contract at age 20.

Contador was one of "Manolo's boys" at the Liberty Seguros squad, a gaggle of new pros barely out of their teens that everyone said would one day dominate Spanish cycling. The others included Luis León Sánchez and Carlos Barredo, but Contador always stood out. His favorite weapon is the 39×17—the gearing he uncorks to make blistering attacks on the steepest climbs of Europe.

"He's a natural-born climber, with long legs and muscles with a light weight," said Discovery Channel team doctor Kepa Zelaia. "He has tremendous capacity to clear out lactate acid, the stuff that causes fatigue. He recovers well, and he has tremendous maturity for a rider his age. Maybe that's from the circumstances he's had to overcome in his life."

Everything was golden about Contador's life until the 2004 Tour of Asturias, a second-tier Spanish race held each May that attracts riders preparing for the Tour de France. Contador was short-listed to make Saíz's Tour team when he crashed heavily after feeling dizzy on a snaking descent along Spain's verdant Costa Verde. Only quick action from a race medic saved Contador from choking to death on his own tongue. He suffered another dizzy spell a few days later. Tests revealed a congenital blood clot in his brain, and doctors said emergency surgery was required to prevent a life-threatening stroke.

Contador went from Tour-bound cyclist to bedridden patient without a secure future, secretly worried that he would end up like his younger brother. While undergoing four months of rehabilitation, he found inspiration from a familiar name, Lance Armstrong. "I didn't think I could ever race my bike again, let alone lead a normal life because doctors said it's never sure what happens after brain surgery," he said. "I was reading Armstrong's biography. That gave me hope to come back."

Contador indeed made a comeback worthy of Armstrong. He found strength from his family, whose motto is *querer es poder*, which loosely translates to "willpower to overcome." By January 2005, Contador was back in the saddle and winning races, his inner drive earning him a great stage win at Australia's Tour Down Under before he ripped through an impressive campaign that included victories at Spain's Setmana Catalana, a stage of Switzerland's Tour de Romandie, and a climbing time trial at Spain's Tour of the Basque Country.

The 2006 Tour was supposed to be Contador's big coming-out party. On the heels of his solid Tour debut a year earlier, he would have freedom to chase the white jersey, and help Liberty Seguros-Würth team captain Vinokourov in the mountains. But Contador's career faced its next serious threat when his name was among nine riders from four teams ejected before the start of the 2006 Tour for alleged links to the blood doping ring at the center of the Puerto investigation. So when Contador slipped into the 2007 Tour's yellow jersey, following Rasmussen's abrupt departure, many were scratching their heads wondering how a rider who was ejected from the previous year's Tour was on the cusp of winning the 2007 edition.

"I was on the wrong team at the wrong time," Contador said. "My name was on this infamous list, but one week later, the UCI had more time to examine the documents, and I was taken off. My relation with Puerto was annulled. I was cleared of any link with the scandal."

Contador's name appeared twice in the 36-page facsimile sent by Spain's Guardia Civil to Tour officials. The summary document, written in Spanish, included the most damning evidence confiscated in police raids in May 2006, but there's not much on Contador. Both references to the young Spaniard are in lists of riders and training programs, without making incriminating references to doping practices that eventually led to confessions from such riders as Ivan Basso, Jörg Jaksche, and Michele Scarponi. A Spanish judge and the UCI both cleared Contador. Even alleged ringleader Dr. Eufemiano Fuentes, speaking on Spanish radio, said he never worked with Contador. But that didn't stop journalists from grilling Contador about whether the world could believe him.

"I'm clean or I wouldn't be here right now," Contador said. "I have passed all my controls, both in and out of competition, without a problem."

Contador also denied any connection with controversial Italian doctor Michele Ferrari, the infamous *preparatore* who worked with Armstrong, and the embattled Vinokourov, who failed blood doping tests after his time trial win at Albi. "I wouldn't recognize Ferrari if I saw him. I've never spoken a word to him," Contador said. "My doctors are the ones from the team. I don't work with anyone else."

Contador may have been secretly happy that he wasn't in the yellow jersey for long. Unlike Rasmussen, who often seemed alone and distant from his teammates and directors, Contador had the confidence-boosting presence of Armstrong and Bruyneel in the Discovery Channel team car trailing him at the final time trial. Even if some skeptics were less than satisfied with his

Puerto answers, he was hailed as a hero in Spain. His return to Madrid was capped with a celebration in the Cibeles fountain that's usually reserved for revelry after key soccer games.

A headline in Spanish sports daily *Marca* declared, "Through the Biggest Door"—a reference to bullfighters leaving the ring through the *puerta grande*. The Madrid daily *El Mundo* declared, "The Triumph of a Dream."

Contador's worst night came after he secured the yellow jersey for good, when just the ceremonial spin into Paris remained. "I was a bundle of nerves and I couldn't sleep," Contador said. "I just wanted it to end." And end it did, with Contador becoming an overnight sensation, five years in the making.

— ◎ —

Two weeks after the finish in Paris, doping remained in the headlines. Patrik Sinkewitz admitted using synthetic testosterone at a pre-Tour training camp; Vinokourov's B-samples did prove positive for blood doping; and Vino's Astana teammate Andrey Kashechkin also came up positive for homologous blood doping following an out-of-competition test while he was on vacation with his family in Belek, Turkey, on August 1.

At the same time, the unemployed Rasmussen was looking for a team so that he could do some end-of-the-season races. But no luck; nobody wanted anything to do with him.

There were also new allegations against Contador and Valverde. It was in this atmosphere that the Tour winner called a press conference in Madrid to defend himself.

Contador's answers during the Tour hadn't quieted all the critics. German antidoping activist Werner Franke—who exposed the rampant abuse of performance-enhancing drugs in the former East Germany—reportedly provided investigators at the World Anti-Doping Agency with documents detailing Contador's work with the notorious doctor. "The name of this Mr. Contador appears on several occasions on the court and police documents," Franke told German television station ZDF on July 30. "All of this has been simply concealed and hidden under the carpet while the name Contador was erased from the list of suspicious riders."

So, on August 10, Contador took the extraordinary step of making a public statement to try to counter the growing media antagonism in the wake of his impressive Tour victory. He was accompanied by Discovery Channel team manager Johan Bruyneel, Spanish sports minister Jaime Lissavetzky, and members of his family. Earlier in the day, Contador had met with Lissavetzky in a closed-door session.

"I have never doped, and I have never participated in an act of doping," said Contador, reading from his prepared statement (reproduced below). "I won the Tour clean. I cannot understand the attacks against me by people that don't even know me. My commitment is absolute, and I will always be ready to collaborate in the fight against doping."

Contador said he has supported efforts by the UCI and by Spanish authorities to crack down on alleged doping practices. He also said he would give a DNA sample if asked to do so by the proper authorities.

His full statement, translated from the Spanish, was the following:

Dear friends, supporters who have cheered me from the grandstands or in front of the television screen, communication media, sponsors, cycling event organizers, and cycling authorities. The events that occurred during the Tour have made me contemplate many things.

All of this is new to me. While I was too focused during the race and on the role that I was supposed to play for my team, I did not realize other things. I was not aware of the real importance of winning this race, even though I had seen it on TV.

I only came to realize this when the race had finished: police protection, crowds of people surrounding me, the phone endlessly ringing, people asking for autographs, and press, lots of press—for the good and for the bad.

Three years ago, when I was going to debut in the Tour, a painful experience due to an illness hampered my start; this almost cost me my life and my professional career.

On top of my health frustration, being involved in a doping scandal that caused my team to exclude me from the Tour of 2006 was not any less frustrating. It was a situation of impotence, sadness, and disillusion that changed my vision of cycling, the sport that I am giving the best years of my life, the sport in which, as mentioned in the letter I wrote last year, I have always practiced cleanly, with zeal, hard work, and a great deal of illusion.

Today, from my position as the winner of the 2007 Tour, the most important race in the world, the race that any cyclist dreams of winning, a race that I won with effort and honesty, I ask you to continue believing in bicycling and in me.

And because I have won this race in a clean way, and because I have greatly enjoyed the presence of the fans, I will promise you that you will be able to continue enjoying my participation since my goal, other than winning the race, is to make bicycling an attractive and admired sport by all.

That is why I find it impossible to comprehend the attacks against me, doubts of my honesty as a sportsman, from people that don't really know me, but who somehow feel capable of judging and evaluating my condition on a TV screen, diagnosing the nature of my physical capacities and my moral tendencies. Some of them even claim to be doctors. The doctors that I know, who made it possible for me to be here after treating my illness, would not talk in public about their patients, not even to mention the patients of other doctors.

I have never committed an act of doping, I have never participated in an act of doping, and those who know me know what I think about it.

My attitude against doping is absolute, and you would always find me willing to collaborate; that's why I have met, in every moment, the standard in bicycling; that's why, year after year I send the UCI the questionnaires of location for being controlled at any moment that this sport's authorities consider is necessary; and that's why I have passed the surprise and programmed drug tests in my own house and at races, and during the off-season, blood and urine tests, which logically are way more than what any other participant of the race has to take.

I have the full support of the UCI, the Spanish cycling federation, and Jaime Lissavetzky state secretary of sports and his Consejo Superior de Deportes—which has endorsed this statement by allowing this conference to take place at its headquarters. Furthermore, I am willing to take part in as many studies as needed for the authorities concerning doping, including my DNA.

I don't know if there's anything left I can do to be considered as a just winner of the race; but if after this appearance, in which I express my absolute collaboration, the defamatory information and attacks still persist, affecting my family, team, sponsors, and peers, I will defer to the legal system and any relevant rule of law. If any immeasurable damage done to me is compensated financially, part of that compensation would go toward the fight against doping.

This is the contribution that Alberto Contador Velasco, winner of the Tour 2007, provides to the credibility and renaissance of the new cycling, which would not be possible without the media, authorities, laws, and supporters.

Thank you to everybody.

Madrid, August 10, 2007

— ◉ —

C ontador's statement didn't silence the critics, in part because he refused to take questions afterward, and in part because reporters had other things to write about. On the same day he was talking to journalists in Madrid, an announcement came from his team headquarters in Austin, Texas: the Discovery team was being disbanded at the end of the year. Riders and staff members would have to look for new employers.

Incredibly, the organization that runs the team, Tailwind Sports, was simply pulling out of cycling. The decision to quit wasn't made because Tailwind was not capable of finding a new title sponsor, its principals said. Instead, the team management—part-owner Armstrong, team director Bruyneel, president Bart Knaggs, general manager/CEO Bill Stapleton, and team founder Thom Weisel—said it did not want to continue running the team.

Tackling the sponsor issue first, Armstrong dismissed the notion that Tailwind was unable to find a replacement for Discovery. "I think we had a firm commitment for three years," he said. "It wasn't signed and sealed, but we were 90 percent there."

The situation was not the same as in 1996, when Motorola ended its six-year sponsorship with U.S. team owner Jim Ochowicz, who was unable to find a replacement despite a two-year search. Ochowicz's previous title sponsor, 7-Eleven, had also supported his pro team for six years.

Motorola did not drop cycling because of any inherent problems with the team or the sport; the sponsorship had simply run its course. The American corporation's goal in sponsoring a pro cycling team was to get its wireless technology brand better known in the European market. That goal was achieved, so there was no need to continue as a sponsor.

Fortunately for American cycling, a year before Ochowicz's team folded, Weisel's Montgomery-Bell squad had just obtained a major title sponsor, the U.S. Postal Service. The new team immediately expanded to the size of a Motorola and gained a wild card slot at the 1997 Tour de France. Postal remained as the title sponsor for nine years, followed by Discovery Channel for three years—a 12-year span that mirrored the Motorola/7-Eleven sponsorship time frame.

In explaining why Tailwind was stopping its activities, Stapleton said, "We can't control the sport and we can't control other teams, and we couldn't in good conscience recommend that a sponsor come in. It's just not an environment conducive to a big investment."

That environment included the continuing power struggle between Tour de France organizer ASO and the UCI, the negative publicity from multiple doping issues—whether it was former riders admitting they once used banned drugs or current stars being caught out by antidoping controls—and the bickering between teams and team groupings.

Armstrong said, "We need some semblance of order. You have to get back to a level of trust among all the interested parties." As an example of the disconnection, he cited the proposal by ASO that it wanted national teams to contest the Tour de France alongside the trade teams. "If ASO decided to go with national teams," said the seven-time Tour winner, "then someone's $15 million investment is worth zero."

The situation could not be compared with the one in 1998 when the Festina team was excluded from the Tour de France because of organized doping. That triggered police raids on the hotels of other teams, two rider protests that disrupted or annulled stages, and the withdrawal from the Tour of all the Spanish teams.

The sport was sullied, but the sponsors remained. In fact, Festina said that its business increased after all the "bad" publicity, and it continued to sponsor a team for another three years. Festina was still the official timing sponsor of the Tour in 2007.

In 1998, no teams lost their title sponsors because of the Festina affair. In 2007, no companies pulled their sponsorships because of the doping scandals at the Tour. ProTour team Unibet.com was not continuing because ASO stopped it from competing in its event for two reasons: ASO accepted only 18 of the 20 ProTour teams to its events; and the French authorities banned the online betting operations of Sweden-based Unibet because of an obscure commercial law. At the same time, Astana, Cofidis, CSC, Milram, and T-Mobile all endorsed their ProTour team sponsorships, despite various doping-related incidents, while Gerolsteiner ultimately decided to honor its sponsorship contract through 2008.

The closest equivalent to Tailwind's ending its team was the demise of the highly successful Mapei team in 2002. But that team was owned and operated by the title sponsor, and when the Mapei company owner, Dr. Giorgio Squinzi, decided to stop the team because he did not approve of the allegedly widespread use of EPO in the peloton, that was it. Mapei, however, continued to own the Mapei Sports Center, which is dedicated to scientific training without recourse to drugs. Cadel Evans is its most famous client.

Despite Tailwind's withdrawal as a team owner, Stapleton said, "I hope that someday we'll return." But that promise didn't help the men and their staff who had just finished the Tour de France. Directeur sportif Sean Yates wrote on his Web site the day after the announcement, as Leipheimer was leading the team into the Tour of Germany: "'Welcome to the morgue.' That's how one of the members of the staff greeted me yesterday when I turned up at the team hotel here in Germany. It was then that the news I had received the previous evening really started to sink in. It was not just a bad dream, it was reality. The team was finished. 'How is that possible?' were the words coming out of most people's mouths. Shock and panic was the mood of the day. I am sure it will sink in soon enough though, and everybody will try and move on. I for one really want to stay in this line of work as you can all imagine, and I have contacted a few teams with that in mind. I am hoping that in the next ten days or so I will have a good idea if that is possible or not. Until then it's knuckle down to it here in Germany; it would be nice to get a result."

Despite the bad news surrounding cycling and the Tour, there were also some notes of optimism. Back in London where the 2007 edition started, Mayor Ken Livingstone and UK Sport, the government agency that enabled the race to start in England, said they were eager to host the Tour again.

The *grand départ* was watched by 4 million spectators and provided an estimated $230 million boost to the British economy. Mayor Livingstone said the city wanted to host the Tour start again in 2013 or 2014, or just a stage or two earlier than that. A UK Sport spokesman told the *Evening Standard*: "We support the efforts to eradicate the drug cheats and we will stand by the sport rather than abandon it. The *grand départ* showed we are able to stage a world-class sporting event in London, and there were two amazing days."

Perhaps there would be more amazing days, and fewer tense ones, at the Tour de France in 2008.

Appendix A

RESULTS

FINAL GENERAL CLASSIFICATION

1. Alberto Contador (Sp), Discovery Channel, 3569.9km in 91:00:26 (39.226kph); **2.** Cadel Evans (Aus), Predictor-Lotto, at 0:23; **3. Levi Leipheimer (USA), Discovery Channel, at 0:31; 4.** Carlos Sastre (Sp), CSC, at 7:08; **5.** Haimar Zubeldia (Sp), Euskaltel-Euskadi, at 8:17; **6.** Alejandro Valverde (Sp), Caisse d'Épargne, at 11:37; **7.** Kim Kirchen (Lux), T-Mobile, at 12:18; **8.** Yaroslav Popovych (Ukr), Discovery Channel, at 12:25; **9.** Mikel Astarloza (Sp), Euskaltel-Euskadi, at 14:14; **10.** Oscar Pereiro (Sp), Caisse d'Épargne, at 14:25; **11.** Juan Mauricio Soler (Col), Barloworld, at 16:51; **12.** Michael Boogerd (Nl), Rabobank, at 21:15; **13.** David Arroyo (Sp), Caisse d'Épargne, at 21:49; **14.** Vladimir Karpets (Rus), Caisse d'Épargne, at 24:15; **15. Chris Horner (USA), Predictor-Lotto, at 25:19; 16.** Iban Mayo (Sp), Saunier Duval-Prodir, at 27:09; **17.** Fränk Schleck (Lux), CSC, at 31:48; **18.** Manuel Beltran (Sp), Liquigas, at 34:14; **19.** Tadej Valjavec (Slo), Lampre-Fondital, at 37:08; **20.** José Cobo (Sp), Saunier Duval-Prodir, at 37:14; **21.** Juan Manuel Garate (Sp), Quick Step-Innergetic, at 38:16; **22.** Ivan Gutierrez (Sp), Caisse d'Épargne, at 45:42; **23.** Amets Txurruka (Sp), Euskaltel-Euskadi, at 49:34; **24. George Hincapie (USA), Discovery Channel, at 54:50; 25. Christian Vande Velde (USA), CSC, at 55:50; 26.** Dmitriy Fofonov (Kaz), Crédit Agricole, at 56:23; **27.** Stéphane Goubert (F), Ag2r Prévoyance, at 1:06:30; **28.** Jens Voigt (G), CSC, at 1:08:22; **29.** Patxi Vila (Sp), Lampre-Fondital, at 1:09:37; **30.** Patrice Halgand (F), Crédit Agricole, at 1:12:45; **31.** Bernhard Kohl (A), Gerolsteiner, at 1:13:27; **32.** Kanstantsin Siutsou (Blr), Barloworld, at 1.15:16; **33.** Alexandre Botcharov (Rus), Crédit Agricole, at 1:22:25; **34.** Markus Fothen (G), Gerolsteiner, at 1:30:12; **35.** Thomas Dekker (Nl), Rabobank, at 1:30:34; **36.** Linus Gerdemann (G), T-Mobile, at 1:30:47; **37.** Christophe Moreau (F), Ag2r Prévoyance, at 1:33:06; **38.** Vladimir Gusev (Rus), Discovery Channel, at 1:33:50; **39.** Moises Duenas (Sp), Agritubel, at 1:36:33; **40.** Bram Tankink (Nl), Quick Step-Innergetic, at 1:36:44; **41.** Marzio Bruseghin (I), Lampre-Fondital, at 1:36:44; **42.** Carlos Barredo (Sp), Quick Step-Innergetic, at 1:36:46; **43.** Iñigo Landaluze (Sp), Euskaltel-Euskadi, at 1:36:50; **44.** Ludovic Turpin (F), Ag2r Prévoyance, at 1:44:54; **45.** Charlie Wegelius (GB), Liquigas, at 1:46:25; **46.** Xavier Florencio (Sp), Bouygues Telecom, at 1:52:19; **47.** Christian Knees (G), Milram, at 1:53:23; **48.** Gorka Verdugo (Sp), Euskaltel-Euskadi, at 1:53:32; **49.** David de la Fuente (Sp), Saunier Duval-Prodir, at 1:54:50; **50.** Ruben Perez (Sp), Euskaltel-Euskadi, at 1:56:15; **51.** Iñigo Cuesta (Sp), CSC, at 1:58:45;

52. José Luis Arrieta (Sp), Ag2r Prévoyance, at 2:00:07; **53.** Iker Camano (Sp), Saunier Duval-Prodir, at 2:05:17; **54.** John Gadret (F), Ag2r Prévoyance, at 2:06:50; **55.** Cédric Vasseur (F), Quick Step-Innergetic, at 2:08:14; **56.** Dario Cioni (I), Predictor-Lotto, at 2:10:42; **57.** Nicolas Portal (F), Caisse d'Épargne, at 2:15:14; **58.** Laurent Lefèvre (F), Bouygues Telecom, at 2:15:17; **59.** Michael Albasini (Swi), Liquigas, at 2:18:35; **60.** Fabian Wegmann (G), Gerolsteiner, at 2:19:36; **61.** Egoï Martinez (Sp), Discovery Channel, at 2:20:16; **62.** Axel Merckx (B), T-Mobile, at 2:21:00; **63.** Johan Van Summeren (B), Predictor-Lotto, at 2:21:57; **64.** Thomas Lövkvist (S), Française des Jeux, at 2:22:50; **65.** Sergio Paulinho (P), Discovery Channel, at 2:23:31; **66.** Thomas Voeckler (F), Bouygues Telecom, at 2:24:34; **67.** Kurt-Asle Arvesen (N), CSC, at 2:24:36; **68.** Jérôme Pineau (F), Bouygues Telecom, at 2:24:59; **69.** David Millar (GB), Saunier Duval-Prodir, at 2:32:07; **70.** Mario Aerts (B), Predictor-Lotto, at 2:32:58; **71.** Sandy Casar (F), Française des Jeux, at 2:33:46; **72.** Francisco Perez Sanchez (Sp), Caisse d'Épargne, at 2:37:25; **73.** Frederik Willems (B), Liquigas, at 2:37:30; **74.** Martin Elmiger (Swi), Ag2r Prévoyance, at 2:37:41; **75.** Daniele Bennati (I), Lampre-Fondital, at 2:38:30; **76.** Kjell Carlström (Fin), Liquigas, at 2:39:34; **77.** Christophe Rinero (F), Saunier Duval-Prodir, at 2:40:59; **78.** Andriy Grivko (Ukr), Milram, at 2:41:41; **79.** Erik Zabel (G), Milram, at 2:42:28; **80.** Juan Miguel Mercado (Sp), Agritubel, at 2:44:27; **81.** Ronny Scholz (G), Gerolsteiner, at 2:44:39; **82.** Jorge Azanza (Sp), Euskaltel-Euskadi, at 2:50:30; **83.** Benoît Vaugrenard (F), Française des Jeux, at 2:50:54; **84.** Pierrick Fédrigo (F), Bouygues Telecom, at 2:53:42; **85.** Juan Antonio Flecha (Sp), Rabobank, at 2:55:58; **86.** Grischa Niermann (Nl), Rabobank, at 2:56:09; **87.** Stefan Schumacher (G), Gerolsteiner, at 2:56:30; **88.** Alessandro Ballan (I), Lampre-Fondital, at 2:57:05; **89.** Aleksandr Kuchynski (Blr), Liquigas, at 2:58:46; **90.** Iñaki Isasi (Sp), Euskaltel-Euskadi, at 2:59:37; **91.** Vicente Garcia Acosta (Sp), Caisse d'Épargne, at 3:00:38; **92.** Nicolas Vogondy (F), Agritubel, at 3:00:50; **93.** Johann Tschopp (Swi), Bouygues Telecom, at 3:07:19; **94.** Simon Gerrans (Aus), Ag2r Prévoyance, at 3:09:19; **95.** Paolo Bossoni (I), Lampre-Fondital, at 3:09:56; **96.** Daniele Righi (I), Lampre-Fondital, at 3:10:35; **97.** Lilian Jegou (F), Française des Jeux, at 3:14:11; **98.** Anthony Geslin (F), Bouygues Telecom, at 3:14:15; **99.** Alexander Efimkin (Rus), Barloworld, at 3:14:19; **100.** Fabian Cancellara (Swi), CSC, at 3:15:48; **101.** Murilo Fischer (Bra), Liquigas, at 3:16:08; **102.** Freddy Bichot (F), Agritubel, at 3:16:58; **103.** David Cañada (Sp), Saunier Duval-Prodir, at 3:17:19; **104.** Sébastien Rosseler (B), Quick Step-Innergetic, at 3:18:25; **105.** Bert Grabsch (G), T-Mobile, at 3:19:58; **106.** Félix Cardenas (Col), Barloworld, at 3:19:58; **107.** Julian Dean (NZ), Crédit Agricole, at 3:21:57; **108.** Matteo Tosatto (I), Quick Step-Innergetic, at 3:22:14; **109.** William Bonnet (F), Crédit Agricole, at 3:22:59; **110.** Leif Hoste (B), Predictor-Lotto, at 3:23:02; **111.** Gianpaolo Cheula (I), Barloworld, at 3:23:11; **112.** Matthieu Ladagnous (F), Française des Jeux, at 3:23:17; **113.** Manuel Quinziato (I), Liquigas, at 3:23:42; **114.** Nicolas Jalabert (F), Agritubel, at 3:24:02; **115.** Benjamin Noval (Sp), Discovery Channel, at 3:24:13; **116.** Ralf Grabsch (G), Milram, at 3:24:35; **117.** Mickaël Delage (F), Française des Jeux, at 3:24:46; **118.** Robbie Hunter (SA), Barloworld, at 3:26:12; **119.** Tom Boonen (B), Quick Step-Innergetic, at 3:26:19; **120.** Marcel Sieberg (G), Milram, at 3:26:48; **121.** Bernhard Eisel (A), T-Mobile, at 3:26:57; **122.** Alessandro Cortinovis (I), Milram, at 3:27:04; **123.** Steven De Jongh (Nl), Quick Step-Innergetic, at 3:27:45; **124.** Paolo Longo (I), Barloworld, at 3:27:48; **125.** Benoît Salmon (F), Agritubel, at 3:28:59; **126.** Claudio Corioni (I), Lampre-Fondital, at 3:29:26; **127.** Marcus Burghardt (G), T-Mobile, at 3:29:37; **128.** Pieter Weening (Nl), Rabobank, at 3:31:49; **129.** Heinrich Haussler (G), Gerolsteiner, at 3:32:30; **130.** Sébastien Chavanel (F), Française des Jeux, at 3:35:25; **131.** Enrico Poitschke (G), Milram, at 3:35:28; **132.** Sébastien Hinault (F), Crédit Agricole, at 3:35:37; **133.** Peter Wrolich (A), Gerolsteiner, at 3:36:05; **134.** Bram De Groot (Nl), Rabobank, at 3:37:46; **135.** Robert Förster (G), Gerolsteiner, at 3:40:10; **136.** Anthony Charteau (F), Crédit Agricole, at 3:40:44; **137.** Sven Krauss (G), Gerolsteiner, at 3:40:51; **138.** Gert Steegmans (B), Quick Step-Innergetic, at 3:41:38; **139.** Thor Hushovd (N), Crédit Agricole, at 3:41:57; **140.** Geraint Thomas (GB), Barloworld, at 3:46:51; **141.** Wim Vansevenant (B), Predictor-Lotto, at 3:52:54.

POINTS CLASSIFICATION

1. Tom Boonen (B), Quick Step-Innergetic, 256; **2.** Robert Hunter (SA), Barloworld, 234; **3.** Erik Zabel (G), Milram, 232; **4.** Thor Hushovd (N), Crédit Agricole, 186; **5.** Sébastien Chavanel (F), Française Des Jeux, 181.

KING OF THE MOUNTAINS CLASSIFICATION

1. Juan Mauricio Soler Hernandez (Col), Barloworld, 206; **2.** Alberto Contador (Sp), Discovery Channel, 128; **3.** Yaroslav Popovych (Ukr), Discovery Channel, 105; **4.** Cadel Evans (Aus), Predictor-Lotto, 92; **5.** Laurent Lefèvre (F), Bouygues Telecom, 85.

BEST YOUNG RIDER CLASSIFICATION

1. Alberto Contador (Sp), Discovery Channel, in 91:00:26; **2.** Juan Mauricio Soler Hernandez (Col), Barloworld, at 16:51; **3.** Amets Txurruka (Sp), Euskaltel-Euskadi, at 49:34; **4.** Bernhard Kohl (A), Gerolsteiner, at 1:13:27; **5.** Kanstantsin Siutsou (Blr), Barloworld, at 1:15:16.

TEAM CLASSIFICATION

1. Discovery Channel (USA), 273:12:52; 2. Caisse d'Épargne (Sp), at 19:36; **3.** CSC (Dk), at 22:10; **4.** Rabobank (Nl), at 36:24; **5.** Euskaltel-Euskadi (Sp), at 46:46.

STAGE WINNERS

Prologue (London): Fabian Cancellara (Swi), CSC, 7.9km in 8:50; **Stage 1** (London to Canterbury): Robbie McEwen (Aus), Predictor-Lotto, 203km in 4:39:01; **Stage 2** (Dunkirk to Ghent): Gert Steegmans (B), Quick Step-Innergetic, 168.5km in 3:48:22; **Stage 3** (Waregem to Compiègne): Fabian Cancellara (Swi), CSC, 236.5km in 6:36:15; **Stage 4** (Villers-Cotterêts to Joigny): Thor Hushovd (N), Crédit Agricole, 193km in 4:37:47; **Stage 5** (Chablis to Autun): Filippo Pozzato (I), Liquigas, 193km in 4:39:01; **Stage 6** (Semur-en-Auxois to Bourg-en-Bresse): Tom Boonen (B), Quick Step-Innergetic, 199.5km in 5:20:59; **Stage 7** (Bourg-en-Bresse to Le Grand Bornand): Linus Gerdemann (G), T-Mobile, 197.5km in 4:53:13; **Stage 8** (Le Grand Bornand to Tignes): Michael Rasmussen (Dk), Rabobank, 165km in 4:49:40; **Stage 9** (Val-d'Isère to Briançon): Juan Mauricio Soler Hernandez (Col), Barloworld, 159.5km in 4:14:24; **Stage 10** (Tallard to Marseille): Cédric Vasseur (F), Quick Step-Innergetic, 229.5km in 5:20:24; **Stage 11** (Marseille to Montpellier): Robbie Hunter (SA), Barloworld, 182.5km in 3:47:50; **Stage 12** (Montpellier to Castres): Tom Boonen (B), Quick Step-Innergetic, 178.5km in 4:25:32; **Stage 13** (Albi, ITT): Alexander Vinokourov (Kaz), Astana, 54km in 1:06:34; **Stage 14** (Mazamet to Plateau de Beille): Alberto Contador (Sp), Discovery Channel, 197km in 5:25:48; **Stage 15** (Foix to Loudenvielle): Alexander Vinokourov (Kaz), Astana, 196km in 5:34:28; **Stage 16** (Orthez to Gourette): Michael Rasmussen (Dk), Rabobank, 218.5km in 6:23:21; **Stage 17** (Pau to Castelsarrasin): Daniele Bennati (I), Lampre-Fondital, 188.5km in 4:14:04; **Stage 18** (Cahors to Angoulême): Sandy Casar (F), Française des Jeux, 211km in 5:13:31; **Stage 19 (Cognac to Angoulême, ITT): Levi Leipheimer (USA), Discovery Channel, 55km in 1:02:44; Stage 20** (Marcoussis to Paris Champs-Élysées): Daniele Bennati (I), Lampre-Fondital.

Appendix B

Records of the Tour de France

THE CHAMPIONS

7 Victories
Lance ARMSTRONG (1999, 2000, 2001, 2002, 2003, 2004, 2005)

5 Victories
Jacques ANQUETIL (1957, 1961, 1962, 1963, 1964)
Eddy MERCKX (1969, 1970, 1971, 1972, 1974)
Bernard HINAULT (1978, 1979, 1981, 1982, 1985)
Miguel INDURÁIN (1991, 1992, 1993, 1994, 1995)

3 Victories
Philippe THYS (1913, 1914, 1920)
Louison BOBET (1953, 1954, 1955)
Greg LEMOND (1986, 1989, 1990)

2 Victories
Lucien PETIT-BRETON (1907, 1908)
Firmin LAMBOT (1919, 1922)
Ottavio BOTTECCHIA (1924, 1925)
Nicolas FRANTZ (1927, 1928)
André LEDUCQ (1930, 1932)
Antonin MAGNE (1931, 1934)
Sylvère MAES (1936, 1939)
Gino BARTALI (1938, 1948)
Fausto COPPI (1949, 1952)
Bernard THÉVENET (1975, 1977)
Laurent FIGNON (1983, 1984)

Number of overall wins by country
36: France
18: Belgium
11: United States
9: Italy
9: Spain
4: Luxembourg
2: Switzerland and the Netherlands
1: Ireland, Denmark, and Germany

Smallest time difference between the winner and second place (since 1947)
8 seconds (1989) between Greg LEMOND (USA) and Laurent FIGNON (F)
23 seconds (2007) between Alberto CONTADOR (Sp) and Cadel EVANS (Aus)
38 seconds (1968) between Jan JANSSEN (Nl) and Herman VAN SPRINGEL (B)
40 seconds (1987) between Stephen ROCHE (Irl) and Pedro DELGADO (Sp)
48 seconds (1977) between Bernard THÉVENET (F) and Hennie KUIPER (Nl)
55 seconds (1964) between Jacques ANQUETIL (F) and Raymond POULIDOR (F)
57 seconds (2006) between Floyd LANDIS (USA) and Oscar PEREIRO (Sp)

Greatest time difference between the winner and second place (since 1947)
28:17 (1952) between Fausto COPPI (I) and Stan OCKERS (B)
26:16 (1948) between Gino BARTALI (I) and Brik SCHOTTE (B)
22:00 (1951) between Hugo KOBLET (Swi) and Raphaël GEMINIANI (F)
17:54 (1969) between Eddy Merckx (B) and Roger PINGEON (F)
15:51 (1973) between Luis OCAÑA (Sp) and Bernard THÉVENET (F)

Number of yellow jersey wearers by country
81: France
53: Belgium
24: Italy
17: The Netherlands
12: Germany
10: Switzerland
10: Spain
6: Denmark
6: Luxembourg
5: United States
4: Great Britain and Australia
3: Ireland
2: Canada
1: Austria, Poland, Portugal, Russia, Estonia, Colombia, Norway, and Ukraine

Number of days in yellow
111: Eddy MERCKX
83: Lance ARMSTRONG
79: Bernard HINAULT
60: Miguel INDURAIN
52: Jacques ANQUETIL

Highest average speed of a Tour winner
41.654kph: Lance ARMSTRONG (USA), 2005
40.940kph: Lance ARMSTRONG (USA), 2003
40.784kph: Floyd LANDIS (USA), 2006
40.553kph: Lance ARMSTRONG (USA), 2004

Fastest stages in Tour history
50.355kph: Laval–Blois (191km) in 1999—Mario CIPOLLINI (I)
49.938kph: Bordeaux–St. Maixent-l'École (202.5km) in 2003—Pablo LASTRAS (Sp)
49.417kph: Evreux–Amiens (158km) in 1993—Johan BRUYNEEL (B)

Fastest time trials (from 20km to 50km)
54.545kph: Versailles–Paris (24.5km) in 1989—Greg LEMOND (USA)
54.361kph: Pornic–Nantes (49km) in 2003—David MILLAR (GB)
50.495kph: Bretigny–Montlhéry (48km) in 1993—Tony ROMINGER (Swi)

In the 2005 Tour, David ZABRISKIE (USA) rode the fastest individual time trial (other than a prologue) in Tour history at a speed of 54.676kph for 19km.

Fastest time trials (longer than 50km)
53.986kph: Freiburg–Mulhouse (58.5km) in 2000—Lance ARMSTRONG (USA)
53.571kph: Cognac–Angoulême (55.5km) in 2007—Levi LEIPHEIMER (USA)
52.349kph: Tours–Blois (64km) in 1992—Miguel INDURAIN (Sp)

Fastest team time trials
57.324kph: Tours–Blois (67.5km) in 2005—Discovery Channel
54.930kph: Mayenne–Alençon (67km) in 1995—Gewiss-Ballan
54.610kph: Berlin–Berlin (40km) in 1987—Carrera

Fastest prologues
55.152kph: Lille (7.2km) in 1994—Chris BOARDMAN (GB)
54.193kph: Dublin (5.6km) in 1998—Chris BOARDMAN (GB)
53.660kph: London (7.9km) in 2007—Fabian CANCELLARA (Swi)

Most stage wins (including time trials)

34: Eddy MERCKX (B)

28: Bernard HINAULT (F)

25: André LEDUCQ (F)

22: André DARRIGADE (F) and Lance ARMSTRONG (USA)

20: Nicolas FRANTZ (Lux)

19: François FABER (Lux)

17: Jean ALAVOINE (F)

16: Charles PÉLISSIER (F), Jacques ANQUETIL (F), and René LE GREVES (F)

Most time trial wins (including prologues)

20: Bernard HINAULT (F), including 5 prologues

16: Eddy MERCKX (B), including 3 prologues

11: Jacques ANQUETIL (F)

11: Lance ARMSTRONG (USA), including 2 prologues

The youngest winners

19 years: Henri CORNET (F) in 1904

21 years: Romain MAES (B) in 1935

22 years: François FABER (Lux) in 1909, Octave LAPIZE (F) in 1910, Philippe THYS (B) in 1913, Felice GIMONDI (I) in 1965, and Laurent FIGNON (F) in 1983

The largest interval between two victories

10 years: Gino BARTALI (I) between 1938 and 1948

Most Tours ridden (since 1947)

16: Joop ZOETEMELK (Nl) (1 win, 6 second places; no abandons)

15: Lucien VAN IMPE (B) (1 win, 1 second place, 3 third places; no abandons); Viatcheslav EKIMOV (Rus) (no wins; no abandons); Guy NULENS (B) (no wins; 2 abandons)

14: André DARRIGADE (F) (no wins; 1 abandon); Raymond POULIDOR (F) (3 second places, 5 third places; 2 abandons); Sean KELLY (Irl) (no wins; 2 abandons)

(Records that changed in 2007 are indicated in boldface type)

Appendix C

Americans at the Tour

THE 32 AMERICANS WHO HAVE RIDDEN THE TOUR

Jonathan Boyer: 1981 (32nd); 1982 (23rd); 1983 (12th); 1984 (31st); 1987 (98th)

Greg LeMond: 1984 (3rd); 1985 (2nd); 1986 (1st); 1989 (1st); 1990 (1st); 1991 (7th); 1992 (DNF); 1994 (DNF)

Doug Shapiro: 1985 (74th); 1986 (DNF)

Andy Hampsten: 1986 (4th); 1987 (16th); 1988 (15th); 1989 (22nd); 1990 (11th); 1991 (8th); 1992 (4th); 1993 (8th)

Bob Roll: 1986 (63rd); 1987 (DNF); 1990 (132nd)

Jeff Pierce: 1986 (80th); 1987 (88th); 1989 (86th)

Ron Kiefel: 1986 (96th); 1987 (82nd); 1988 (69th); 1989 (73rd); 1990 (83rd); 1991 (138th); 1992 (DNF)

Eric Heiden: 1986 (DNF)

Alexi Grewal: 1986 (DNF)

Davis Phinney: 1986 (DNF); 1987 (DNF); 1988 (105th); 1990 (153rd)

Chris Carmichael: 1986 (DNF)

Jeff Bradley: 1987 (DNF)

Andy Bishop: 1988 (135th); 1990 (116th); 1991 (126th); 1992 (DNF)

Norman Alvis: 1990 (142nd)

Roy Knickman: 1989 (DNF)

Michael Carter: 1991 (DNF)

Frankie Andreu: 1992 (110th); 1993 (89th); 1994 (89th); 1995 (82nd); 1996 (111th); 1997 (79th); 1998 (58th); 1999 (65th); 2000 (110th)

Lance Armstrong: 1993 (DNF); 1994 (DNF); 1995 (36th); 1996 (DNF); 1999 (1st); 2000 (1st); 2001 (1st); 2002 (1st); 2003 (1st); 2004 (1st); 2005 (1st)

George Hincapie: 1996 (DNF); 1997 (104th); 1998 (53rd); 1999 (78th); 2000 (65th); 2001 (71st); 2002 (59th); 2003 (47th); 2004 (33rd); 2005 (14th); 2006 (32nd); 2007 (24th)

Bobby Julich: 1997 (17th); 1998 (3rd); 1999 (DNF); 2000 (48th); 2001 (18th); 2002 (37th); 2004 (40th); 2005 (17th); 2006 (DNF)

Kevin Livingston: 1997 (38th); 1998 (17th); 1999 (36th); 2000 (37th); 2001 (43rd); 2002 (56th)

Tyler Hamilton: 1997 (69th); 1998 (51st); 1999 (13th); 2000 (25th); 2001 (94th); 2002 (15th); 2003 (4th); 2004 (DNF)

Marty Jemison: 1997 (96th); 1998 (48th)

Christian Vande Velde: 1999 (85th); 2001 (DNF); 2004 (56th); 2006 (24th); 2007 (25th)

Jonathan Vaughters: 1999 (DNF); 2000 (DNF); 2001 (DNF); 2002 (DNF)

Fred Rodriguez: 2000 (86th); 2001 (DNF); 2002 (DNF); 2005 (132nd); 2006 (DNF); 2007 (DNF)

Chann McRae: 2000 (DNF)

Floyd Landis: 2002 (61st); 2003 (77th); 2004 (23rd); 2005 (9th); 2006 (1st)

Levi Leipheimer: 2002 (8th); 2003 (DNF); 2004 (9th); 2005 (6th); 2006 (13th); 2007 (3rd)

Chris Horner: 2005 (33rd); 2006 (64th); 2007 (15th)

Guido Trenti: 2005 (149th)

Dave Zabriskie: 2005 (DNF); 2006 (74th); 2007 (DNF)

(Riders in bold competed at the 2007 Tour.)

Appendix D

2008 Tour de France: No Prologue in Brittany

The 95th Tour de France takes place from July 5 to 27, 2008, on a course to be announced in Paris on October 25, 2007. What is known is that the race will start in Brest in the far west of France, and head counterclockwise around the country, with the race passing through the Pyrénées and then the Alps before the finish in Paris.

In contrast to the 2007 Tour start in London, with a prologue on a spectacular city-center course, there will be no opening time trial in 2008. This is because for the first time in the history of the Tour, a whole region (Brittany) has bought the rights to the *grand départ*. As a result, the Tour is opening with three straight road stages that will crisscross the four *départements* that make up the Breton peninsula.

Stage 1 starts in the naval port of Brest and heads southeast over the rolling hills of the Monts d'Arrée to an uphill finish on the Cadoudal hill in the village of Plumelec, just north of Vannes. Stage 2 goes from Auray, a village west of Vannes, and heads north through central Brittany, over the infamously steep Mur de Bretagne to a probable finish in downtown St. Brieuc. Stage 3 starts from the ancient ramparts of St. Malo, on the northern coast, and heads south to an as yet unnamed destination—most likely the city of Nantes or a town nearby. The hope is that stage 4 will be a team time trial, one of the Tour's most popular disciplines, which was absent from the 2006 and 2007 editions.

Officially, every Tour since 1967 has started with a prologue; but there was one exception. When the race started at La Baule in southern Brittany in 1988, the opener was a so-called prelude that did not count toward the general classification. Just one rider from each of the 16 teams raced the straight 1km course along the Atlantic beachfront, with the Italian Guido Bontempi taking the win.

About the Authors

John Wilcockson is the editorial director of *VeloNews* and the author of more than a dozen books. He has been writing about cycling since 1968, and in 2007 he reported on the Tour de France for the thirty-ninth year. He has appeared on CNN, MSNBC, ESPN, CBS, and OLN, and has reported for NPR, BBC, ESPN radio, and many other stations. He lives in Boulder, Colorado.

Andrew Hood is the European correspondent of *VeloNews*, and has been reporting on the Tour de France since 1996. He lives in León, Spain.

Neal Rogers is the senior writer of *VeloNews*; he reported on the Tour de France for the third time in 2007. **Ben Delaney** is the editor of *VeloNews*; he reported on the Tour de France for the first time in 2007. **Matt Pacocha** is the technical editor of *VeloNews*, he reported on the Tour de France for the first time in 2007. **Charles Pelkey** is the editor of velonews.com.